THE BIG RADIO COMEDY PROGRAM

EDITED BY ROSS FIRESTONE

cbi Contemporary Books, Inc.
Chicago

For
My Mother and Father
and
Gail and Simon

Library of Congress Cataloging in Publication Data

Firestone, Ross.
　The big radio comedy program.

　　1. Radio plays—United States.　　2. American wit and
humor.　　I. Title.
PN6120.R2F484　　　　791.44′7　　　　78-8402
ISBN 0-8092-7909-6
ISBN 0-8092-7908-8 pbk.

Copyright © 1978 by Ross Firestone
All rights reserved
Published by Contemporary Books, Inc.
180 North Michigan Avenue, Chicago, Illinois 60601
Manufactured in the United States of America
Library of Congress Catalog Card Number: 78-8402
International Standard Book Number: 0-8092-7909-6 (cloth)
　　　　　　　　　　　　　　　　　　0-8092-7908-8 (paper

Published simultaneously in Canada by
Beaverbooks
953 Dillingham Road
Pickering, Ontario L1W 1Z7
Canada

CONTENTS

ACKNOWLEDGMENTS

"Baron Munchausen's Circus" is printed by permission of Jack Pearl.

"Jake, A Business Man" is printed by permission of Lewis W. Berg.

"Mr. Dempsey and Mr. Tunney Meet in a Cigar Store" is from *The Small House Half-way Up in the Next Block: Paul Rhymer's Vic and Sade*, edited by Mary Frances Rhymer, Copyright © 1972. Used with permission of McGraw-Hill Book Co.

"Hollywood Agents" is copyrighted © by the Radiola Company, Box C, Sandy Hook, Connecticut 06482. It is transcribed from *Groucho on Radio*, Radiola Release # 72.

"Fire In The Home" is copyrighted © by W. C. Fields Productions, Inc., 1977.

"Allen's Alley: Used Cars" and "Reminiscing With Jack Benny" are from *Treadmill to Oblivion*, by Fred Allen, Copyright © 1954. Reprinted by permission of William Morris Agency, Inc.

"California and New York" and "The Bullfight" are printed by permission of Marilyn Cantor Baker.

"The Grasshopper and the Ant," "The Physiology Lesson," and "At The Newsstand" are printed by permission of Edgar Bergen.

"The Visit" is printed by permission of Si Rose.

"At the Naval Air Station at Los Alamitos" is copyrighted © 1973 by Joe Morella, Edward Z. Epstein, and Eleanor Clark. Taken from *The Amazing Careers of Bob Hope*, published by Arlington House. All rights reserved. Used with permission.

"On The Atcheson, Topeka and Santa Fe" and "The Big Game" are printed by permission of Bob Hope.

"The Hunting Trip" is printed by permission of Garry Moore.

"Jane Goes to a Psychiatrist" is from *Ladies and Gentlemen, Easy Aces*, by Goodman Ace. Copyright © by Goodman Ace. Reprinted by permission of Doubleday & Company, Inc.

"A Commercial" and "Long Distance" are printed by permission of Henry Morgan.

"Person-of-the-Month Club" and "Bob and Ray Reunite the Whirleys" are from *Write if You Get Work: The Best of Bob and Ray*, by Bob Elliott and Ray Goulding. Copyright © 1975 by Robert B. Elliott and Raymond W. Goulding. Reprinted by permission of Random House, Inc.

INTRODUCTION

At the beginning—like now—radio was mostly music. Eddie Cantor and Ed Wynn had brought their comedy to the air as early as 1921 and 1922, just two and three years after scheduled commercial broadcasting started, but these were only isolated experiments. It took another full decade before they could be heard with any regularity.

By the early 1930s, though, the comedians had arrived in force and were beginning to dominate the medium. America was in the depths of the Great Depression, and laughter proved a valuable commodity, with the power to attract listeners and advertising revenues to the newly formed radio networks. The Depression had also hurt vaudeville badly, and even the most successful vaudeville comedians were responsive to the medium's need for new talent and fresh programming. For less successful performers, the opportunities offered by radio were a godsend.

By 1933 one could move across the dial and tune in comedians like Cantor, Wynn, Jack Pearl, the Marx Brothers, Jack Benny, George Burns and Gracie Allen and Fred Allen, as well as such comedy dramas as *Amos 'n' Andy*, *The Goldbergs*, *Vic and Sade* and *Easy Aces*. Within the next few years they were joined by Bob Hope, Edgar Bergen, *Fibber McGee and Molly*, Jimmy Durante, Abbott and Costello and all the others who come to mind whenever one thinks of radio's so-called Golden Age.

And once they came, most of them stayed, taking over the prime evening hours with their shows. For all the notorious fickleness of public taste, the top radio comedians had extraordinary longevity. As Erik Barnouw tells us in his *History of Broadcasting in the United States*, "The cluster of comedians heading the ratings remained remarkably constant. They seemed to cut across age groups and socio-economic strata. They provided universal therapy." Such therapy continued past the Depression and into World War II and the postwar years. The comedy only faded in the 1950s, when it was lured over to the newly emergent medium of television. Then, once again, radio returned to the music with which it began.

This book celebrates those twenty years or so when comedy flourished on the air by bringing together some of the funniest moments broadcast by most of the best performers and shows.

The pieces have been selected from recordings and tapes of the original shows, previously published books on broadcasting and actual radio scripts that somehow survived the years. Sometimes I have included entire programs. More often, I have selected self-contained episodes and scenes that express the essence of a performer's art.

In searching out this material, I have looked for pieces that still seem as funny now as they must have been then. The judgment is admittedly subjective, but if a script didn't wear well with time, I chose to omit it. A few performers who probably ought to be here are missing because I couldn't find the right shows. A few others aren't here because I couldn't obtain the necessary clearances.

I also looked for pieces that would come through on the printed page. Radio comedy worked by the interaction between words and the listener's imagination, so it reads much better than transcripts from film or television or live performances, where what you see can carry as much of the meaning as what you hear. Still, to get as close as possible to the experience of the actual broadcasts, I have stylized the way the words appear on the page to reflect the tempo, rhythm, inflection and timing of a performer's delivery. Those of you familiar with *Breaking It Up!*, my earlier book on stand-up comedy, will recognize the format. As I stated there, if the result looks something like poetry, the resemblance isn't entirely coincidental. The comedian compares to the poet in his sensitivity to the creative possibilities of language and in his ability to deploy it with precision, economy and effect.

My introductions to each performer and show are indebted to three basic books on the subject: John Dunning's encyclopedic *Tune In Yesterday*, Frank Buxton's and Bill Owen's *The Big Broadcast: 1920–1950* and Jim Harmon's *The Great Radio Comedians*. I thank the authors for their information and insights.

I would also like to thank some of the many others who helped make this book possible: Jeff Atterton, Marilyn Cantor Baker, Lewis W. Berg, Edgar Bergen, Mel Berger, Marilyn Dean, Leopold Fechtner, William C. Fields III, Gail Firestone, Joe Franklin, Bill Gaines, George V. Garabedian, J. David Goldin, Ward Grant, Catharine Heinz, Bob Hope, Sydelle Kramer, Juliet Lewis, Lester Lewis, Garry Moore, Henry Morgan, Jack Pearl, Mary Romano, Michael Rophone, Si Rose, Bill Sampson, Nat Sobel, Art Spiegelman, Bhob Stewart, Judith Weber and Elihu Winer. My special gratitude to the Lincoln Center Library of the Performing Arts in New York and the Broadcast Pioneers Library in Washington, D.C.

ED WYNN

Ed Wynn was one of the first established stage comedians to try his hand at the new medium of radio. If you count the 1922 broadcast of his Broadway review *The Perfect Fool*, he was perhaps the very first. There were no networks yet, just local stations, and Wynn brought his show to New Jersey's WJZ for the first, only partially successful, two-hour experiment in coast-to-coast transmission. Eleven years later he attempted to create his own radio network, the Amalgamated Broadcasting System. The venture failed, but the key New York station, WNEW, still operates today, the E and W in its call letters standing for Ed Wynn's own initials.

Before coming to radio, Wynn was an enormously successful vaudevillian, a headliner as early as 1902 who went on to star in the *Ziegfeld Follies* and his own productions. His busy theatrical career as well as his awareness that his humor was essentially visual kept him away from appearing on the air regularly until 1932, the year he began *The Fire Chief* show for Texaco Gasoline. To put himself at ease in the sterile confines of the broadcasting studio, Wynn wore stage makeup and costumes and pioneered the use of a live studio audience. The show achieved immediate popularity, rivaling the already established Eddie Cantor and Jack Pearl, and Wynn's high, lisping voice was heard throughout the country every Tuesday night until 1935. Wynn wrote the show himself with the assistance of Eddie Preble. His announcer and straight man was Graham McNamee, historically important figure in his own right for his early sports and newscasting.

One of *The Fire Chief*'s regular features was Wynn's retelling of such operas as the *Carmen* printed here. These "operas," which sometimes carried names like *When You Were Eight and I Was Nine and We Were Seventeen*, were a fusillade of outrageous puns and gags, punctuated with Wynn's trademark catchphrase, "Soooooo-o-o-o-o." The fun of their wordplay was a verbal equivalent to the funny hats and outlandish costumes and props Wynn used on the stage and brought with him to the studio.

In 1935 Wynn moved on to a new show called *Gulliver*. It was followed two years later by *The Perfect Fool*, the title of his earlier stage hit and the epithet by which he himself was known. In 1944 he began the last of his weekly series, *The Happy Island*. In his son Keenan's words, "*Happy Island* came straight out of Dad's daydreams of what he would like to be in the best of all possible worlds. He played King Bubbles in a lollipop land where refugees flocked from Worry Park. His costume included a court outfit with leg-of-mutton sleeves and a midget crown that came from any nursery-tale picture of Old King Cole."

Carmen with Graham McNamee   (1932)

Wynn:

As the curtain goes up on the opera *Carmen*,
you see Carmen, the heroine of the opera.
She is very pretty but very thin.
She is so thin she's just like a bone.
In fact, her own dog buried her
three times in one week.
The opera is all about gypsies,
and gypsies, as you know,
are not very clean people.

Graham:

What do you mean, Chief?
Don't they wash themselves?

Wynn:

Oh, yes.
They wash clean,
but they dry dirty.
And in the first scene
Carmen says to her father,
"Papa, your wash is back;

the laundry refused it."
Her father is the king of the gypsies,
and he is a very old man.
He's so old he gets winded playing checkers.
He decides to go fishing.
It seems he can only eat soft foods
as he has a pullman mouth.

Graham:

A pullman mouth?

Wynn:

Yes, a pullman mouth.
My goodness, Graham,
don't you know what a pullman mouth is?
No lowers and very few uppers.
He is fond of mussels
and is going fishing for them.
Carmen says,
"Are you going fishing, Papa?"
and the old man says,
"Yes, I'm going to fish for mussels."

1

The next scene shows the
mussel-bound old man
going to the river.

Soooooo-o-o-o-o . . .
The gypsies gather around the fire
just as the hero enters.
His name is Joesay.

Graham:

You mean "Hosay."
It isn't pronounced "J" in Spanish;
it's pronounced "H."

Wynn:

Oh, that's ridiculous, Graham.
According to that,
if you saw a donkey pulling a carriage
in Spain,
you'd call it a "hack-ass."

Well, all right, Graham,
I'll say Hosay,
but it sounds silly to me.

The king returns with the fish
for the evening meal.
He picks out the biggest fish for himself.
Just as he sits down,
a cat jumps on the table
and eats the king's fish.
This makes the king mad.
So to get back at the cat
the king goes over to the cat's saucer
and drinks the cat's milk.

The second act takes place in New York
on Sixth Avenue.
Carmen has rented a small store

and is now a gypsy fortune teller.
She's a mind reader.
She is writing her diary,
and being a mind reader
she is writing her diary
two weeks in advance.

As she writes she is singing and laughing.
A stranger walks in.
He says, "Are you a mind reader?"
She says, "Yes."
He says, "Then you're a medium?"
She says, "Yes."
And he slaps her in the face.
Carmen says, "What are you doing?"
And the man says,
"I'm taking my father's advice.
He said I'd be a success
if I could strike a happy medium."

This appeals to Carmen
and she says, "Who are you?"
And he says,
"I'm a bullfighter from Brooklyn."
And Carmen says, "What's your name?"
He says,
"Well, my father gave me a Spanish name,
but I don't know what it is
because I can't speak Spanish."

Carmen says, "Come sit on my right hand."
He does but jumps right up again
because she had a large ring on.
She says, "So you are a bullfighter?
Have you any scars on you?"
He says, "No, I have no scars on me,
but I can let you have a cigarette."

Sooooooo-o-o-o-o . . .
Carmen lights the cigarette
and the way she smokes
fascinates the bullfighter.
He says, "You are lovely.
Will you kiss me?"
And Carmen kisses him
but she forgets to take
the cigarette out of her mouth.
What an exciting scene that is, Graham.

This kindles a spark in the bullfighter,
and he realizes he loves Carmen
and he proposes to her.
Nine different times he asks her
to marry him,
and still he keeps on asking her.
He will not take "yes" for an answer.
He realizes he is hooked
unless he finds a way out.
He racks his brain.
The mental strain is terrific.
All of a sudden something snaps.
It's his garter.

Sooooooo-o-o-o-o . . .
he fixes his garter
and Carmen asks him to call.
That night the bullfighter calls
to see Carmen.
He has on a tuxedo suit which he rented,
but the rent is in the wrong place.
Like all bullfighters, he is stout
and has very short legs.
Carmen sees the funny-looking man
in the tuxedo and faints.
She thinks he is a penguin.

The last act of the opera takes place
in Madrid, Spain.
It is the day before the bullfight.
The bullfighter from Brooklyn,
who we now know as Escamillo,
has left a call at his hotel
to be awakened at eight o'clock.
The clerk calls him at six o'clock
to let him know
he has two hours more to sleep.
As this is his last day of training,
he decides to work very hard.
He starts shadow boxing
but stands perfectly still for half an hour.
He is waiting for his shadow to hit him first.

The door opens.
It is Hosay,
Carmen's sweetheart of the first act.
He says to Escamillo,
"How dare you try to steal
the love of my Carmen!"
And Escamillo says, "Your Carmen?"
And Hosay says,
"Yes, I've known her for years.
She sat on my lap when she was a child."
And Escamillo says,
"Well, I know her better than you do.
She sat on my lap last night."

Sooooooo-o-o-o-o . . .
Hosay rushes out of the room
down to the cigar factory
where Carmen works.
He sees her.
She has on a Havana wrapper.
He says,
"Carmen, how can you treat me like this?
After all, I have given you

3

the ten best years of my life."
And Carmen says,
"My goodness, were they your best?"

Hosay says,
"I will fix your new sweetheart.
I will put the toughest bull in Spain
in the arena against him.
This bull is so tough
that even cyclones ask
permission to pass him."

The next scene is the bullfight.
The arena is gaily decorated.
Royalty and peasants are turning out
for the great battle of the year.
A carriage drives up to the entrance.
A nobleman steps out.
He is a pillar of society.
The crowd knows this
and they lean on him.

He is the Earl of Wintergreen.
He buys five bags of peanuts
to take in the royal box with him.
He hates peanuts,
but he loves to blow up
the bags and break them.

Carmen, too, is in the royal box.
It is a day when rich and poor mingle.
In fact, you see Carmen, the cigarette girl,
rubbing shoulders with
the Earl of Wintergreen.

Soooooo-o-o-o-o . . .
in his dressing room,
Escamillo is pacing the floor.
His toreador's costume
hasn't come back from the cleaners.
The spectators are yelling for Escamillo.
He cannot wait for his costume to come,
so he rushes into the arena in his underwear
and the bull sees red.

Escamillo wins the fight,
and so he will not also win Carmen.
Hosay shoots her but she does not die.
That night she calls up Escamillo and says,
"Did you read in the paper
that I have been killed?"
And he says,
"Yes, I know you're dead.
Which place are you calling from?"

JACK PEARL

John Dunning's *Tune In Yesterday* calls Jack Pearl "the first truly great dialectician of the air." The particular dialect Pearl employed so brilliantly was comic German, a staple of the vaudeville and burlesque knockabout in which he had served his apprenticeship as an entertainer. What was special was the character he created with it: the ebullient Baron Munchausen, fabricator of fantastical tall tales and equally outrageous puns and gags. Pearl got the name for his character from an actual historical figure, an eighteenth-century German soldier and traveler. The extravagant book of "memoirs" named after him, *Baron Munchausen's Travels*, also provided Pearl with a model for the high-flown fables that made him one of the top stars of early radio. For much of his career, Pearl worked with Cliff Hall as his straight man. Hall would provide the occasion for the Baron's stories, and his skepticism about their truthfulness would inevitably provoke the comedian into the question, "Vas you dere, Sharlie?," which became one of the most widely quoted catchphrases of its time.

Pearl made his radio debut in 1932 on Ed Sullivan's interview show, a program that also introduced Jack Benny, Irving Berlin and George M. Cohan to the radio audience during the brief season it remained on the air. Later that same year he appeared frequently on the equally short-lived *Ziegfeld Follies of the Air*, along with such stars as Fanny Brice, Will Rogers and Billie Burke, and he began his own one-hour series with Walter O'Keefe for Lucky Strike Cigarettes. In 1933 Pearl moved on to *The Jack Pearl Show*, an extremely popular half-hour sponsored by Royal Gelatin, and made numerous appearances with Rudy Vallee on *The Fleischmann Hour*. According to Jim Harmon in *The Great Radio Comedians*, the rise of Hitler in the mid-1930s made funny Germans suddenly not so funny any more, and Pearl's popularity began to slip badly. Although he tried out different formats and roles, Baron Munchausen remained his classic characterization, and he revived it frequently over the years. The performance included here was originally broadcast in 1939 in a guest appearance with music critic Deems Taylor, who took over the part of Cliff Hall's straight man.

Baron Munchausen's Circus with Deems Taylor (1939)

Taylor:

It's Jack Pearl!

(APPLAUSE)

Pearl:

Never I see much a man—
(Sneeze)

Taylor:

Just a minute, Baron.

Pearl:

(Sneeze . . . sneeze)

Taylor:

Say, you've got a bad cold.

Pearl:

(Sneeze)
I'm sick as a dog.

Taylor:

Where did you catch that cold?

Pearl:

I drank some beer out of a damp glass.

Taylor:

Who ever heard of catching a cold
drinking beer out of a damp glass?

Pearl:

It was draught beer.

Taylor:

I see.
Well, Baron,
what have you been doing lately?

Pearl:

. . . Sure.
I been making a leopard
give me a leopard skin.

Taylor:

A leopard give you a leopard skin?

Pearl:

Yes sir!
But—

Taylor:

But what?

Pearl:

I had to shoot him to get it!

Taylor:

Oh, that's different.
You killed him?

Pearl:

Sure—
You don't think I got it
while he was changing his underwear,
do you?

Taylor:

Hardly . . .
Leopards are hard to locate,
aren't they, Baron?

Pearl:

Not for me!
I know all their spots!

Taylor:

You know all the leopard's spots?

Pearl:

Sure—
It's a great spot spotting their spots.

Taylor:

Ah ha!
So it's going to be that kind of a night!

Pearl:

What kind of a night?

Taylor:

Spotty!

Pearl:

Sure—
(Laugh)
—In spots!

Taylor:

Well, it's spot time!

Pearl:

Yes, it's—
(Laugh)
Let's talk about tigers!

Taylor:

Do you know anything about tigers?

Pearl:

Do I?—
(Laugh)
I know more about tigers than—
than tigers know about tigers!

Taylor:

I expected you to say something
along those lines.

Pearl:

Yes, I—
NOT LIONS.
TIGERS!

Taylor:

Tigers!

Pearl:

Yes sir—
But I am also a big lion man!

Taylor:

Everybody knows that!

Pearl:

Sure, I—
THE SUBJECT IS TIGERS!

Taylor:

All right, the *lion* is out!

Pearl:

Yes sir!
Tonight there is no lion!

Taylor:

Thank goodness for that!

Pearl:

Yes—
TIGERS!

Taylor:

All right.
Get back to the tigers.

Pearl:

Sure—
I got a tiger in my circus what is—

Taylor:

Do you own a circus?

Pearl:

A bigger one as the Gong-Gong Cousins!

Taylor:

The Gong-Gong Cousins?

Pearl:

The Ding-Dong Nephews—
The Tinkle-Tinkle Sisters—

Taylor:

Do you by any chance mean
the Ringling Brothers?

Pearl:

That's it!
The Ring-a-ling Brothers!

Taylor:

The greatest circus on earth!

Pearl:

(Laugh)
A Punch-and-Judy show.

Taylor:

A Punch-and-Judy show?

Pearl:

Sure—
In my circus I got zixteen hundred acrobats!

Taylor:

Sixteen hundred acrobats?

Pearl:

Yes sir!

Taylor:

How's tricks?

Pearl:

It's—

Take a tumble to yourself!

Also I got twelve hundred

and forty trapeezers!

Eight hundred and thirty-five

rareback biters!

Taylor:

Rareback biters?

Pearl:

(Laugh)

Bareback riders—

(Laugh)

I had the horse in front of the back! . . .

Three thousand zix hundred and ninety-fife

animal trainers,

fourteen thousand animals—

Taylor:

Now you're clowning!

Pearl:

I—

No sir!

For clowning I got nine hundred clowns!

Taylor:

A good clown has to be

silly, foolish, act like an idiot.

Pearl:

Sure—

(Laugh)

Do you want a job?

Taylor:

No—

(Laugh)

You can have it!

Pearl:

Thanks, I—

LAUGH, CLOWN, LAUGH!

Taylor:

Your circus must be

a stupendous combination!

Pearl:

—HELLO!

Taylor:

A marvelous, mammoth, enormous,

gigantic, colossal, spectacular aggregation,

embodied with consubstantial ensembles!

Pearl:

—ALLY OOP!

Taylor:

Your menagerie must be monstrous!

Pearl:

Such monstrous!

I got every kind of dumb animal but one.

Taylor:

Your Cousin Hugo!

Pearl:

Ye—please!

My Cousin Hugo is not dumb like an animal!

Taylor:

I apologize.

Pearl:

You don't have to!

Taylor:

Why not?

Pearl:

(Laugh)
He's dumber!
Also I got smart animals—
That Prince, is he smart!

Taylor:

Who's Prince?

Pearl:

A tiger—
He weighs a ton!

Taylor:

Ah—a Princeton tiger!

Pearl:

Sure, he—
HOLD 'EM, YALE!

Taylor:

Come on, Baron, kick off!

Pearl:

I got an ant what is twenty-two feet high
and it is—

Taylor:

Whoa!
An *ant* twenty-two feet high!

Pearl:

And four inches!
It is—

Taylor:

What in the world kind of an ant is it?

Pearl:

It's a—
Lemme see—
I got it!
The first name is Ella!

Taylor:

Ella?

Pearl:

Yes—
Ella-phant.

Taylor:

An elephant.
A mammal of the genus Elephas,
group Proposcidea.

Pearl:

(Laugh)
Still an elephant!
He weighs eighty-fife tons!

Taylor:

Eighty-five tons?

Pearl:

Without a trunk or suitcase!
Last week I needed a white elephant,
so I had him whitewashed.

Taylor:

Whitewashed!

Pearl:

Yes—

It took a hundred men twelve days
to whitewash—

Taylor:

Ridiculous!
Absurd!
Preposterous!
You can't make me believe
you have an elephant
weighing eighty-five tons
that was whitewashed!

Pearl:

WASH you there, Deems?

Taylor:

I *WASH* not!

Pearl:

(Laugh)
I didn't think you did. . . .
While he was being whitewashed,
he backed up and stepped on my foot!

Taylor:

An eighty-five ton elephant
stepped on your foot?

Pearl:

Yes—
And I realized he was
too big a proposition for me.

Taylor:

You had a white elephant on your hands!

Pearl:

Sure—
ON MY *FOOT!*

Oh, did I get so mad!
I picked him up and—

Taylor:

Now hold on, Baron!
You couldn't possibly pick up an elephant.

Pearl:

Didn't I ask you if you was there?

Taylor:

Yes.

Pearl:

And didn't you say you was *not?*

Taylor:

Yes.

Pearl:

SO I PICKED UP THE ELEPHANT!

Taylor:

All right, you picked up the elephant!

Pearl:

And a couple of
hip-o-pots-on-top-oh-the-busses!

Taylor:

And three or four kangaroos,
a few giraffes
and a rhinoceros!

Pearl:

(Laugh)
Always fooling me.

Taylor:

What do you mean, fooling you?

Pearl:

You was there all the time!

Taylor:

Tell me, Baron—
have you any freaks with your circus?

Pearl:

Sure—
from the five corners of the world!

Taylor:

FIVE corners?
There are only four!

Pearl:

(Laugh)
I found a new one!

Taylor:

I suppose you have a two-headed calf,
fat man, fat girl, living skeleton,
bearded lady, Siamese twins—

Pearl:

Only *one* I got.

Taylor:

One Siamese twin?
How come?

Pearl:

They had an argument and split!
And I got fire-eaters, sword swallowers,
and, oh, have I got an India rubber man!

Taylor:

An India rubber man?

Pearl:

The best!
He can stretch his neck out fifteen feet,
his hands twenty feet
and his feet fifty feet!

Taylor:

Hold on, Baron—

Pearl:

You don't believe it?

Taylor:

No—
that's stretching things too far!

Pearl:

Sure—
get the stretcher!

Taylor:

What other freaks have you?

Pearl:

I got a feller what is tattooed all over—
but I won't have him long!

Taylor:

Why not?

Pearl:

He's a marked man!

Taylor:

He's a—
Make that two stretchers!

Pearl:

My feature freak is a talking baboon!

Taylor:

A talking baboon!

Pearl:

Yes—

AND I DON'T MEAN MY COUSIN HUGO!

Taylor:

Let's forget about Hugo.

Pearl:

Sure—

From now on

there will be no more insulting Hugo!

Taylor:

Fine!

Pearl:

Well sir, he was born on the desert.

Taylor:

Hugo?

Pearl:

No—

(Laugh)

The *other* baboon!

Taylor:

The baboon was born on the desert?

Pearl:

Yes!

Taylor:

Where it's barren?

Pearl:

Sure, it's—

Did you call me?

Taylor:

No, I said barren!

Barren—meaning destitute of all things . . .

empty, useless, flat!

Pearl:

(Laugh)

I should get mad at you—

but I'll consider the worcestershire!

Taylor:

The worcestershire?

Pearl:

(Laugh)

The sauce! . . .

The day I ran into the flock of baboons,

they got frightened and ran away.

Taylor:

Let 'em go.

Pearl:

They went!

I followed them to the yungles!

Taylor:

Jungles!

Pearl:

Yungles!

Taylor:

Not yung.

Jung—jung!

Pearl:

Yung—gung—st—

I FOLLOWED THEM TO THE WOODS!

Taylor:

Have it your way.

Pearl:

Zuddenly I saw a horse flying!

He was—

Taylor:

Pardon me, Baron.

Horses don't fly!

Pearl:

You never saw a horse fly?

Taylor:

Never!

Pearl:

(Laugh)

Sometime you must come to my house!

THE GOLDBERGS

T
he Goldbergs was the creation of Gertrude Berg, one of radio's true auteurs. She not only wrote, directed and produced the show but played the leading role of Molly Goldberg, a character she became virtually identified with over the course of her long career.

Under the title *The Rise of the Goldbergs*, the comedy serial made its debut on November 20, 1929, as an unsponsored weekly show sustained by NBC. It had no particular time slot of its own but was scheduled differently from week to week according to the network's programming needs. This was hardly calculated to build an audience, but somehow its listeners managed to keep track of it, and by 1931 it was being broadcast nightly on a regular basis under the sponsorship of Pepsodent Toothpaste. Except for a three-year gap in the mid-'30s, it remained on the air until 1945. In 1948, Mrs. Berg took her characters to the Broadway stage in *Molly and Me*, then in the next few years over to television, back to radio, then on to film in the 1951 feature *Molly*.

The original popularity of *The Goldbergs* probably had something to do with the fractured English spoken by Molly and her husband Jake. As an aural medium, radio was particularly suited to the comic distortions of dialect humor. One is reminded of the early success of such other dialecticians as Freeman Gosden and Charles Correll (Amos and Andy) and Chester Lauch and Norris Goff (Lum and Abner), as well as Jack Pearl.

Yet *The Goldbergs'* unusual longevity, as well as the special affection and esteem in which it was held, suggests that its appeal was grounded on something deeper and more meaningful. What Gertrude Berg offered her audiences was an essentially realistic depiction of the immigrant experience in the United States. The Goldbergs happened to be European Jews transplanted to New York's Lower East Side, but the underlying truth of their lives was recognizable to listeners of all ethnic backgrounds. Mrs. Berg translated the life of her own family into her scripts, and in reading them today one is struck by the authenticity of her perceptions, particularly in respect to the varied impact America had on the different immigrant generations.

Focusing in on the possibilities for economic self-improvement the New World has to offer, Jake Goldberg gives himself over totally to hard work and rises from poor tailor to (at times) prosperous manufacturer. The two children, Rosalie and Sammy, at home in American society in a way their parents can never be, join the Girl and Boy Scouts, correct their parents' English and grudgingly put up with the music lessons that are their mother's symbols of cultural advancement. Presiding over the family is Molly, smoothing over the inevitable tensions between the generations, delighting in the newness of the New World while reaffirming her connections to the Old. Molly is a wonderfully realized character, no doubt the single most important reason for the show's success. If rather too loving and wise for today's more jaded tastes, she is drawn with at least as much accuracy as the satiric caricature of the Jewish mother that has become all too familiar in recent years.

Jake Goldberg was played by James R. Waters, and Rosalie and Sammy by Roslyn Siber and a very young Alfred Ryder. At various times the cast also included such well-known performers as Everett Sloane, Menasha Skulnick, Arnold Stang, Marjorie Main, Joseph Cotton, Keenan Wynn, Minerva Pious, Van Heflin and George Tobias.

Jake, A Businessman (1931)

Molly:

Jake—it's *Shabbes*—

you must go to voik also today?

Jake:

Molly, how many times must I toll you,

I go to beezness,

not to voik.

Molly:

Bot Jake,

don't you alvays tell me

you're voiking hard?

Jake:

Yes, Molly,

bot vhen it's far yourself,

it's beezness.

Molly, I'm a contractor.

I'm a beezness man.

Molly:

Oy, vat beezness!

Saturday, Sonday, holledays.

Plain talking all de time!

Vhy don't you buy a bed

and slip dere and finished!

And dat's beezness?

It's a slavery—
jost like in Oncle Tom's Cabinet!

Rosalie:

Cabin, mama!

Molly:

Ulleright,
let be cabinet.

Jake:

Don't vorry, Molly.
Soch slavery is a pleazure.

Molly:

Bot before you vas a beezness man,
ve used to go out a liddle.
I also knew vat vas going on in de voild.
Far seex monts
ve didn't even go to a moving picture.

Jake:

Who's got de head far such foolishness?
Did you efer!—
moving pictures—
can you emagine vat's laying in her head?

Molly:

Vat's so foolish?
You farget alleready
how you used to lofe de movies, ha?
Don't you remember dot vonderful picture,
Oy, Vot a Fool I Am,
by Ruddy Kipland?

Rosalie:

Ma, you mean *A Fool There Was,*
by Rudyard Kipling.

Sammy:

(Laughs)

Molly:

Let be like you say.
And Jake, de *Ten Commanders*—
dot vas some picture, ha?

Rosalie:

Ten Commandments, ma.

Sammy:

(Laughs again)

Molly:

So let be commandments.

Jake:

Ef you vant to go to a show, Molly,
take Rosie and go.
Do you need me I shall take you?

Molly:

You'll soon become
like a boarder in de house,
slipping and itting, ha?
You got a partner
and you can't even take off
a half-day Saturday, ha?

Jake:

A partner?
Mendel—who is Mendel?
Don't you 'derstand, Molly,
I'm de brains from de foim.
So far as I'm concerned,
he's a silence partner.

Molly:

Vat's dot, a silence partner?

Jake:

A silence partner, Molly, is—

vell, I'll gif you a far instance.

Take de void—

let me see—

take far instance my name, Jake,

J-A-K-E.

De E is silence.

It's dere und it ain't dere—

you don't even hear it at all.

Dot's a silence partner.

Jake could be Jake vidout de E—

get de point?

You 'derstand now?

Vat's de use talkink, Molly,

I'm de whull beezness.

Soon anodder season like dis

und I'll be a menufacturer.

Molly:

Ulleright, ulleright!

Far me is enoff ulleready.

Don't fly too high vid de foist vind, Jake.

Sammy:

Papa, can I have a bicycle for my birthday?

Jake:

A bicycle!

Vat's a *bicycle*?

Ef I'll get de order from Simon and Simon

I'll buy you a *tri*cycle.

Molly:

Batter buy him a good wiolin;

de vun he's got is from soap tickets.

Oy, since you're in de beezness

you didn't even hear Sammy playink.

Oy, Jake, take a liddle pleasure

vid your voik,

Sammy, qvick,

while papa is itting de breakfast,

play for him someding.

(MUSIC: VIOLIN SOLO BEGINS)

Molly:

Jake, open de vindow

and let Mrs. Bloom hear

how is beautiful.

At least ef she ain't got no pleasure

from her own children,

let her take pleasure from ours.

(MUSIC: VIOLIN SOLO ENDS)

Jake:

Ulleright, Sammy, dot's vonderful.

Molly, *you* leesen to de feenish.

T-t-t-t—it's eight o'clock ulleready—

it's late—

Molly:

Jake, it don't take no qvicker

ef you stend up und itt.

Vhipe off your mustache,

it's full of coffee;

you got coffee ull over.

Oy, Jake, you'll maybe get

a noivous breakop, I'm afraid.

Jake:

Molly, I told you last week

to look far rooms uptown;

it don't look good far de boss

of de Mollie Cloik and Soot Company

to leeve here in Pike Strit on de fift floor.

Be sure it's vid a helewator
und cemetrary plombing.
Mendel's brodder is got four rooms
from on Honerd and Nineteent Strit.
De vay he says,
dey most be simple gorgeous.

Molly:

Ulleright, ulleright,
I'll look, I'll look.
Here's your coit.
Remember, Jake,
a fader most not only have a home,
bot a home most have a fader.

Jake:

Don't vorry,
you'll soon have turkey rogs
and flowers in de vinter time
like your brodder Joe.
Vhere's my het, Molly?

Molly:

Sammy, vhere's papa's het?

Sammy:

How should I know?

Molly:

Dot's how you enswer beck?
Go look in de hall!

Jake:

Oy, dot makes me so noivous.
Every day de same ting.
Ef I put my het on de mantelpiece
Vhy do you always take it avay, ha?

Molly:

Vell, Sammy!
Did you find de het?

Sammy:

I don't see it.

Molly:

Look vid your eyes,
you'll find it!

Sammy:

What else am I looking with?

Jake:

Close de fresh mout, Sammy!
One flavor I'll esk you, Molly;
when I'll put de het on de mantelpiece,
leave it on de mantelpiece, please!

Molly:

Ulleright! Ulleright!
Don't get oxcited!

Jake:

Rosie!
Vhat are you stending!
Vhy don't you look for de het?

Molly:

Hold yourself in a liddle!
Don't liv out de temper on de child!

Rosalie:

(Laughs)
Papa, the hat's on your head!

Jake:

(Sheepishly)
Nu, did you efer?

Molly:

Thanks God, ull de oxcitement far notting.

Oy, horry op, horry op;

you're a boss!

Jake:

Good-bye, good-bye!

I'll be in de office overtime.

Don't keep supper far me.

Mr. Finger from Finger und Hendel

is giving me a blowop.

He's got a proposition to talk over.

Good-bye.

(SOUND: DOOR SLAMS)

Molly:

Sammy, now to de wiolin, please.

Sammy:

Ma, can't I practice

when I come home from the scout meeting?

Molly:

No, mine child,

foist de moosic, den de scotch.

Sammy:

Ah, all right!

Come on, Rose,

let's get it over.

Molly:

Let's get it over, ha?

It's like poison to you, ha?

Oy, vait und see when you'll grow op

how vonderful you'll fill

vhen you'll go to a party

und dey'll esk who knows how to play

und dey'll look at you and say,

"Uf course,

Sammy Goldberg und his sister, Rosie."

Ain't dat batter dan you shall fill shamed

und seet in de corner

und be a flower on de vall?

Oy, ef you children vould only know

vat it minns to have a chence in life.

Sammy:

(Growling)

Give me an A.

(SOUND: PIANO KEY TAPPED)

Rosalie:

Here's A.

Anything else?

Takes you a year to tune up.

(MUSIC: VIOLIN AND PIANO PLAYING TOGETHER . . . TUNE ENDS)

Molly:

Rosie, go over to Tante Elke.

She got a letter from Europe,

und I like to know vat's going on at home.

Rosalie:

Tell Sammy to go, ma,

so I can help you wash the dishes.

Sammy:

Ma told you first, didn't she?

I always have to be the goat.

I won't go, mama!

I'm telling you, and that's all!

Molly:

Quiet!

Leesen, Samalla;

ef you had brodders und seesters

und an old mama tousander miles away,

und ef came a letter frum across de hocean,

vouldn't you—

Sammy:

All right, all right.

What am I supposed to do—cry?

You always pull that sob stuff on me

'cause you know I have a soft heart.

But, gee, Rosie, wait till I get you after.

Molly:

Sammy!

Sammy:

But you told her, didn't yuh?

Molly:

Here's your het.

Botton op your neck,

you shouldn't ketch a colt.

Sammy:

Oh, leave me alone.

It's too tight.

Good-bye.

Molly:

You got a handkerchief hair?

Tell Tante Elke to comm over a liddle efter.

Sammy:

All right!

Will you let me go already?

I only hope Tante Elke don't kiss me.

(SOUND: DOOR SLAMS)

22

Molly:

Vot a femely it's becoming!

You fader a boss,

Semmy a boy scotch.

Rosalie, vhat are you?

Rosalie:

I'm a girl scout, and it's wonderful!

You learn so many things!

Molly:

Ah, so? . . .

Maybe you can make someding from me, too.

Rosalie:

Where's the dishrag, ma?

Molly:

Never mind, liv de dishes,

you'll spoil your hends.

Rosalie:

Then I can go now, mama?

Molly:

Yes, vhy not?

Put on your nice coit,

pull op your stockings,

bot be careful,

don't scretch op your new shoes.

Rosalie:

All right, mama, darling!

Don't be lonesome—no? Ha?

Good-bye, I won't be late.

Molly:

Vy should I be longsome?

It's de foist time I'm alone?
Go, darlink, have a good time.

Rosalie:

Good-bye!

Molly:

Good-bye!

(MUSIC BRIDGE)

Molly:

(Calling up the dumbwaiter)
Mrs. Bloom!
Oohoo, Mrs. Bloom!
Mrs. Bloom, vhata matter
you didn't comm op a liddle
lest night efter sopper?
Ha?
I vas tired, too!
How vas de cheeken
you got by Rosen, de butcher?
Mine vas herd like a stone.
Your bargains!
Batter don't look far bargains next time.
Did you get a latter frum Dora
since she got married?
Hm, hm, soch a beautiful goil vat she was,
sooch a chences vat she hed!
Ef ve could only put our heads
on de children's shoulders,
'tvould be a difference sturry to tell. . . .

(SOUND: DOORBELL RINGS)

Molly:

Vait vun minute, Mrs. Bloom,
dot's mine doorbell.
Most be de iceman.

It starts to ring de bell in de morning;
you can go crazy.
(shouts) No ice today, Joe!
Tomorrow!
Oy, yes, like I vas saying, Mrs. Bloom,
don't vorry;
maybe it'll be ulleright.
Ef Dora lofes him so moch
und he lofes her,
vhat else?
He don't make a lifing?
Dey're younk pipple!
Oy, a piece of bleck bread, Mrs. Bloom,
bot only younk!
You know vhat?
I'm beginning to tink dat it's de stroggle
vat put taste in de life.
Believe me, I know.

(SOUND: DOORBELL RINGS)

Molly:

Oy, oy, de doorbell again!
Vun minute, Mrs. Bloom.

Sammy:

Tante Elke said she'd bring the letter herself;
she wants to read it to uncle first.

Molly:

Vhere you ronning, vhere you ronning?
Vait a minute!
It's a fire someplace?

Sammy:

Oh, ma, I'm late, I got to go!
Say, ma, can I have a nickel?

Molly:

Here's ten cents;
buy yourself a malted.

Sammy:

Good-bye, ma!

Molly:

Good-bye, don't ron like a Indian!
No vonder you're skinny like a stick. . . .

(SOUND: DOOR SLAMS)

Molly:

I vas gonna tell you, Mrs. Bloom,
my Jake vants I should mofe optown.
I hesk you, vat vill I do optown?
I'm so used here ulleready.
Op dere it'll be jost like
I came frum de old country—
a greenhorn.
Here I got you, Mrs. Finkelstein
und de grocery lady,
bot he says it don't look nice far him.
He's gonna be a menufecturer soon,
mine Jake.
You should see, Mrs. Bloom,
he makes his own monneh ulleready.
He got a book,
und he writes Jacob Goldberg
on a piece frum paper,
und dat's all—und it's monneh—
real monneh—cash!

(SOUND: DOORBELL RINGS)

Molly:

Excuse me, excuse me,
mine bell is ringing.

Comm op a liddle efter, yes? . . .
(Calling) Who's dat?

Man:

Telephone man,
New York Telephone Company.

Molly:

Vhat?

Man:

I got an order
to put a telephone in your apartment, ma'am.

Molly:

No, you got a mestake, man.

Man:

Is this Goldberg's,
Jacob Goldberg's?

Molly:

Yes, sure, certainly.

Man:

Well, it's for you.

Molly:

(At the dumbwaiter)
Yoo-hoo! Mrs. Bloom!
Comm op qvick!
Is coming by me a telephon!

Man:

Say, lady, I ain't got all day!
Where do you want me to put this?

Molly:

Mr. Telephon Man, I tink
you shall batter put it outside de hull

so de neighbors shouldn't ring too moch
mine bell.

Man:

You should have ordered a booth,
'stead of a private wire.

Molly:

Mr. Telephon Company,
vhere do you put de nickels?

Man:

You don't put in any nickels.

Molly:

In Fishman's drugstore
dey got a regular slots machine. . . .
Oy, dis is a beautiful vun!

Look all de rope!
Ken you emagine,
you put your mout here
und you give talk, "hulloh!"
und right avay it henswers you beck!
Soch a brains vat pipple got!

Man:

Say, don't make me laugh, missus;
I got a split lip!
That's the part you put near your ear.
See, like this.

Molly:

Nu, I bet Mrs. Bloom
vill make a mestake, too.
Dis is a contry full frum supprises!

VIC AND SADE

G ertrude Berg's *The Goldbergs* mirrors the experiences of a generation of immigrants
coming to terms with the new world of possibilities that was America. Berg's theme
is change and the inevitable tensions it gives rise to as new ways rub against the old,
poverty looks to the promise of prosperity and sons and daughters matter-of-factly
enter into the mainstream of American life while parents stand hesitantly to one side, a bit
awed by all this strangeness.

Paul Rhymer's *Vic and Sade* celebrates a different America. It is set not in the dynamic
tenements of New York's Lower East Side but in the placid small town of Crooper, Illinois,
"forty miles from Peoria," where life stays pretty much the same from one day to the next. It
is a quiet, stable, middle-class world, comforting if a little dull in its familiarity and routine.
Vic Gook goes off to his bookkeeper's job at Plant Number 14 of the Consolidated Kitchen-
ware Company. His wife Sade takes care of the house. Their son Rush goes to school and
hangs out with his pals, Bluetooth Johnson and Smelly Clark. The dramatized high points are
a letter from a relative, a phone call with a friend, a neighbor's appendectomy reported in
the evening paper, preparations for the annual Fourth of July picnic.

In Ray Bradbury's words, Rhymer "collected bits and pieces of mediocrity from all our commonplace occupations, all our inane conversations, all our bored afternoons and long evenings where all we could think of to do was trot down to the YMCA to watch the Fat Men Play Handball." Yet out of this humdrum, essentially undramatic material, he was able to fashion one of the undisputed triumphs of radio comedy. "Comedy" is perhaps not the right word. You will find no gags or belly laughs here. What Rhymer gives us is a gentle, affectionate, yet off-center humor springing directly out of the interaction of character and situation. Any potential sentimentality is controlled by his wonderfully original imagination, which penetrates the surreal quirks and eccentricities which, as Sherwood Anderson also knew, underlie the surface blandness of small-town life.

Vic and Sade ran fifteen minutes a day, five days a week, from 1932 to 1944, and Rhymer wrote every word of it. Given the phalanx of idea men, writers, rewriters and polishers it takes to do even a single half-hour situation comedy today, such productivity seems extraordinary. Even more extraordinary is the sustained high quality of Rhymer's work. Broadcast in the afternoon in the midst of the lugubrious procession of soap operas, it was, as Jean Shepherd puts it, "as though *Death of a Salesman* and *Our Town* debuted on a typical Wednesday afternoon between *As the World Turns* and *Against the Storm*, following *The Hollywood Squares*." I don't know about *Death of a Salesman*, but the comparison to *Our Town* seems very much to the point. One thinks also of *Ah, Wilderness!*, *Winesburg, Ohio*, Booth Tarkington's Penrod stories.

Credit must also be given to the four splendid actors whose voices became synonymous with "radio's homefolks" in "the little house halfway up in the next block." Vic was played by Art Van Harvey, a former grain dealer and advertising man. Bernadine Flynn was Sade. Billy Idelson, now a television producer, was the original Rush. In 1940 Clarence Hartzell joined the cast as Uncle Fletcher, till then known only indirectly from his letters to the Gooks and family anecdotes.

Vic and Sade appeared on both NBC and CBS. Its longtime sponsor was Proctor and Gamble's Crisco.

Mr. Dempsey and Mr. Tunney Meet in a Cigar Store   (1932)

Rush:

(Wails from his bedroom)

Sade:

(Waking up)
Vic! Vic!

Vic:

(Wakes up)
What is it, Sade?

Sade:

I heard something.

Vic:

What?

Sade:

I don't know what.
A noise.

Vic:

Aw, you been dreamin' prob'ly.
G'wan back to sleep.

Sade:

Oh, I never can go back to sleep

once I wake up in the middle of the night.

Vic:

Well, I can.

Sade:

I know I heard something.

Vic:

Your imagination.
Wonder what time it is.

Sade:

I don't know.

(SOUND: CLOCK STRIKES ONE)

Vic:

One o'clock.

Sade:

Or half-past something.
I wish I knew.

Vic:

Why?

Sade:

Well, if it's only one o'clock
I know I can go back to sleep
because it's so early.
But if it's later
I'll get the idea there's no use
trying to go back to sleep
it's so late and . . .

Vic:

Aw, I never heard such nonsense.
Now if you'll excuse me

I think I'll just sneak on back to dreamland.
I . . .

Sade:

Please see what time it is first,
won't you, Vic?

Vic:

Aw, why don't ya just figure it's one o'clock
and go back to sleep?
Gosh, I . . .

Sade:

Oh, lean on your elbow
and look at your wristwatch
on the little table.

Vic:

Aw, thunder. . . .
(Raises himself)
It's . . . it's three-thirty.

Sade:

Oh, now I know I'll never go back to sleep.
Wish you hadn't told me what time it was.

Vic:

Well, you asked, Sade.
I'd like to talk all this over with you
a little later . . .
say about daylight.
Right now I'm bein' paged
in the land of dreams and . . .

Rush:

(Wails)

Vic:

Now what?

Sade:

That's what I heard.
It's Rush.

Vic:

Yellin' in his sleep.
Maybe we oughta gag him.

Sade:

Maybe he's sick.

Vic:

Aw, if he was we'd know it quick enough.

Sade:

Better go see, Vic.

Vic:

Aw, Sade . . .
what's the sense in traipsin' around
in the middle of the night?
For Gosh sakes, I . . .

Rush:

(Wails again)

Sade:

Go see, Vic.

Vic:

(Getting up and out)
Oh, all right.
Golly, I wonder
if there's any other poor dub in the world
got a family like mine.
(Calling to Rush)
S'matter, son?

Sade:

(Calling after him)

If he's just talking in his sleep, Vic,
don't wake him up.

Vic:

(Softly)
Oh, Rush, son . . . awake?

Rush:

Yeah, gov.

Vic:

What's the matter?

Rush:

I got a stomach-ache.

Vic:

Stomach-ache, huh?

Rush:

Yeah . . .
hurts awful.

Vic:

Wanta go to the . . .

Rush:

No.
(Moans a little)

Vic:

Well, why don't you try to go to sleep, Rush?

Rush:

I don't want to go to sleep.

Vic:

Why not?

29

Rush:

My sick stomach
makes me have awful bad dreams.
Scary ones.
Gee, gov, I was dreamin' that there was
a great big snake on my neck
and some lions with false teeth in my lap
and . . .

Sade:

(Calling in)
What is it, Vic?

Vic:

(Calls back)
Stomach-ache.

Rush:

Don't tell mom I got a stomach-ache, gov.

Vic:

Why not?

Rush:

'Cause I ate a whole lot of strawberries,
and she *said* I'd get a stomach-ache,
and I said I wouldn't,
and . . .

Sade:

Want *me*?

Vic:

No, Sade.
We'll be all right.
(To Rush)
I won't tell her, son.
You better try goin' back to sleep, boy.
You'll be right as a rivet by mornin'.

Rush:

I'm afraid to go back to sleep, gov.

Vic:

'Fraid of bad dreams, huh?

Rush:

Yeah.
(Moans a little)
Gee, my stomach hurts, gov.
Gov?

Vic:

Yeah, son?

Rush:

Can I come to bed with you 'n mom?

Vic:

What for?

Rush:

I think I could go to sleep
and not dream bad dreams
if I was sleepin' with you 'n mom.

Vic:

Three in a bed's altogether too many, Rush.
Besides, you kick.

Rush:

I won't kick, gov.
I'll be still as anything.
C'mon, let me.
My stomach hurts so.

Vic:

Well . . .

don't want you in here suffering alone, Rush.
We'll see what mom says.

Rush:

I wish you would, gov.
I won't even *stir* if you let me.

Vic:

(Calls)
Sade, Rush wants to come in our bed.

Sade:

In our bed?
Why?

Vic:

Oh, he isn't feeling so hot.
Has bad dreams.
Wants company.

Sade:

Oh, lands.
Well, bring him.

Vic:

C'mon, Rush . . .
get on my back.

Rush:

Gee, you're a sport, gov.

Vic:

(As they go)
You won't think I'm such a sport
if you go to kickin' me in bed.
I'll break you in little pieces.

Sade:

What's the matter, Rush?

Rush:

I ain't feelin' very well, mom.
My . . . my elbow . . .

Sade:

Elbow nothing!
That box of strawberries . . .
Well, guess there's no use rubbing it in
about that box of strawberries.
If you're sick, you've learned your lesson.

Vic:

Move over, Sade.
I'll dump this bag of uselessness
in the middle.

Sade:

Now you gotta lie quiet, Rush.
Gov and mom've got to go to sleep.

Rush:

I will, mom.

Sade:

Ooh, your feet are cold, Rush.
Get 'em over.

Rush:

Wanta get 'em warm, mom.

Sade:

Well, wait till gov comes back
and use *his* feet for a stove.
(Calling)
Oh, Vic,
while you're in the bathroom,
get those pills. . . .

Rush:

Aw, mom.

Sade:

Get those pills on the top shelf
and a glass of water.
D'ya hear, Vic?

Vic:

(From bathroom)
Yeah.
The pink pills?

Sade:

Yes.
Two.

Vic:

Okay.

Rush:

Aw, mom, I don't want no pills.
It's my elbow. . . .

Sade:

Elbow nothing.
Listen, child,
you just be quiet about that sick elbow
and I'll not say a single word
about that box of strawberries.

Rush:

Gosh, mom, my stomach.
(Moans)

Sade:

Well, as soon as you've taken your pills
you go to sleep.

Vic:

(Comes in)
Here y'are, son.
Two snappy delicious pink pills.
Just the thing for the stomach-ache.

Rush:

Aw, I . . .

Sade:

Take 'em, Rush,
or back to your own bed you go.
Take 'em.

Vic:

And don't spill any water
on my side of the bed.

Rush:

Aw . . .
(Takes pills)
Nasty!
Gimme the water.

Vic:

Here it is.
Be careful now.
(Rush drinks)
Gimme back the glass.

Sade:

You'll feel lots better in the morning.

Rush:

Gee, them pills are awful.
Rather have the stomach-ache a darn sight.

Vic:

Now mooch over.

There's another party got a reservation
in this bed.
And that party's *me*.

Rush:

Can *you* move over a little, mom?

Sade:

No, I can't.

Vic:

(Crawling in)
Rush, get your feet over.

Rush:

Mom, get *your* feet over.

Vic:

Well, here we are.
And I gotta get some sleep.
Of course it's a great pleasure
to be in bed with so many dear old friends,
but I'm in favor of
cutting out jolly conversation
and settlin' down to some good old shut-eye.

Sade:

Me too.
Rush, stop wiggling.

Rush:

(Moans a little)
My stomach hurts.

Vic:

Rush, you said you'd be quiet
if we let you come in bed with us.

Sade:

He can't help it if he's suffering, can he?

Vic:

No, I s'pose not.
Try to lie still, Rush, will ya?

Rush:

Yeah, gov.
I'm going right to sleep.

(Little pause)

Vic:

(Grunts suddenly)
Aw, I knew you'd begin to *kick*.
Listen, I'm gonna go sleep in the little bed.

Rush:

It's too short for you, gov.
Your feet'll stick out the end.

Vic:

Anything's better'n this.

Rush:

Aw, don't go, gov.

Vic:

But I got to get some sleep, Rush.
Work in the morning.

Sade:

That's right, Rush.
You better let gov go sleep in your bed.

Rush:

Gov, if you'd tell me a little story—

just a little one—
I'd go to sleep and never *budge* till tomorrow.

Vic:

I should be telling stories
at pretty near four o'clock in the morning?

Rush:

Please, gov.

Sade:

Go on, Vic.
Maybe it would put me to sleep, too.

Vic:

Well, what'll I tell about?

Rush:

Tell about one of your funny dreams.

Vic:

I'd like to be *having* a funny dream . . .
'stead of entertainin' my family
in the middle of the night.

Sade:

Go on, Vic.

Vic:

Well, lemme see.
Well, the other night I was dreamin'
that I was going to a party
and I wore Mis' Fisher's nightshirt,
only it had wheels on it,
and I took a bobsled
and hitched it onto Mr. Bucksaddle
and we got to going so fast
Mr. Bucksaddle couldn't stop
and . . .

Rush:

You oughta of put a *brake* on the bobsled,
gov.

Sade:

Or one on Mr. Bucksaddle.

Vic:

Listen, who's telling about this dream?
You two go to sleep instead of buttin' in.
Well, when we got to the party
I found out the party wasn't a party at all
but a funeral.
Well sir, they wanted to have the funeral
but they didn't have any corpse handy
so I volunteered.

Rush:

Why didn't you use Mr. Bucksaddle?
He'd make a nice corpse.

Sade:

(Giggling)
Aw, Rush.

Vic:

Listen, I quit.
I'm going to sleep.

Sade:

Go on with the story, Vic.
We'll be still.

Rush:

Yeah, gov.
While you were telling about your dream
I forgot all about my stomach.
Didn't hurt a bit.
Hurts *now*, though.
(Moans a little)

Vic:

Nope, I'm through storytellin'.
I'm going to sleep.
Let mom tell you a story.

Rush:

Will ya, mom?

Sade:

Will you promise to go to sleep if I do?

Rush:

Yes.

Sade:

All right, then.
But first, get your foot away.

Vic:

Has he got a foot stabbin' you too?
Rush, get your feet in the middle of the bed.

Rush:

All right, gov.
Tell me the story, mom.

Sade:

Well, one time there were three bears:
a big bear, a middle-sized bear and . . .

Rush:

I know that story.

Sade:

Well, let's see.
How's this?
Once upon a time
there was a beautiful princess
and she . . .

Rush:

Is this the one where she went to sleep
and didn't wake up for fifty years?

Sade:

Yes.
Gee, you've heard all my stories.

Vic:

I wish to thunder *I* was a beautiful princess
and could go to sleep for fifty years.
Let's cut out the storytellin' and be quiet.
You can go to sleep if you try, Rush.

Rush:

No, I can't.

Sade:

Try, Rush.

Rush:

I did try.
Hey, I bet I know how I could go to sleep.

Vic:

How! . . . for goodness' sake!

Rush:

Well, both of you tell a story
at the same time.
Gov, you can be somebody,
and mom, *you* can be somebody.
And talk back and forth.

Vic:

No soap, son.
Mom and me
ain't puttin' on no three-act plays
at this time of night.

Rush:

Aw, please.

I know who you could be.

Sade:

Who, Rush?

Rush:

Well, mom, you could be Jack Dempsey.

Sade:

Jack Dempsey, huh?

Rush:

Yes.

And gov can be Gene Tunney.

Vic:

Want us to put on a six-round battle

right here in bed, huh?

Nonsense.

Go to sleep, and no more foolishness.

Rush:

Aw, please.

Listen . . .

mom, you're Jack Dempsey, see.

And you meet Gene Tunney—

that's gov—

in a cigar store.

And he accidentally steps on your foot,

and . . .

Vic:

Have a heart, son.

I got to go to work in the morning.

Sade:

Let's do it, Vic.

We might as well do that

as lie here bawling each other out.

C'mon.

I'm Jack Dempsey and you're Gene Tunney:

Rush:

And ya just met in a cigar store

and Gene Tunney accidentally

steps on Jack Dempsey's foot.

Vic:

Aw, criminy.

Who'm I?

Sade:

You're Gene Tunney.

And you accidentally step on my foot.

We're in a cigar store.

(Chuckles)

Vic:

All right.

'Morning, Mr. Dempsey.

Sade:

Good morning, Mr. Tunney.

Get off my foot.

(Giggles)

Rush:

(Laughs)

Vic:

I ain't on your foot, Mr. Dempsey.

Sade:

You are, too.

Look, Mr. Tunney.

Vic:

Well, gosh, Mr. Dempsey,

I'm awful sorry.

I . . .

Rush:

Aw, gov.

Gene Tunney's an awful tough fella.

He wouldn't apologize

for stepping on somebody's foot.

Vic:

Well, what if I *am* on your foot, Dempsey.

Don't ya like it?

Sade:

No, I don't like it.

I think I'll give you a hit in the face.

Rush:

Aw, mom,

Jack Dempsey wouldn't say that.

He'd say "a sock on the beezer."

Sade:

No, I don't like it.

I think I'll give you a sock on the beezer.

Vic:

Oh, yeah?

Well, looka here, Dempsey,

I got half a notion

to lay one up-side your jaw.

Sade:

You just try it, Gene Tunney,

and I'll give you a biff on the snoot.

Rush:

(Laughs)

That's it, mom, that's it!

Vic:

Now, is this putting you to sleep or isn't it?

Rush:

Sure, sure.

I'm almost asleep.

Vic:

You were never wider awake in your life.

I'm quittin' this stuff.

You just have to round yourself up

another Gene Tunney.

Sade:

You're *not* going to sleep, Rush.

Rush:

Aw, please be Jack Dempsey

and Gene Tunney

a little while longer.

I'll go to sleep in no time.

Vic:

Listen, Rush,

if you'll promise not to open your trap

till the clock strikes four . . .

not say a single word . . .

we'll go on with this.

Do you promise?

Rush:

Yes, gov.

Vic:

All right, then . . .

not another word.
Aw . . . Mr. Dempsey.

Sade:

Yes, Mr. Tunney.

Vic:

I think I'll smash you in the jaw.

Sade:

You just try it
and see what you get, Mr. Tunney.

Vic:

Aw, what'll I get, ya flathead?

Sade:

You'll get a smack in the coco,
that's what you'll get.

Vic:

(Lowering his voice somnolently)
Say, Mr. Dempsey.

Sade:

I don't want none of your lip, Mr. Tunney.

Vic:

Mr. Dempsey,
I was down by the stockyards the other day
and I saw some sheep.

Sade:

Is that so, Mr. Tunney?

Vic:

Yes, Mr. Dempsey.
They were coming out of a barn

one at a time.
First I saw *one* sheep.

Sade: *(Giggling)*
Uh-huh, Mr. Tunney.
And then I bet you saw *two* sheep.

Vic:
Uh-huh.
And three sheep.

(Softly and slowly)

Sade:
And four sheep.

Vic:
And five sheep.

Sade:
And six sheep.

Vic:
And seven sheep.

Sade:
And eight sheep.

Vic:
And nine sheep.

Sade:
And ten sheep.

Vic:
And eleven . . .

Rush:
(Sighs deeply)

Vic:

And eleven sheep.

Sade:

And twelve sheep.

Vic:

And thirteen sheep.

Sade:

And fourteen sheep.

Vic:

And fifteen . . . sh.
(Giggles)

Sade:

(Whispering)
Is he asleep?

Vic:

Dead to the world.

Sade:

Good night, Mr. Tunney.

Vic:

Night, Mr. Dempsey.

(SOUND: CLOCK STRIKES FOUR TIMES)

GEORGE BURNS AND GRACIE ALLEN

By the time George Burns and Gracie Allen made their first radio appearance, they were already veteran vaudevillians. Not that they were really that old. Gracie was already working on the stage by the time she was three as part of her father's song-and-dance act. Burns had also been a child entertainer, singing in saloons as one-quarter of the Peewee Quartet. They began working together in 1922, when she was seventeen and he was twenty-four, and married four years later. At the beginning of the partnership, Gracie was the straight man and Burns told the jokes; but since Gracie was the one who seemed to get most of the laughs, they soon exchanged roles, setting the basic format for a joint career that lasted until 1964, the year of Gracie's death.

Burns and Allen were vaudeville headliners by 1930, the year they made their radio debuts on the BBC while vacationing in London. The next year they did their first radio broadcast together in the United States on Rudy Vallee's *Fleischmann Hour*. Vallee had a formidable record as a discoverer of talent for the new medium. Other performers he helped establish through exposure on his show include Alice Faye, Milton Berle, Phil Baker, Joe Penner, Bob Burns and Edgar Bergen. In 1932 Burns and Allen began their own half-hour comedy-variety series with Guy Lombardo, *The Robert Burns Panatela Program*. They continued in radio for various sponsors on both the CBS and NBC networks until 1949, when they made a successful transition to television.

Throughout the years, the main appeal of their shows was Gracie's giddy, fast-talking, scatterbrained characterization. Burns largely limited himself to setting up Gracie's malapropisms and non sequiturs, a job his peerless timing enabled him to do brilliantly. He was perhaps the best straight man in the business, as well as a splendid comedian in his own right, as became apparent when he took up a solo career after his wife's death. Curiously, although Gracie was the acknowledged star of the show, she seemed to have little interest in it off-microphone. Burns was the one who supervised the writing, saw to it that the high quality was maintained, and established the program's overall direction. When it temporarily lost its audience in the early 1940s, Burns correctly analyzed the problem: the jokes no longer reflected their actual ages. The necessary changes were made to show them as the middle-aged married couple they were, and they once again resumed their usual high ratings.

Burns and Allen made particularly effective use of the running joke. One of the earliest and most elaborate was Gracie's search for her "missing" brother. According to Frank Buxton and Bill Owen in *The Big Broadcast*, it was essentially a CBS publicity gimmick to help build the audience for the show with Lombardo, and it worked spectacularly well. Gracie's search led her to pop up unannounced in the middle of all sorts of other programs on the network and culminated in an appearance with Rudy Vallee on his NBC series. The rival network was so incensed by the free publicity the visit generated for its CBS competition that it pulled Vallee off the air, which of course only generated further publicity. Other running gags included Gracie's stories about her seemingly endless number of relatives, her infatuation (to George's predictable discomfort) with matinee idol Charles Boyer and her inexplicable enthusiasm for her husband's singing. Their long-standing theme song, "Love Nest," as well as Burns's familiar sign-off, "Say good night, Gracie," added to their audience's pleasure of recognition.

The show was also notable for its particularly strong cast of supporting players. At various times George and Gracie were joined by the ubiquitous Mel Blanc as the sad-voiced Happy Postman; Gale Gordon; Hans Conried; bandleaders Ray Noble and Meredith Willson, both of whom had a good way with comic dialogue; and announcers Ted Husing, Harry Von Zell, Jimmy Wallington and Bill Goodwin. At one point their director was Ed Gardner, who later went on to star as Archie in his own series, *Duffy's Tavern*.

Gracie's Anniversary Gift to Guy Lombardo (1933)

Gracie:

Now, listen, Sargie,

I could do this by myself

if Guy Lombardo and George Burns

were here to help me.

But they're not here,

so I guess I'll have to do it by myself.

Sergeant:

Listen, lady, I'll do anything you want . . .

but first put that gun down!

It's loaded!

Gracie:

Certainly!

Hello, George;
hello, Guy.
Isn't Sargie Jones silly!

George:

What's going on here?

Guy:

Gracie, this marine doesn't happen to be
your missing brother?

Gracie:

Oh, there you go!
This big fraidy cat is scared
just because I'm pointing
a loaded gun at him,
and anybody knows
you can't be hurt with a loaded gun!

Guy:

You can't be hurt with a loaded gun?

Gracie:

Certainly!
I read that General Pershing said:
"More men are killed
with empty guns every year
than with loaded guns!"

George:

Gracie, give me the gun . . .
and what is all this about?

Sergeant:

Thanks!
I'm Sergeant Jones of the U.S. Marine Corps
and I know this must look silly for you
to find me here being held up
by this little girl . . .

and if this ever gets out,
I might as well quit the Corps.
I'll never live it down!

George:

Now wait a minute.
This is Guy Lombardo.
I'm George Burns.
We've had a little trouble, too!
What happened and how did you get here?

Sergeant:

I was standing in front of the recruiting tent
and I heard a scream.
"Help! Help!"
And you know the marines
are always the first to fight . . .
so I looked around
and this lady said,
"Quick, follow me!"

Guy:

Gracie, was somebody bothering you
that you needed help?

Gracie:

No, George told me to do it!

George:

Told you to do what, Gracie?

Gracie:

When I told you I was going to write a book
for Guy Lombardo . . .
you told me to tell it to the marines.
And I couldn't talk to him
on a windy street corner!

George:

I see! . . .
So you brought him home.
Listen, Gracie,
"tell it to the marines"
is just an expression.
It means, don't bother me,
tell it to somebody else.

Gracie:

I'll be glad to!
Listen, Guy,
I'm writing a book
for your Canadian Anniversary!

Guy:

Canadian Anniversary?

Gracie:

Well, of course, maybe in Canada
they don't use books in their anniversaries,
but I don't know how
anybody can learn anything
in an anniversary that hasn't got a book.

George:

An anniversary that hasn't got a book?

Gracie:

Well, you don't think my brother went to
the Anniversary of Southern California
for nothing, do you?

George:

Guy, next year you'll be celebrating
your fifth university.

Guy:

Gracie, do you mean to say
your brother actually went through college?

Gracie:

How do you think he got to be worth
fifty thousand dollars
if he didn't go through college?
He went through Southern California.

George:

I know . . .
he came out with three gold watches
and about three hundred dollars in cash.

Gracie:

That's when he went through
public school . . .
but when he went through college . . .

George:

Don't bother with it.

Gracie:

Oh, there you go!
Really, George, my brother went to college.
And now he's worth fifty thousand dollars.
You see, he heard they had a man there
who taught you how to play football . . .

Guy:

You mean the coach.

Gracie:

Well, if you want to change the subject. . . .
Anyway, my brother heard
this man who teaches football
was worth forty thousand dollars. . . .

George:

Do you mean to say
your brother went to college
to take football?

Gracie:

Why should he take the football?
He took the man who teaches it.
And now my brother's worth
thirty thousand dollars in California.
And Oklahoma is offering
ten thousand dollars for him.
And in Texas he's worth
three thousand dollars. . . .
But we're going to give him to Oklahoma—
that'll be a seven-thousand-dollar profit to us
and a ten-thousand-dollar loss to Oklahoma,
which will teach Texas a good lesson. . . .
Don't you think so?

George:

I think so.

Guy:

Listen, George,
I've really got an important date.
I, for one, have to go.

Sergeant:

I have to go, too!

George:

And I have to go three!

Gracie:

One, two, three . . .
I'm always last.
Well, I guess I'll go four.
I don't know what I'm going for.
But I'll go four.

George:

Whatever you're going for—
go for days or go for years.

But no matter what you're going for . . .
we'll stay.

Gracie:

Well, I don't know what game you're playing
but if you're coaxing me to stay,
I'll stay.

George:

Guy, I think we were better
off with that book!

Gracie:

Oh, yes, that book, Guy.
As long as I'm going to write a book for you,
I'd like to write one you like.
Now . . .
do you like a book with a lot of people in it
or do you like a book
with only just a few people in it?
Or do you like a book?

Guy:

Well, that depends on the story, Gracie.

Gracie:

Well, I'm reading a book now
with so many people in it
that I can't keep track of the story.

Guy:

What's the name of the book?

Gracie:

It's that new book,
the Suburban Telephone Directory.

George:

Gracie, forget the whole thing.
I just dropped in to ask you a question.

Gracie:

I wouldn't do that, George.
My uncle asked a question once
and the police came and got him.

George:

Don't be silly!
They can't arrest a man
for asking a question.

Gracie:

Well, you see, he was a stranger.

George:

Who . . . your uncle?

Gracie:

No . . . the man who lost his watch.

George:

A man lost his watch?

Gracie:

Yeah . . .
my uncle asked the man what time it was
and his watch disappeared.

George:

His watch disappeared?

Gracie:

And the policeman
turned out to be a magician.

Guy:

What policeman turned out to be a magician?

Gracie:

The policeman that came

and made my uncle disappear.
We haven't seen him for six months.

George:

Forget the whole thing, Gracie!
As long as Guy is here
there's no use making any secret of it.
Let's do something for his anniversary.
And an anniversary is not a college.
It's a birthday.
You know what a birthday is.

Gracie:

My little baby sister
just had a birthday in December
and we named her after Christmas.

George:

Yeah, I know.
You named your sister after Christmas—
Mary Christmas!

Gracie:

Mary Christmas?
You're silly.
What would that mean?
We waited until after Christmas
to name my little baby sister
because we wanted to see
what presents would come in.

Guy:

But, Gracie . . .
how did the people know
what name to put on the presents?

Gracie:

We don't know how they knew.
That's what's so marvelous.
The family sent in a lot of little towels

45

and knives and forks
and a few plates . . .

George:

Well, what's unusual about that?

Gracie:

Well, it said on the presents . . . Hotel Statler
So we named the baby Hotel Statler Allen.

George:

But Gracie, don't you know
there's a Hotel Statler in Buffalo
and there's a Hotel Statler in Cleveland
and there's a Hotel Statler in Detroit . . .

Gracie:

Well, it can't be my little baby sister
because I've been home
ever since she was born
and if she's gone to any of those places
she'd have sent us a postcard.

George:

I wish you'd go someplace
and never send me a postcard
and never come back.

Gracie:

Oh, George,
I'll bet you tell that to all the girls!

Guy:

Really, George, I for one have got to go.

Sergeant:

I've got to go, too.

Gracie:

And George has to go three
and I have to go four.

George:

Guy, you started that.
Now listen, Gracie,
Guy is going to have an anniversary
and anniversaries are celebrated
the same way we celebrate Christmas.

Gracie:

Christmas—
well, believe me,
I'm never going to do that again.
Catch me hanging up my stocking again!

Guy:

Why, Gracie,
didn't you get anything last year?

Gracie:

I should say I did!
I got a backache that I had for three weeks
and a pain in the neck
and a twisted ankle.

George:

You got a backache,
a pain in the neck and a twisted ankle
from hanging up your stocking?

Gracie:

Yeah, I forgot to take it off.

Guy:

Well, George, I for one have got to go.

Gracie:

I'll go two.
I'm not going to go fourth again.

George:

Gracie, you go two and three
and I'll go fourth
and never come back!

Gracie:

Then I'll go two!

George:

Oh, all right, Gracie.
You've got to do more for Guy's anniversary
than write a book.
What do you know about books?

Gracie:

Well, I've written a dime novel.

George:

A dime novel?

Gracie:

Yeah!
And when I've written nine more
I'll get a dollar.

George:

But Gracie, Guy gave us a lovely present
for Christmas.
Don't you remember that fancy box
all tied up with
holly ribbon and sealing wax?

Gracie:

Oh there you go.
Ceiling wax.
Who ever heard of ceiling wax?
It's floor wax.
Nobody waxes the ceiling.

George:

All right, Gracie,
floor wax, ceiling wax, beeswax . . .
what do I care!

Gracie:

Well, we care about beeswax.
Once we kept a bee for six years
and it didn't give a bit of wax.

Guy:

Really, George, I've got to go.
I'm very busy.
I've got to . . . ah . . .
I've got to buy some candles for my
anniversary cake.

Gracie:

Well, if you're going to have a cake
made out of candles . . .

George:

Gracie . . .
putting candles on an anniversary cake
is a ceremony.
Like hanging holly at Christmas.
Don't you hang holly at Christmas?

Gracie:

Why should we hang holly
when my brother's been hanging
for twenty years?

George:

Your brother's been hanging
for twenty years?

Gracie:

Yeah.

Hanging around poolrooms.
But we think he'll come home soon.

George:

Well . . . that'll be nice!
What are you planning to do
when your brother comes home?

Gracie:

My father is going to help my brother
comb his hair.

Guy:

Comb his hair?

Gracie:

Yeah.
I heard my father say,
"When that brother of yours comes home
from the poolroom
I'm going to take one of his cues
and part his hair with it."

Guy:

Gracie, it looks pretty bad for your brother.
Your father must be a pretty hotheaded man.
Has he got red hair?

Gracie:

We don't know.
He never takes his toupee off.

George:

Let me talk to her, Guy!
Gracie, let's stop all this silly talk
about Guy's anniversary.
Capturing marines . . .
writing books . . .
parting your brother's hair.

That isn't what people do for anniversaries.
They give presents.
And I've got one for Guy.

Gracie:

Well, why didn't you say that?
I've got one for Guy, too!

George:

What is it?

Gracie:

What is it that hangs from a ceiling
and whistles?

George:

I don't know!

Gracie:

A herring!

George:

Gracie, a herring
doesn't hang from the ceiling
and it doesn't whistle.

Gracie:

Well, is that my fault?

Sergeant:

Hands up!
Stand where you are!
Don't move!
Or I promise I'll shoot.
I can't stand any more of this.
I've got to get out of here!
Stand back from that door.
I'll get out if I have to kill all three of you!

Gracie:

Wait a minute, Sargie . . .
you wouldn't go
without your mother's picture!

George:

His mother's picture?

Gracie:

Yeah . . .
here it is right in the back of his wallet!

Guy:

George, quick!
Get some water for the sergeant.
I think he's fainted.

George:

All right, Guy . . .

MILTON BERLE

Milton Berle achieved his greatest success not on radio but on television as the presiding comic spirit of the *Texaco Star Theater*. The show went on the air in 1949, and from the beginning the response to Berle was extraordinary. Every Tuesday evening at eight, America dropped whatever else it was doing to tune in on the special brand of madness presented by this brash, manic, try-anything-for-a-laugh entertainer.

Though television brought him his fullest national fame, Berle had been a successful performer from the time he was a small child and appeared as a kiddie actor in silent films. During the 1930s and '40s he starred as a stand-up comic in vaudeville and nightclubs and acted in a number of Hollywood movies. The one medium he did not work in, contrary to common belief based on his love of slapstick, was burlesque.

Berle first appeared on radio in 1934, when he was twenty-six years old. Between 1934 and 1949 he was a regular on at least six different shows. These included the *Gillette Original Community Sing* excerpted here, *Stop Me If You've Heard This One*, *Let Yourself Go*, and *The Milton Berle Show*. Each tried out a different format, and none lasted for much more than a year. As

Berle himself acknowledges in his recent autobiography, he was primarily a visual performer, and radio was probably not the best setting for his talents. Certainly he never meshed with the medium with the force of a Jack Benny or Bob Hope. Yet on the evidence of surviving scripts and tapes, he was very good indeed, demonstrating the same zany comic virtues that made him such a wonderfully effective entertainer on television. Curiously, our experience of Berle on television may actually enhance our appreciation of his earlier work on radio. Through our imaginations, we can fill in the visual goofiness, knockabout and mugging that are impossible to communicate through sound alone.

Berle the Athlete with Wendell Hall, Dan Seymour, and Eileen Barton as Jolly (1936)

Hall:

And here he is once more . . .
your favorite funnyman—
MILTON BERLE!

Berle:

Thank you, Wendell. . . .
The whole world
seemed to be singing with us
on that last chorus.
Everybody seemed to be in tune
except one fellow in a fishing boat
down in Florida.
He was OFF KEY—WEST!

Ooh!
Why did I TAMPA with that joke?

Really, this singing
puts me in a sentimental mood.
You know, during that last song
I was touched.
Really, Dan Seymour touched me
for five dollars!

Folks, if I sound a little tired tonight
it's because I got to bed rather late.

Wendell Hall and I were out last night.
We had a lot of fun.
We went to the Paradise Restaurant.
There's a restaurant.
They've got three waiters to each table.
One gives you the check . . .
and the other two revive you!

It was so late
I didn't want to go uptown.
So Wendell invited me to sleep at his home.
He said, "Milton, you sleep with me
and you'll be purty comfortable.
It's a feather bed."
So at two o'clock in the morning I woke him.
I said, "Move over, Wendell.
It's my turn to sleep on the feather!"

The funniest experience I ever had
with sleeping . . .
Huh, I gotta tell you this. . . .
I checked into the same hotel
that Frank Buck lives in.
And during the night
one of his pet baboons
came into my room.
So I called down to the clerk.

51

I said, "Clerk, there's a baboon in my room."
So the clerk said,
"He'll have to come down and register!"

Seymour:
Well, Milton . . .
did you register?

Berle:
Haha, that was Dan Seymour . . .
an announcer with a great following.

Seymour:
Right, Milton . . .

Berle:
A wonderful following:
three sheriffs . . .
a house detective . . .
and the finance company!

Danny, why do you hound me?
Here I am . . .
working my head to the bone—
I mean my fingers!
Why, I've been working so hard . . .
my *mother's* tired!

(PLANTED APPLAUSE)

Thanks, Mom!
Mom was right on cue . . .
just the way we rehearsed it!

Seymour:
(Laughs)
Yes sir, Milton.
You've certainly got to hand it
to your mother!

Berle:
You're darn right.
And after I hand it to her . . .
huh . . . she deposits it!

Seymour:
You hope!

Berle:
But, Danny . . .
you're not insinuating
that I am a momma's boy!

Seymour:
I should say you're not a momma's boy . . .

Berle:
You're darn right. . . .

Seymour:
(Mutters)
You sissy!

Berle:
(Dopey voice)
You big bully!
You—you—you—

Seymour & Berle:
(Singing)
"You!
Gee, but you're wonderful!
You!"

Hall:
Milton, you're crazy.

Berle:
I'm crazy?
Maybe I am.

After all,

this is a coast-to-coast nutwork!

(crying)

Always picking on me. . . .

You'll be sorry, you fellows. . . .

Seymour:

Who'll be sorry?

Berle:

You'll be!

You know what Abraham Lincoln said:

He said—he said—he said—

Seymour:

(Whispers)

Berle . . .

what Abraham Lincoln said

is on the next page!

Berle:

(Whispers)

Thanks, bud.

Abraham Lincoln said:

You can fool some of the people

some of the time,

and you can fool some of the people

some of the time.

But some of the people—WATCH OUT!

And not only that . . .

I'm not clowning now. . . .

When Harry Richman and Dick Merrill

were forced down in their airplane

in Newfoundland . . .

who did they send for to help them?

WHO? . . . WHO?

Seymour:

Eddie Rickenbacker!

Berle:

Right!—

No, they sent for Berle!

When Richman and Merrill

were forced down,

they sent for me.

Seymour:

Well, they were smart, sending for *you.*

Berle:

I'll say they were smart.

Seymour:

Sure, they needed some extra gas!

Berle:

That was a wow!

That was a scream!

You know something, Seymour?

You'd make a *wonderful* stranger!

You're talking to the all-American Berle.

Take those rough-and-ready sports.

Take wrestling, for instance.

Take marathon running.

Take football.

Take hockey.

You take them!

I'll take checkers.

As a matter of fact,

most of the actors I know

are interested in sports—

they're athletic.

Rudy Vallee . . .

huh . . . Rudy Vallee plays with the *Yankees*!
Phil Baker . . . he's known for his good *Gulf*!
Major Bowes . . . he has wonderful *amateur*
standing!
Joe Penner . . . world's greatest *duck* hunter!
Greta Garbo has two great *feats* to her credit!
Jack Benny's been running for five years . . .
and nobody can *touch* him!
And last . . . but certainly not least . . .
poor Eddie Cantor.
Cantor spends most of his life outdoors
and he still can't get the *sun*!
They're all athletic!
See you later!

(*AUDIENCE SINGS THREE SONGS*)

Berle:

Thank you, Wendell.
(*Laughs*)
Y'know, as I was saying a few minutes ago
before I was interrupted
by twenty or thirty millions of people
who suddenly started to sing . . .
athletics are really great for you!
And to be a top-notch athlete
I found out that you've got to eat
the three most important foods.
The three most important foods. . . .
Breakfast. . . .
Lunch. . . .
And dinner!

Seymour:

(*Laughing*)
Berle . . . the athlete.
Any great athletes in your family?

Berle:

Are there?
Danny, you take my brother—

Seymour:

Who needs him?
We've got a dog!

Berle:

I mean my brother's a terrific swimmer!
He should be a great swimmer.
He's had enough practice. . . .
He used to be an ambulance chaser
in Venice!

I had a terrible ordeal the other day
while I was swimming.
A man was drowning.
I swam out to him . . .
struggled with him for three hours,
and finally I brought him to shore.

Seymour:

Wonderful, Milton.

Berle:

It was nothing.
I shouldn't have had to struggle.
All I should have done
was throw him a Gillette razor.
You know why, Danny?

Seymour:

Certainly.
Because a Gillette razor
is a life shaver!

Berle:

Yeah—huh?

(Whispers)

Danny, there's something wrong here.
It says in the script
that I was supposed to take that line.

Seymour:

Pardon me, Milton.
Go ahead—you take it.
No hard feelings.

Berle:

Okay.
Ready?
*Because a Gillette razor
is a life shaver!*

*(COMPLETE SILENCE IN THE
AUDIENCE)*

*Because a Gillette razor
is a life shaver. . . .
Because . . .*

Seymour:

Milton.

Berle:

Yes?

Seymour:

It was funnier when I said it.

Berle:

Oh yeah, you're a wow!
You're a scream!
I like this program.
It's so peaceful . . .
so *jolly!*

Jolly:

Hello!

Berle:

Things were bad before,
but now—
Oh, it's Jolly,
the sponsor's daughter!

(APPLAUSE)

Seymour:

Now, Milton, be careful.
Don't say the wrong thing.
You know what happened last Sunday.

Berle:

You said it. . . .
I opened my mouth and put my foot in it!
Now, Jolly—no trouble with you tonight!
I'm not in the mood.

Jolly:

What's the matter Mr. Berle?

Berle:

Nothing—
except this morning
I woke up with an awful grouch!

Jolly:

Oh?
You sleep with your twin brother?

Berle:

Jolly, let's have a truce.
If you leave me alone I'll be nice to you.
What can I do to make you laugh?

Jolly:

Tune in Fred Allen!

Berle:

Jolly, *why* did you come here?

Jolly:

My daddy sent me!

Berle:

I knew it!

It's a frame-up!

Jolly:

My daddy said I should ask you

for your autograph.

Berle:

My autograph?

Sure!

With pleasure . . .

Jolly:

No . . . with this pen.

Would you please write in this book?

Berle:

Okay—let's have the pen.

(SOUND: SCRATCHING NOISES)

Berle:

Where did you get this pen . . .

in the post office?

There you are . . .

my signature . . .

Milton Berle.

Jolly:

HOORAY!

I *WIN!* I *WIN!*

Berle:

What do you mean . . . you win?

You win what?

Jolly:

Well—my daddy bet me a lollipop

that you couldn't write!

Berle:

Well, I'm glad you won the lollipop.

That was a sucker bet!

That's a wow!

Your daddy said I can't write.

Jolly:

Well—that's what my daddy said.

Berle:

You know, Jolly—

if ANYBODY ELSE said I couldn't write—

I might resent it.

But if YOUR DADDY says it—

I think it's witty!

I think it's clever!

Jolly:

You'd better!

My daddy's the sponsor!

Berle:

(Crying)

Some treatment I get.

All abuse!

There are *some* people

who think I'm something!
In fact, Jolly—
there is one young fellow on
this program who's popular.
A fellow who *grows on people.*
GROWS ON PEOPLE. . . .
Who do I mean?

Jolly:

HARE!

Berle:

Yeah—Ernie HARE . . . NO!
I'M THE POPULAR GUY.
I grow on people.

Jolly:

That's right . . . my daddy told me.

Berle:

Oh, your daddy *knows I grow* on people?

Jolly:

Yeah—
he said you're a WART!

Berle:

(Laughs)
Well . . . who cares what your daddy says?

Jolly:

You do.

Berle:

WHY?

Jolly & Berle:

MY DADDY'S THE SPONSOR!

Berle:

Good-bye . . . Jolly. . . .

(APPLAUSE)

THE MARX BROTHERS

G roucho Marx was the longest-delayed success in radio. It wasn't until 1947, when he was well into his fifties, that he finally broke through as host of the quiz show *You Bet Your Life*. On the face of it, running a quiz program would seem a rather depressing conclusion to a career that had encompassed so many triumphs in vaudeville and film, but Groucho's interviews with the contestants proved to be the ideal vehicle for his spontaneous wit and humorous insults. The show achieved enormous popularity and remained on the air until 1959. Because of the relatively simple and inexpensive production required by its format, it made the transition to television with ease, extending Groucho's career even further into the new medium.

You Bet Your Life was far from Groucho's first attempt to establish himself in radio. In 1937 he and his brother Chico played a pair of shyster lawyers on NBC's *Flywheel, Shyster and Flywheel*, but the series lasted only thirteen weeks. The next year they tried again on CBS with *The Marx Brothers Show*. The "Hollywood Agents" sketch broadcast on that series is ample evidence of their ability to bring their comedy to radio with all its outrageous lunacy intact— it plays like one of their better movie routines—but that show also failed. (One may assume that Harpo, the speechless third member of the triumvirate, didn't take part in these endeavors for reasons that are entirely self-evident; committed as he was to a persona that never spoke, his radio work was essentially limited to a few guest spots where he played the harp or whistled.)

Despite these failures, Groucho continued to nurture the idea of his own radio series. Arthur Marx tells us in his book *Son of Groucho* that his father was convinced that radio was the medium of the future and that it offered a better way to make a living than the physically demanding roughhouse comedy of the Marx Brothers movies. The pay was good, there was no makeup or costumes to bother with, and you didn't have to memorize your lines. In 1939 he and Chico tried it a third time when they joined the cast of *The Circle*, an innovative, largely spontaneous talk and entertainment show that anticipated what Jack Paar and Johnny Carson would be doing on television many years later. The other regulars included Ronald Colman, Cary Grant and Carole Lombard, but even this extraordinary assemblage of talent wasn't enough to get the program through its first season.

In the early 1940s Groucho turned up as a frequent guest on *The Rudy Vallee-Joan Davis Show*, did occasional spots with Bob Hope and Bing Crosby and even appeared in Norman Corwin's radio drama *The Undecided Molecule*, along with Robert Benchley and Vincent Price. Finally, in 1943, he got his own series, *Blue Ribbon Town*, a half-hour variety show sponsored by Pabst beer, which featured Kenny Baker, Virginia O'Brien and announcer Ken Niles. The Marx Brothers had dissolved their partnership by then, and Chico was leading the orchestra on *The Fitch Bandwagon*, with a very young Mel Torme as his singer. *Blue Ribbon Town* lasted one season. Robert Dunning writes in *Tune In Yesterday* that the problem was that Groucho hadn't yet developed the bite and verbal sting that would serve him so well on *You Bet Your Life*. Arthur Marx considers the possibility that his father's outrageousness off-microphone might have had something to do with the show's cancellation. While Pabst was considering whether or not to renew, Groucho attended the brewery's centennial celebration in Milwaukee and took the eighty-year-old son of the founder into a saloon for a beer. When the bartender asked him what brand, he promptly answered, "Miller's High Life! . . . And Mr. Pabst will have the same." In any case, the firm decided to replace him with Danny Kaye, and it took another four years before Groucho at long last made his mark over the air.

Hollywood Agents (1938)

Announcer:

And here's the office of

the Square Deal Amusement Company,

operated by Groucho and Chico Marx,

representatives of talents of the screen,

sellers of sensational stars.

Also headquarters for slot machines,

pinball games, turkey raffles

and marked cards.

Here they are—

Chico and Groucho!

(MUSIC CUE AND APPLAUSE)

Groucho:

Very irksome, very irksome.

I don't understand it.

We've got a business.

We've got a marvelous office here.

But nobody comes in.

I wonder why they stay away?

Chico, did you put up that sign on the door?

Chico:

Yeah . . .

but I couldn't find a sign that said Marx.

The nearest thing I could get
was a sign that said Mumps.

Groucho:
A fine office!
Where's my secretary?

Chico:
Out to lunch.

Groucho:
What time did she leave?

Chico:
October.

Groucho:
If she's not back by next March,
I'll give her two weeks' notice.
A fine office!—
Or did I say that?
Chico, why don't you go out
and drum up some business?

Chico:
I would.
Only I don't know what business we're in.

Groucho:
Why, we're Hollywood agents.
We get people jobs in pictures.

Chico:
Do we?

Groucho:
Don't change the subject.

Chico:
But why do we want
to get-a people jobs in pictures?

Groucho:
Well, we get ten percent of their salaries.

Chico:
Don't we haveta do anything for the money?

Groucho:
No.
We're *agents*.

Chico:
I know, but what do we do?

Groucho:
Nothing.
We're *agents!*

Chico:
Say, I been an agent for years.

Groucho:
Of course.
You should be great as a picture agent.
You've never been able
to get yourself a job in pictures.

Chico:
Well, I nearly got a job one time.
In a picture called *The Human Race.*

Groucho:
Yeah?
What happened?

Chico:
Aw, they said I wasn't the type.

Groucho:

Well, then you'll certainly make a fine agent.

Chico:

All right.
Where do you get-a these people
you put into pictures?
How do you find actors?

Groucho:

Just carry a roast beef sandwich
down the street
and sign up anybody who snaps at it. . . .
Now go out and sign up some stars.

Chico:

Say, I got a great idea.
I'll get-a Jean Harlow up in the office
and sign her up.

Groucho:

Wait a minute.
Jean Harlow has an agent.

Chico:

Yeah, but it'll be a lotta fun
getting her up in the office. . . .
Say, boss,
do we charge the ladies
the same ten-percent commission?

Groucho:

We take ten percent
of everything an actress gets.

Chico:

Y'know, I'm only afraid of one thing.

Groucho:

What's that?

Chico:

Twins.

Groucho:

Chico, you're a dreamer. . . .
C'mon, I'll try you out as an agent.
For example,
if you walked into a producer's office,
how would you sell him Kate Smith?

Chico:

I dunno.

Groucho:

Why, you'd say,
"This little lady can sing,
play the piano . . .
and in an emergency, move it."

Chico:

Oh, I see.
I got-a the idea.
C'mon, try me again.

Groucho:

All right.
Suppose the studio calls you up
and wants a leading man like Clark Gable.
What would you do?

Chico:

Well, you say,
"This little lady can sing,
play the piano
and in an emergency, move it."

Groucho:

The trouble with you is
you can't get your mind off of Jean Harlow.

(SOUND: DOOR OPENS AND CLOSES)

Actress:

Pardon me.
Are you the Mumps Brothers?

Groucho:

Chico, you don't have to answer that.

Actress:

You needn't be afraid of me.
I've had the mumps.

Chico:

Yeah, but you haven't had
the Marx Brothers.

Groucho:

Away with false modesty.
What's your name, madam?

Actress:

Sadie Thompson.

Chico:

Hey, what's-a your racket, Miss Thompson?

Actress:

I was in the California company of *Rain*.

Groucho:

I don't remember that.
What was it called?

Actress:

Local Showers.

Groucho:

Enough of this pitter-patter.
Tell me, my little blood orange,
what do you do?

Actress:

Well, you see,
I can sing,
play the piano—

Groucho & Chico:

And in an emergency, move it.

Groucho:

Miss Thompson,
you're wasting our valuable time and jokes.
Would you like to sign up with us?

Actress:

I should say not.
Don't you remember?
I was in here a month ago.
I gave you my name and address,
but you never got me a job.
What are you gonna do about it?

Groucho:

I'll give you back your name and address.

Actress:

Gee, thanks very much.
Gee, I think you're swell.

Groucho:

Aw, we're not swell.

Actress:

I say yes, you're swell.

I'll never forget ya for this.

I think you're both swell.

Chico:

We think-a you're swell, too.

Groucho:

I don't think we're nearly as swell as she is.

You are. . . .

But I certainly am not.

Chico:

Well-a, it's certainly swell of you to say that.

Actress:

Well, good-bye.

It was swell seein' ya.

Groucho:

Well, it was swell seeing you too.

Swell up and see us again some time.

(SOUND: DOOR OPENS AND CLOSES)

Groucho:

This is a fine location.

With the type of people we're getting in here,

our main entrance must be on an alley.

(SOUND: DOOR OPENS AND CLOSES)

Comic:

Hello, fellas.

Groucho:

Ah, an actor—

Or does my nose deceive me?

Chico:

Say, this guy looks-a swell, too.

Groucho:

No, that's not swell.

It's the past tense—swollen.

Comic:

My name is Cookie Johnson.

Groucho:

Oh, another piano mover—

or is it just a piano?

What do you do for a living?—

If you call that living.

Comic:

I'm a radio comedian.

Groucho:

Oh, a radio comedian, eh?

Well, you came to the right place.

There's gonna be fireworks around here,

and we'll need a punk like you.

Comic:

Are you the man who

gets people jobs in pictures?

Groucho:

No, I'm a Hollywood agent.

But this is no time for the truth. . . .

Tell me, why do you want to leave the radio to go into pictures?

Comic:

Well, pictures is high class.

Groucho:

Yeah, isn't they?

Chico:

(Laughs)

Groucho:

Oh, you liked that, eh?

Chico:

No.

Comic:

Who's that?

Groucho:

Oh, this is my partner, Chico Marx.

Comic:

Any relation to laundry marks?
(Cracks himself up)

Groucho:

Chico, put on your brass knuckles
and shake hands with Mr. Johnson.

Chico:

How do ya do?
The name is familiar,
but I don't know how to do with-a your face.

Groucho:

I got a couple of suggestions.

Comic:

I don't know if I want you
guys for my agents.
I don't know if I want an agent.
You can't depend on 'em.
I read in the paper the other day
about an agent who committed suicide
by jumping off a roof.

Groucho:

Oh, don't pay any attention to that.

Comic:

Why not?

Groucho:

That was me.
It was a publicity stunt.

Comic:

I'm gettin' out of here.

Groucho:

Quick, Chico, lock the door.

Comic:

Wait a minute.
What do you agents charge for commission?

Chico:

Well, ten percent is our fee.

Comic:

Well, if it's fee,

why do you charge ten percent?
(Cracks himself up)

Groucho:

Quick, Chico, *open* the door.

Chico:

Y'know, I don't like him.

Comic:

Another thing,
how much salary will you guarantee me?

Groucho:

Chico, get a contract ready
and write in the salary we'll guarantee him.

Chico:

Okay, how do ya spell "salary"?

Comic:

And it's got to be a legal contract.

Groucho:

You can trust us, Mr. Johnson.
We're an old established firm. . . .
We've been in this location
since a quarter past seven. . . .
Here, I'll draw up the contract.
How's this:
"Whereas you think you're a comedian
and whereas we think we're agents
and we think we can get you a job in movies
(of course, we're not sure whereas),
for this consideration, you as a claimant
whereas waive retainer thereof whereas."

Chico:

That's-a the trouble with this country—
too many foreigners.

Comic:

Lemme see that contract.
Hey, what do I pay ya this ten percent for?

Chico:

That's for overhead.

Comic:

Yeah, but what's this other ten percent for?

Chico:

That's for underwear.

Comic:

See here, haven't you guys
got any underwear?

Groucho:

Yes, but you know
we live in a changing world.

Comic:

Now let's get this straight right now.
Mr. Marx, how much commission
do you want?

Groucho:

How much money do you need to live?

Comic:

Hey, wait, here's another ten percent!

Chico:

Yeah, that's-a for overcoats.

Comic:

Well, I'm not gonna sign this.

Groucho:

Listen, tub of butter,

when you say that, smile.

Chico:

Yeah.

You know what-a happened to the last guy

who didn't sign with us?

Comic:

No, what?

Groucho:

He's now a star at MGM.

Comic:

I'll tell ya what I'll do.

You get me a job for

five thousand dollars a week

and I'll give ya fifty dollars.

Chico:

Huh!

You get us a job for

five thousand dollars a week

and we give *you* a hundred dollars.

Comic:

Well, that seems fair enough.

Groucho:

Fine.

Sign here and we'll take you right over

to Mr. Pincus's office at the Miracle Studio

and get you started on a new picture

called *Strike Me Pincus.*

Comic:

Okay.

But you gotta put a clause in the contract

guaranteeing me work.

Groucho:

Okay, how's this:

"Whereas if we don't get you a job

in four consecutive months

or four consecutive jobs

in one consecutive month,

you're an old maid."

Now sign.

Comic:

Now wait a minute.

Take it easy.

I can't sign right away with you.

You're strangers.

Chico:

Strangers?

You're crazy.

I've known Groucho for years.

Comic:

Well, that's different.

I'll sign.

Where's your pen?

Chico:

Alcatraz.

Groucho:

Not your home.

The pen, he means.

Here you are.

Comic:

Thanks.

Groucho:

Wait, there's no pen point in this pen.

Comic:

That doesn't matter.

I can't write.

(Cracks himself up)

Groucho:

Then we're even. . . .

We can't read.

JUDY CANOVA

The twangy country drawl was one of the more persistent of the many regional and ethnic dialects that proved so popular from the early days of radio comedy. There were Lum and Abner, proprietors of the Jot 'Em Down Store in Pine Ridge, Arkansas, who also ran their own very successful series from 1931 to 1953. There was Arkansas Traveler Bob Burns, who was introduced on radio by Rudy Vallee in 1935, then followed a six-year spot with Bing Crosby on *The Kraft Music Hall* with his own *Bob Burns Show*, which remained on the air from 1941 to 1947. The two big country-music programs each had their resident comedians. Minnie Pearl talked about life in Grinder's Switch on the *Grand Ole Opry*, which also featured Whitey Ford as the Duke of Paducah. In the early 1940s Pat Buttram spun his tall tales on *The National Barn Dance* and was a permanent hired hand on *Gene Autry's Melody Ranch*.

Judy Canova was very much part of this tradition. With her calico dress and pigtails and backcountry astonishment at the fancy ways of the big city, she was perhaps the living archetype of the radio hillbilly. Peculiarly enough, she started out as an opera singer and established her hillbilly persona in New York City, where she played clubs and appeared in the 1936 edition of the *Ziegfeld Follies* along with Fanny Brice, Bob Hope and Josephine Baker. But then, Chester Lauck and Norris Goff, Lum and Abner's creators, were actually college graduates and began as blackface comics. And before taking up his stovepipe bazooka and hillbilly character, Bob Burns was a political humorist in the vein of Will Rogers.

Like Bob Burns and so many other performers, Judy Canova made her radio debut on Rudy Vallee's *Fleischmann Hour*. In the late 1930s she worked on the air with her sister Annie and brother Zeke. They had their own musical series, *The Canovas*, and appeared as guests with Edgar Bergen and Paul Whiteman, doing sketches like the one printed here. In 1943 she began her period of greatest popularity with *The Judy Canova Show*, a situation comedy with music, which ran for ten years on CBS and then NBC, mostly in the half-hour spot leading into *Grand Ole Opry*. Canova was given strong support by a cast that included Hans Conried, Verna Felton and Sheldon Leonard. The most memorable character on the show was probably Mel Blanc's Pedro, a comic Mexican who always announced his appearances with his popular catchphrase, "Pardon me for talking in your face, senorita."

Flying to New York with Zeke and Annie Canova and Paul Whiteman (c. 1939)

Announcer:

It's that old trouble of Paul Whiteman's,

that menace of the mountains . . .

Judy Canova

with her sister Annie

and her brother Zeke.

(APPLAUSE)

Judy:

Howdy, Mr. P. W.

Whiteman:

Hello, Judy.

Zeke:

Good evenin', ever'body.

Annie:

Good night, ever'body.

Whiteman:

Well, I see you finally got to New York, Judy.

Judy:

We sure did, Mr. P. W.

And we'd have got here sooner

only we came from Fort Worth by airyplane.

Whiteman:

Airplane!

But that's the fastest way you could travel.

Judy:

I know,

but Zeke made a mistake

and bought us tickets to Los Angeles.

Whiteman:

Why on earth did he do that?

Judy:

The tickets to Los Angeles

was two dollars cheaper.

Whiteman:

You mean that you went

all the way to Los Angeles
in order to get to New York?

Judy:

That's nothing.
We met a woman
who was going all the way to Reno
just so she could get to Niagara Falls

Whiteman:

Well, tell me about the trip, Judy.

Judy:

We went up ten thousand feet.

Whiteman:

Were you frightened, Judy?

Judy:

No, I wasn't skeered.

Zeke:

Then why was your teeth a-chatterin'?

Judy:

I brushed 'em that morning
and I couldn't do a thing with 'em.

Whiteman:

Were Zeke and Annie affected by the height?

Judy:

Lordy, yes.
Zeke was so skeered he wouldn't sit down.

Whiteman:

Wouldn't sit down?
Why not?

Zeke:

That airyplane was too shaky
to set all my weight down on it.

Annie:

I asked the pilot
if they had many wrecks on that airyplane.

Whiteman:

What did he say, Annie?

Annie:

He said the worst one they ever had
was Judy. . . .

Judy:

That'll do, Annie.
Go get your hat and coat.

Whiteman:

Personally, I never travel by air.
I guess I'm not built for flying.

Judy:

You're tellin' I!
You know, Mr. P. W.,
I went up and spoke to the pilot.
I asked him what made us
keep going higher and higher all the time.
He said it was the elevator.
So I said, if the dang thing has an elevator,
ring it and let me off at the ground floor.

Whiteman:

But Judy, didn't you get a thrill
out of looking down at the beautiful panorama
below?

Judy:

There was a fella—
looking at what?

Whiteman:

The beautiful panorama.

Judy:

I'll bet you laid awake nights
thinking of that one.
Hey, Zeke, what's a panorama?

Zeke:

A panorama is a soft straw hat.

Judy:

Dog take me, Zeke,
you sure are smart.

Whiteman:

(Chuckle)
You didn't finish telling me
about your airplane trip. . . .
What else happened?

Judy:

Well, the only time we was really skeered
was when the airyplane come sailing
over Newark.
We sure was high up.
I looked out the window
and asked the hostess
what that little bungalow was
down there below.

Whiteman:

What was it?

Judy:

She said it was the Empire State Building.

Whiteman:

But isn't it remarkable
how gently they bring you down?

Judy:

That's what you think.
The hostess said,
"We are now twenty thousand
feet over Newark. . . .
Climb out . . . we're down."
I said, "Well, wait a minute
till my stomach gets here."

Whiteman:

Well, anyway, you're here safe and sound.
Tell me, Judy,
was that the longest trip you ever took?

Judy:

No indeedy.
One time I and Annie
went from Atlanta to . . .
no, we didn't go from Atlanta either. . . .

Zeke:

It was me that went from Atlanta.

Annie:

Yeah, and they're still after you, Zeke.

Judy:

Get under the house. . . .

Whiteman:

By the way, Judy . . .

did you see this story in the paper
about you coming back to New York?

Judy:

Why, no.
Lemme see it, Mr. P. W.

Whiteman:

Here it is, right here.

Judy:

Lordy, it sure is purty, ain't it?
Zeke, read what it says.

Zeke:

All right, Judy.
Which part do I read—
the black or the white?

Judy:

Read the white—
there's more of it.

Whiteman:

No, no, Zeke, read the second column.

Judy:

Read what?

Whiteman:

The second column.

Judy:

I don't see nothing like that.
Zeke, what's a column?

Zeke:

Column is how you feel
when you ain't excited.

Judy:

Listen to that, Mr. P. W.
Wouldn't you think
Zeke had been to college? . . .
You know we none of us
feel very good tonight, Mr. P. W.

Whiteman:

Why, what's the trouble, Judy?

Judy:

Well, we got a tellygram
that our grandpappy died.

Whiteman:

Why, that's too bad.
I'm awfully sorry.

Judy:

You know, grandpappy
was a famous scientist.

Whiteman:

Is that so?

Judy:

Yes, sir.
He discovered
seventy-six new kinds of insects
in his lifetime.

Whiteman:

Why, that's remarkable.
I suppose he had to search all over the world.

Judy:

Nope,
he found 'em the day
he combed out his whiskers.

72

Whiteman:

How old was he when he died?

Judy:

A hundred and ten.

Whiteman:

A hundred and ten!
Just think of that.
What caused his death?

Judy:

Women and liquor.

Whiteman:

Women and liquor?

Judy:

Yep,
he couldn't get either one,
so he just laid down and died.

W. C. FIELDS

W. C. Fields's transit through radio was a relatively brief but productive part of a career that spanned half a century. His success in vaudeville and film led to numerous invitations to star in his own radio show in the early 1930s, but he didn't make his actual debut until 1937. That year, while recuperating from a near-fatal illness, he participated in an all-star radio tribute to Adolph Zukor, the film magnate. Fields was so ill that he had to broadcast his portion of the program from his hospital bed, yet his voice came through in all its distracted comic grandeur. After he returned home a few weeks later, he began a series of memorable guest appearances with Edgar Bergen and Charlie McCarthy on *The Chase and Sanborn Hour*. They were so well received that Fields became virtually a permanent member of the cast until 1939, when he left to try out his own series for Lucky Strike Cigarettes. According to Fields's grandson Ronald, he was attracted to radio during these years because it was less demanding than film making and allowed him to stay active and bring in a sizable income while his health mended.

The appearances with Bergen were notable for the stylized exchanges of invective between Fields and the ventriloquist's dummy. Fields and Charlie McCarthy were nicely matched combatants. One was as caustic and outspoken as the other. Each had humorous vulnerabilities that the other was quick to exploit. Charlie picked on Fields for his drinking ("Here comes W. C. Boy, what an ad for black coffee!") and for the red, bulbous nose that was one of its more visible side effects ("W. C. Fields! The fellow with the one-thousand-watt beezer!"). Fields's retaliations took the form of letting Charlie have it for being, despite all his impudence, only a dummy made of wood: "Silence, you frustrated hitching post, or I'll cut you down to a pair of shoe trees!" Off the air, Fields and Charlie's creator were close personal friends, sharing a mutual respect for each other's talent. One is puzzled what to make of the bizarre anecdote related by Jim Harmon in *The Great Radio Comedians.* "Fields thought of Charlie as a separate, living human being, and on a few occasions Bergen actually had to restrain Fields from damaging the valuable dummy in a fit of rage."

Fields did much of his own writing for the Bergen show and his weekly series for Lucky Strike, which is the source of the piece included here. (Larson E. Whipsnade, the name of the character he plays in "Fire in the Home," reappears in his film *You Can't Cheat an Honest Man.*) A notoriously idiosyncratic and irreverent individual, Fields squabbled constantly with his sponsors and producers, which probably accounts for the series' short life. Robert Lewis Taylor tells us that there were continuous arguments over money, material, time and personnel, culminating in a fight over Fields's wish to lampoon his sponsor on the air. Lucky Strike never got over the fact that Fields's frequent, seemingly innocent references to his fictive son "Chester" were in fact veiled allusions to one of their chief competitors.

By 1939 Fields had recovered his health and was primarily occupied with making his last great series of films for Universal: *You Can't Cheat an Honest Man, My Little Chickadee, The Bank Dick* and *Never Give a Sucker an Even Break.* After completing two seasons of his own show, he gradually phased himself out of radio and its attendant aggravations. For the next few years, he limited himself to reunions with Bergen and occasional guest appearances on a few other programs. He made his final broadcast in 1943, three years before "the fellow in the bright pajamas" took him away.

Fire in the Home (1939)

Announcer:

And now, ladies and gentlemen,

we come to the dramatic highlight

of the evening,

where we trace the weekly adventures

of Mr. Whipsnade

at work and at play.

Tonight we find him very much at play.

Fields:

Tell 'em who plays the part.

Announcer:

Huh?

Oh, yes.

W. C. Fields plays the part

of Larceny Whipsnade.

Fields:

Not Larceny Whipsnade.

Larson *E.* Whipsnade.

Break it up.

Announcer:

If you'll just take a moment

to get into character, Mr. Fields,

I'll go on and set the scene.

Fields:

Okay, okay . . .

75

Announcer:

Tonight Mr. Whipsnade is giving a party
in celebration of having just
inherited a department store.
But it seems that his legal adviser
has more serious things on his mind.
As our curtain rises,
we look into the quiet suburban home
of his attorney.
He's reading the paper.
His wife is knitting.

Mrs. Bigelow:

Chauncey, dear,
I think the house is on fire.

Bigelow:

Think?
Don't you know?

Mrs. Bigelow:

I smell something funny.
Can't you?

Bigelow:

Yes, yes, Jean.
What is it?

Mrs. Bigelow:

Well, better have a look.

(SOUND: DOOR OPENS AND CLOSES)

Mrs. Bigelow:

Chauncey!
The hall is full of smoke!
And it's the cook's night out!

Bigelow:

Now that's a silly remark.

Mrs. Bigelow:

Chauncey, hurry, hurry!
Do something!

Bigelow:

Well, the first thing to do
is phone the fire department.

Mrs. Bigelow:

But the phone is in the hall.
You can't get to it.
You'll suffocate in all that smoke.

Bigelow:

I'll get to it all right!
(Coughs)

(SOUND: TELEPHONE RINGS)

Mrs. Bigelow:

Oh, that'll be the fire department calling us.
They must have seen the smoke.

*(FADE OUT ON THE BIGELOWS. FADE IN
ON THE PARTY AT WHIPSNADE'S
HOUSE.)*

Carousers:

(Singing)
"For he's a jolly good fellow,
For he's a jolly good fellow . . . "

Fields:

Quiet, quiet.
Quiet!

Can't hear the phone at all.
Hello.

Bigelow:

Hello, is this the fire department?

Fields:

Hello, is that you, Bigelow?

Bigelow:

Yes . . .

Fields:

Bigelow?

Bigelow:

Yes, yes, it's me.

Fields:

Guess who this is?
Larson E., your old friend.
Larson E. Whipsnade.

Bigelow:

Yeah, how do you do!
Will you please get off the wire!

Fields:

Well, how's everything, Bigelow?
All quiet along the Wang Poo?

(SOUND: JIGGLES THE RECEIVER)

Fields:

I was cut off.
Here, I'll call him back.

(SOUND: DIALS THE PHONE)

Bigelow:

(Coughs)
Hello!

Fields:

Hello, it's Whipsnade again.
Hey, I'll tell ya why I called you up.
I was thinkin' about
getting away from all this, Bigelow.

Bigelow:

Mr. Whipsnade! . . .

Fields:

The call of the open road.
Get into a trailer
and take along only
the bare necessities of life:
food, clothing and a blonde.

Bigelow:

(Coughs)
Mr. Whipsnade, I beseech you!
Get off the line!

Fields:

Yas, I have one in mind.
She's a softball player.
Plays with the Dipsy Doodle Dairy Company.
Plays catcher.
A little on the heavy side
around the ankles . . .
from sliding into bases, I suppose.

Bigelow:

Look, look, Mr. Whipsnade!
I've got to report a fire!

Fields:

Yas, she's got a lot of fire.

Unusual for a blonde . . .

Bigelow:

Mr. Whipsnade!

Fields:

Huh?

Bigelow:

I'm afraid you'll have to hang up!

Fields:

Hang it up?

Not a chance in the world.

My Aunt Mae Whipsnade died.

Choked to death eating a cream puff.

Left me half-interest in a department store

and a quarter-interest in a distillery. . . .

Bigelow:

Look, you'll have to—

Fields:

Yas, too bad it wasn't the other way around.

Yas.

Bigelow:

(Coughs)

Fields:

Yas, they want to make me manager . . .

janitor or something. . . .

Hello?

(SOUND: JIGGLES PHONE)

Fields:

I was cut off again.

That operator must be drunk.

Here, I'll call him back.

(SOUND: DIALS PHONE)

Bigelow:

(Coughs)

Hello!

Fields:

Whipsnade again.

Want your advice, Bigelow.

Do ya think I'll be happier

in a department store or a brewery?

Bigelow:

Yes, yes! . . .

Fields:

More work in a department store

is my guess.

Bigelow:

(Coughs)

Fields:

That's a fancy cough you got there, Bigelow.

Reminds me of one I picked up in Budapest.

Bigelow:

(Coughs)

Mr. Whipsnade, listen!

Fields:

I am listening.

It's really good.

You're coughing better.

Bigelow:

Listen to what I'm trying to say!

Fields:

Huh?

Bigelow:

Our house is on fire!

Fields:

Your house?

Bigelow:

Yes!

Fields:

Your house is on fire?

Bigelow:

Yes!

Fields:

Well, where are you talking from?

Bigelow:

From the house!
(Coughs)

Fields:

From the house that's on fire?

Bigelow:

Yes!
(Coughs)

Fields:

Godfrey Daniel!
Are you doing anything about it?
You should be calling the fire department.

Bigelow:

I *will* if you clear the line!

(SOUND: DOOR OPENS)

Carousers:
(Singing)
"Sweet Adeline . . .
For you I pine. . . . "

Fields:

Hey, shut that door, will ya.

(SOUND: DOOR SHUTS)

Fields:

I'll serve those yaps sasparilla from now on.

Bigelow:

Look here, Mr. Whipsnade!

Fields:

Fire . . .
one of the scourges of mankind.
Of course, a fire at sea is even more dreadful.
I remember seven years ago . . .
my first trip down to the Antipodes . . .

Bigelow:

Look, Mr. Whipsnade!

Fields:

Huh?

Bigelow:

Mr. Whipsnade,
this is no time for anecodotes!

Fields:

Artichokes?

Yas, in abundance.

Got 'em from

the California Fruitgrowers' Association.

Fire at sea. . . .

We had fun through it all, though. . . .

Even the captain got seasick.

Bigelow:

Mr. Whipsnade, would you please—

Ohh!

Mrs. Bigelow:

Mr. Whipsnade!

Fields:

Oh, is that you, Mrs. Bigelow?

Mrs. Bigelow:

Yes!

Fields:

Good evening.

Long time no see.

Why dontcha drop over and meet the mob?

Mrs. Bigelow:

We are having a fire at present.

Fields:

Oh, couldn't ya get over

for just a little while?

Mrs. Bigelow:

If you know what's good for you,

you'll get off of this wire!

We wish to call the fire department!

Fields:

Oh, certainly, Mrs. Bigelow.

You'll find them a noble body of men . . .

the fire laddies, the smoke eaters . . .

day or night, always ready

with a clang, clang, clang. . . .

Mrs. Bigelow:

Will you please hang up?

Fields:

Oh, absolutely. . . .

Now listen,

if there's anything else I can do,

Mrs. Bigelow,

don't hesitate to phone me.

If your phone is on fire,

just telegram.

Poor Mr. and Mrs. Bigelow. . . .

I better get 'em again.

(SOUND: DIALS PHONE)

Bigelow:

(Coughs)

Hello!

Fields:

Hello, Bigelow!

Bigelow:

Oh! . . .

Fields:

Didja call the fire department yet?

Bigelow:

I don't get a chance to.

You keep calling back.

Look, Mr. Whipsnade,
my hall is filled with smoke!
My lungs are filled with smoke!

Fields:

What brand are you smoking?

Bigelow:

My wife has disappeared!

Fields:

How's the roof holding up?

Bigelow:

I don't know!

Fields:

Sounds like you could use some help.
I say, Bigelow,
do you know the technique
of calling the fire department?

Bigelow:

Ohh!

Fields:

You can usually find the number draped
under the front cover of the telephone book.

Bigelow:

With what may be my last breath,
Mr. Whipsnade,
I implore you—

Fields:

Yeah, I know. . . .
I'll get the phone book
and look up the number for you.
Poor devil. . . .

The book's right here.
I can reach it easily.

(SOUND: LOUD CRASH)

Fields:

Glasswear . . .
knocked over nearly a full quart, too.
Only two drinks out of that bottle . . .
very curious thing.
There was a Persian cat
laying right on top of my book phone.
Don't own a cat, either.
Must belong to the neighbors.
Might've been a big rat with long fur.
I know we have rats. . . .

Bigelow:

Look here—
(Coughs)

Fields:

Ah, here's the book.
Wait a minute, let me see . . .
Emergency Call.
Now listen attentively:
"Either call or dial Operator."
Hey, Bigelow, that's it in a nutshell.
You simply call the Operator. . . .
Where is he?
Hello, hello, hel-lo?

(SOUND: JIGGLES THE PHONE)

Fields:

Bet the wires are down, too.
I'll get the Operator myself.

(SOUND: DIALS OPERATOR)

Operator:

Operator.

Fields:

Huh?

Operator:

Operator.

Fields:

That you, Operator?

Operator:

Yey-ess.

Fields:

I thought it was
that chair squeaking again. . . .
Say, Operator, can I report a fire
by saying to you I want to report a fire?

Operator:

Yey-ess.

Fields:

Wonderful . . .
What an improvement over the old way
of running out in the street
and yelling fire till your lungs give out.

Operator:

What's your street number, pul-eeze?

Fields:

Street number?
605 North Bluebird.

Operator:

605 North Bluebird?

Fields:

Yes.

Operator:

Thank you.

(SOUND: HANGS UP PHONE)

Fields:

Wonder what she wanted *my* number for?

(SOUND: FIRE ENGINES, CROWD NOISES, HEAVY BANGING ON THE DOOR)

Fields:

Ah, somebody tapping on the door.
We have company. . . .
It's the fire company.
What's that?
Oh, a hook and ladder.

Fireman:

Say, where's the fire?
I don't even smell smoke.

Fields:

Ah yes, fire.
I know where there's a good fire. . . .
Over at my lawyer's house.
Just let me make a call here
and I'll find plenty of work for you tonight.

(SOUND: DIALS PHONE)

Bigelow:

(Coughs)

Hello!

Fields:

Hello, Bigelow!

Bigelow:

Oh! . . .

(Coughs)

Fields:

Yas, I'd know your cough in a million.

This is Whipsnade.

Say, I've got the fire department

at my house.

Bigelow:

Oh, I knew it would be you!

Fields:

Say, you wouldn't like to come over

for a cocktail

and ride back on a hook and ladder with us,

would you? . . .

Or are you too busy?

Mrs. Bigelow:

Mr. Whipsnade, all our belongings are gone!

All our clothes are burned up!

Fields:

Your clothes are burned up?

Aren't you cold? . . .

You'll get pneumonia

running around a damp house

without any clothes on. . . .

Good gracious, fire in the home . . .

BUD ABBOTT AND LOU COSTELLO

Abbott and Costello made their radio debut in 1938 on *The Kate Smith Show*, the program that also introduced Henny Youngman and *The Aldrich Family* to the broadcasting audience. On their first appearance, they performed their classic "Who's on First?" routine and were an immediate hit. The skit was closely associated with them throughout their careers, and they repeated it frequently in movies, nightclubs and their own radio and television series. "Who's on First?" was developed, polished and given its definitive performance by the team, but they didn't actually write it themselves. According to Jim Mulholland in *The Abbott and Costello Book*, the piece was an old burlesque standby whose roots go back to the very beginnings of burlesque in the early years of this century.

Burlesque was also Abbott and Costello's own roots. Bud Abbott was born into a show business family, and his father was one of the organizers of the first burlesque circuit in the United States. Abbott started working in burlesque himself in 1911 at the age of sixteen, first as an assistant treasurer, then as producer and finally as performer. Eventually, he became the top straight man for Harold Minsky. Lou Costello, ten years younger than his partner, began in burlesque in 1930 and soon became a highly regarded comic. They teamed up in

1937 and, after touring together for a year in *Life Begins at Minsky's*, became so popular that they moved on to more lucrative bookings in vaudeville and nightclubs. They were discovered for radio by Henny Youngman, who was looking for someone to replace him on *The Kate Smith Show* so he could accept the offer of a screen test at Paramount Pictures.

Grounded as Abbott and Costello were in burlesque, their comedy never moved very far from it. To the delight of their fans and the scorn of highbrow critics, they maintained the archetypal roles of straight man and comic butt throughout their careers, engaging in verbal knockabout full of puns and double entendres that had been cleansed of any sexual connotations. Not that there was any reason for them to change. They complemented each other beautifully in these roles, even in their physical appearance. Abbott was tall, thin and dapper; Costello was short and fat and wore clothes that never quite seemed to fit. Abbott played the self-assured, rather stern and demanding father figure; Costello was the confused, vulnerable child.

Although Abbott was unsurpassed as straight man, a difficult part that warranted his billing ahead of his partner and his initial sixty percent of their salary (the straight man's traditional share), it was Costello's childlike quality that probably accounted for the team's success. There was something wonderfully sweet and touching about his naive, fumbling inability to penetrate the mysteries of the adult world. Children watching their old movies on television today still respond to Costello's catchphrase "I'm a *ba-a-a-ad* boy!" with affection and empathy, as do those grownups who have managed not to deny the child part of their own natures. Interestingly, Jim Mulholland tells us that the pair's actual personalities were just the reverse of their dramatic personas: "Bud was quiet and introverted. Lou was the driving force in the team: outgoing, energetic and industrious."

Abbott and Costello remained a regular feature of *The Kate Smith Show* for a year and a half, doing weekly ten-minute spots such as the one included here. In 1941 they began their own weekly series for NBC, *The Abbott and Costello Program*. That same year *Buck Privates*, their first starring film, was released. Shot on a low budget of two hundred thousand dollars the picture was a huge success, catapulting them into stardom of the first magnitude and saving Universal Studios from financial ruin. Over the years Abbott and Costello made a total of thirty-six films, but their radio program remained the foundation of their career.

The Abbott and Costello Program continued on NBC for six seasons and was always one of the top-rated shows. The first-class supporting cast included Mel Blanc, Artie Auerbach ("Mr. Kitzel"), double-talker Al Kelly and Sid Fields, who was also one of their writers. The show usually featured Hollywood stars such as Veronica Lake and Cary Grant, who participated in the skits and plugged their current films. In 1946 they moved their show to ABC, where they remained on the air until 1951, when they switched over to television.

The Turkey Dinner (1938)

Lou:

(Sings)

"Jingle bells, jingle bells,

Jingle all the way.

Three more days till Christmas

And then what bills to pay."

Bud:

Costello, you're certainly in a happy mood.

I suppose you're all through

with your Christmas shopping.

Hey! What's that string tied around your

finger for?

Lou:

That's to remind me to remind my wife
to ask me if I forgot something
she told me to remember.

Bud:

Which reminds me.
I forgot to get my wife a nutcracker.

Lou:

What kind?
Flatiron or rolling pin?

Bud:

Talk sense.
What did you forget?

Lou:

A present for my Uncle Bumblebee.

Bud:

What a name.
Uncle Bumblebee.

Lou:

Yeah.
That's because everybody he touches
gets stung.
I'm gonna buy him
a shaving brush and a razor.

Bud:

Has he got a mug?

Lou:

Oh, boy!
You should see her.

Bud:

Well, all I need now is my Christmas turkey.

Lou:

Abbott, was I lucky!
I got my turkey for running.

Bud:

Who did you beat?

Lou:

The butcher and two policemen.

Bud:

Costello, you'll end up
by spending Christmas in the police station.

Lou:

Well, that's all right in a pinch.
Hey, Abbott, come over to the house
Christmas
and eat some turkey.

Bud:

Why should I have to eat turkey
on Christmas?
Maybe I'd like chicken.

Lou:

I haven't got any chicken.
I got turkey.

Bud:

Well, is that my fault?
Why didn't you ask me what I'd like
before you invited me over?
If I want chicken,
why should you force me to eat turkey?

Lou:

Who's forcing you to eat turkey?

Don't eat it.

Bud:

I see.

Now I shouldn't eat it.

I should go hungry while you stuff yourself.

Lou:

Who wants you to go hungry?

Aw, I'll go out and steal a chicken.

Bud:

And what happens to the turkey?

Lou:

I'll give it to the dog.

Bud:

That's fine.

You feed the dog turkey

and want me to eat chicken.

Lou:

Look, Abbott, what do you keep arguing for?

Look at me.

I'm congenial.

Bud:

Oh, now you're using an assumed name.

Who are you to travel incognito?

Lou:

Who's traveling in magneto?

I ain't using a consumed name.

I use my own name.

You can find it on my front door.

Bud:

Why should I look for your name?

I know what it is.

Lou:

Then don't look for it.

Bud:

I see.

I shouldn't look for your name.

I should walk into somebody else's house

by mistake

and get shot for a burglar.

Lou:

Ah, I don't want you to get shot.

I'm trying to tell you,

you're welcome at my house.

The door is always open for you.

Bud:

Now you're going to leave the door open.

You want me to sit in a draft and catch cold.

Lou:

Who wants you to catch cold?

I'll close the door.

I'll lock the door.

Bud:

And what am I supposed to do?

Crawl in the window?

Lou:

What do you mean, crawl in the window?

I'll bring you into the house.

Bud:

Oh, you'll bring me in.

What's the matter,
don't you think I can walk?
Do you expect me to come over inebriated?

Lou:

Who cares if you're inebriated?
You don't have to be inebriated.
You can wear anything you want.
I just want you to have
some nice young turkey.

Bud:

How do you know it's a young turkey?
How can you tell a turkey's age?

Lou:

By the teeth.

Bud:

A turkey has no teeth.

Lou:

No, but I have.

Bud:

Is the turkey dressed?

Lou:

Did you ever see a turkey
running around the street
without any clothes on?
Certainly it's dressed.
It has on a suit of feathers.

Bud:

If it has feathers on,
then it isn't dressed.

Lou:

How do you like that?
If it has feathers, it isn't dressed.
Look, I'm talking about a turkey,
not a fan dancer.

Bud:

So am I talking about a turkey,
and if it has feathers on, it isn't dressed.

Lou:

Well, what do you want it to wear—
a shirtwaist and panties?
Or do you want me to take it to my tailor
and say,
"Make my turkey a cutaway suit.
He's going out for Christmas dinner"?

Bud:

That's not necessary.
I thought maybe the butcher
dressed the turkey.

Lou:

That's ridiculous.
Do you think the butcher has time
to put clothes on animals?

Bud:

No.

Lou:

Do you think he says to his customer,
"How would you like your turkey dressed,
as Snow White or one of the Seven Dwarfs?"

Bud:

You don't understand.

When I say, "Is the turkey dressed?"
I don't mean, is the turkey dressed?

Lou:

No?
What do you mean?

Bud:

I mean, is the turkey dressed?

Lou:

Ah, this thing is getting
too complicated for me.
I shoulda stole a hot dog.

Bud:

Then why did you steal the turkey
in the first place?

Lou:

Who stole it in the first place?
I had to try three places before I got it.

Bud:

Well, what I'm trying to find out is this:
did *you* pick its feathers?

Lou:

Did I pick its feathers?
I never saw the turkey before.
Do you think I know
the style in turkey feathers?
It picked its own feathers.

Bud:

That's impossible.
It couldn't pick its own feathers.

Lou:

All right, then its mother chose them for it.

Bud:

Costello, when I say, "Pick its feathers,"
I don't mean, pick its feathers.

Lou:

I know.
You mean, pick its feathers.
This thing gets sillier all the time.

Bud:

There's nothing silly about it.
You've got to pick its feathers.
They're good for quills.

Lou:

Well, who's got quills?
I haven't been sick a day in five years.

Bud:

Costello, I'm trying to tell you
that you can't cook that turkey
with its feathers on.

Lou:

Are you kidding?

Bud:

Certainly not.
You've got to pick the feathers.

Lou:

I'll let my wife pick them.
She picks everything else I get.

Bud:

Does she pick your clothes?

Lou:

Only the pockets.

Bud:

That's fine.
You get mad if your wife picks your pockets,
but it's all right for you to steal a turkey.
You don't care
if the momma and papa turkey
sit in their coop all day on Christmas and cry
because you're having their baby turkey
for dinner.

Lou:

I'm a *ba-a-ad* boy!

Bud:

You are a *bad* boy.

Lou:

I'm the kind of boy
my mother didn't want me to associate with.

Bud:

You bet you are.

Lou:

I shouldn't be allowed
to carve the turkey on Christmas.

Bud:

You won't be allowed.
I'll carve the turkey.
I'll hand out the portions.

Lou:

Then I'll probably end up with the wishbone.

Bud:

What's the matter with the wishbone?
It's lucky.

Lou:

Yeah?
Well, the turkey had it,
and it didn't do *him* any good.

Bud:

Keep quiet while I figure out
how I'll serve the turkey.
Now, I'll take the two legs.

Lou:

Look, Abbott, I'd like to have one of the legs.

Bud:

Sure, the turkey has only two legs,
and you want a leg.
You're the most selfish person I've ever met.

Lou:

Oh, I'm a wanton.

Bud:

What do you mean, you're a wanton?

Lou:

I'm a wanton one of those turkey legs.

Bud:

Never mind that.
I'll take the two legs.
My wife will take the two wings. . . .

Lou:

Well, could I sit under the table
and pick up the crumbs?

Bud:

I'll take care of your share later.
Let me see.
That's the two legs and wings,
and your wife will take the white meat,
your uncle the heart and liver.

Lou:

Look, Abbott, could I lick the plate?
I gotta come out of this with something.

Bud:

Will you stop butting in!
Now that takes care of the legs,
wings, white meat, heart, liver
and, oh yes, your mother-in-law
gets the neck and giblets,
and you . . .

Lou:

Aw, never mind me.
I'll sit on the fence
and grab mine as it goes by!

FIBBER McGEE AND MOLLY

F*ibber McGee and Molly* was written by Don Quinn, a former cartoonist from Grand Rapids, and starred Jim and Marian Jordan, a pair of failed vaudevillians from Peoria who finally broke through in radio in the late 1920s. The show was created out of the partnership between Quinn and the Jordans and precisely reflected where they had come from and what they had been. It was a kind of extended vaudeville sketch about a neighborhoodful of middle-class, small-town midwesterners who might have come right out of the Sunday funnies. It was also one of the best-written and best-played shows on the air. In *The Big Broadcast*, Frank Buxton and Bill Owen include Don Quinn along with Fred Allen and *Vic and Sade's* Paul Rhymer in their choice of radio's three most significant contributors to American comedy. Quinn may have lacked Rhymer's subtlety and lightness of touch, but he shared with his fellow midwesterner a feel for the life of a particular time and place as well as the ability to give that feel skillful dramatic expression.

Unlike most comedy shows, *Fibber McGee and Molly* was not a sequence of unrelated comedy turns but a completely integrated half-hour play. In these mini-dramas, Quinn tended to follow a certain structural formula that proved extremely effective, for all its eventual predictability. Set in or near the McGee residence at 79 Wistful Vista, the action was usually generated by McGee's bungled efforts to implement some dubious bright idea or accomplish some simple task like mailing a letter or chopping down the dead tree in his backyard. As he tried to extricate himself from the inevitable difficulties, he would be visited by a procession of neighbors whose unsolicited conversations would only increase the irritability and sense of frustration that were the comic hallmarks of his character.

There would be Hal Peary's Throckmorton P. Gildersleeve, whose smug superiority would provoke McGee into the exchanges of invective that seemed to be the glue that bound their friendship together. Gildersleeve became so popular that in 1941 he was spun off into his own series.

There would be Bill Thompson's garrulous Old Timer, who made every encounter an occasion for one of his stories, invariably introduced by his catchphrase, "That ain't the way I heered it." At some point in the show Thompson would return as the henpecked Wallace Wimple to complain about "Sweety Pie, my big fat wife."

Isabel Randolph's snobbish Abigail Uppington could also be expected to put in an appearance. So could announcer Harlow Wilcox, who would come by in the middle of the show to sneak in a commercial for Johnson's Wax. There would even be some sort of conversation with Myrt, the telephone operator who was never heard directly.

In later years, other passersby included Arthur Q. Bryan's Doc Gamble, Gale Gordon's Mayor La Trivia and Marlin Hurt's Beulah, a black woman played by a white man, who was the other character on the program to be given a separate series.

Presiding over all these encounters, soothing ruffled feelings and maintaining some semblance of reason was Marian Jordan's Molly, about the only character on the show not possessed by some private obsession. She also played the little girl Teeny, another regular visitor, whose ultimate sweetness also had the effect of penetrating McGee's stubborn peevishness.

The cumulative effect of all these comings and goings was of a small town brimming over with life, a place where everyone knew everyone else's business and often got in each other's way, yet with an undeniable sense of community that would always be restored by the time McGee resolved his problems as the show ended and Molly delivered her sign-off, "Good night, all."

Fibber McGee and Molly was the outgrowth of an earlier collaboration between Quinn and the Jordans, a series called *Smackout* that was broadcast from 1931 to 1935. Jim Jordan played a grocer who was "smackout of everything but tall tales." The "tall tales" part of the character carried over to McGee and accounted for the choice of his first name, but though the name stayed, that aspect of his personality was gradually phased out. *Fibber McGee and Molly* was first aired over NBC in 1935 with Johnson's Wax as the sponsor. According to John Dunning's *Tune In Yesterday*, it started out slowly, gradually built up an enthusiastic audience and in 1941 achieved the distinction of being the top-rated show in the country. It continued to be heard every Tuesday night at nine-thirty until 1953, when it switched to a five-day-a-week quarter-hour format that lasted until 1957.

The Man in the Street (1941)

Wilcox:

A man can fool some of the people
all the time
and all the people some of the time
and his wife almost *none* of the time.

So when our hero seems
unusually gay and lighthearted,
laughing at anything,
his better half suspects the worst.
In other words,

when a guy doesn't grouse,
his spouse smells a mouse.
That's the way it is tonight with . . .
Fibber McGee and Molly!

(APPLAUSE)

Fibber:

(Laughing like everything)
So when I seen Egghead Vanderveen there
in front of Joe's Tavern,
I walks up to him. . . .
(Laughs)
"Hiyah, Egghead," I says.
"What's cookin'?"
(Laughs)
. . . And he says, "*I* am! . . .
They just gimme the hotfoot!"
(Laughs)
Well, sir,
that just about tore my upholstery,
because Egghead is the kind of a guy
who . . .

Molly:

McGee.

Fibber:

. . . the kind of guy who . . .
Er . . . eh?

Molly:

What's the matter with you?
You're as merry as a grig over nothing.
What's on your mind?

Fibber:

On my mind?

Why . . . er . . . why, nothing.
But lemme tell you about Egghead.
(Laughs heartily)
So I says to Egghead, I says . . .

Molly:

I don't want to hear about Egghead.
I want to know about *you*.
You always act like this
when you're covering up something.
Look—did you mail
that special delivery letter for me
yesterday morning?

Fibber:

Special deliv . . . oh, that!
Don't give it a thought, Molly.
But to get back
to what I says to Egghead . . .

Molly:

Did you mail that letter?

Fibber:

Why, Molly!
Am I the kind of guy who,
when you tell him
to do something you want done,
don't mail it?

Molly:

Never mind that.
I just asked a simple questi . . .

Fibber:

Did you ever ask me to do anything

that I wasn't only too glad
to cooperate into doing it?
No, sir!

Molly:

McGee!
Did you mail that letter?

Fibber:

(Pause)
No.

Molly:

Well, the reason I wanted to know is . . .

Fibber:

. . . But I'll do it right away.
Wait'll I get my coat
(Fade)
 and as soon as
I can run across the street,
I'll . . .

Molly:

But McGee, let me . . .

Fibber:

No, I'll do it. . . .
Should o' done it yesterday! . . .
(Fade in)
Sorry I forgot,
but you can consider the error rectifried!

(SOUND: DOOR OPENS)

Molly:

(Off-mike)
Wait a minute, McGee,
that letter is . . .

Fibber:

(Laughs)
I'll just dash across the street
to the mailbox, Molly.
Be right back!

*(SOUND: FOOTSTEPS ON STEPS . . .
SIDEWALK . . . FAST)*

Molly:

(Way off-mike)
McGee!!
Wait a minute!!
I didn't . . . !!!
Oh, dear . . .

Fibber:

(Laughing)
Sometimes I wonder why
the government always puts
mailboxes on the corner
where somebody else lives!
If I had my way, I'd—
Hiyah, Gildersleeve!

Gildersleeve:

(Off-mike)
Hello, McGee!
Hey, don't run across that pavement!!
Can't you see they've just . . .

Fibber:

Aw . . . go bounce a meatball, you big ape!
(Fade)
I know what I'm . . .

*(SOUND: SUCKING NOISE, AS COW-
HOOFS IN MUD)*

95

Fibber:

Hey, what the . . .

What is this?

Fresh tar!

Gildersleeve:

Get out of there, McGee!!

They've just resurfaced that pavement. . . .

You'll get stuck!

Fibber:

Whaddye mean, *get* stuck . . .

I *am* stuck!

Why didn't you warn me, you dumbbell?

Gildersleeve:

(Off-mike)

I tried to, you little twerp!

If you hadn't . . .

Ah there, Mrs. McGee!

Molly:

Hello, Mr. Gildersleeve.

McGee!

Come out of that this minute!

Fibber:

I can't . . . can't pick up my feet.

What *is* this, anyway—tar?

Gildersleeve:

No . . .

it's a new patent paving material

they're trying out.

(Laughs)

You like it?

Fibber:

I love it!

96

In fact, I'm stuck on it!

Well, dad-rat it, *do* something.

Get me outa here!

Molly:

Can't you pull your feet up, dearie?

Fibber:

No . . .

wait . . . lemme try again.

(SOUND: SUCKING NOISE)

Fibber:

Nope . . . it's no use. . . .

Harder I try, the deeper I get in!

Gildersleeve:

You see, Mrs. McGee?

(Laughs)

Confidentially, he sinks!

Fibber:

Dad-rat it, Gildersleeve,

if you don't . . .

Molly:

Now, now, now . . .

let's all keep calm and think this thing out.

McGee . . . can you slip out of your shoes?

Fibber:

Yes, but I ain't gonna.

I just had 'em half-soled.

Molly:

Come on, McGee . . .

don't stand there arguing. . . .
You're attracting a crowd.
Take your shoes off and start running.

Fibber:

Okay . . .
(Grunts . . . again)
Okay . . . here I come!

(SOUND: SUCKING NOISES . . . PAUSE)

Gildersleeve:

Well . . . come on!

Fibber:

Can't.
I'm stuck again!

Molly:

Take off your socks and start over.

Fibber:

Okay . . . I'll try anything.
(Grunts . . . again.)
Now!

(SOUND: SUCKING NOISES . . . PAUSE)

Fibber:

Well . . . what do I do now—
take off my feet?

Molly:

Oh, dear!!!!
Who should I call, dearie?
The street commissioner,
the fire department . . .
the police—
or the Gallup Poll?

Fibber:

Whaddye mean, the Gallup Poll?

Molly:

Well, you're the man in the street, all right.
What shall we do, Mr. Gildersleeve?

Gildersleeve:

(Laughs heartily)
I don't know what *you're* going to do,
Mrs. McGee,
but *I'm* going home
and get my movie camera.
(Laughs)
By George,
I never saw anything so funny in my life!

Fibber:

Dad-rat it!
You stay where you darn are, Gildersleeve,
you big heel!

Gildersleeve:

Ohhhhhhhh!!

Molly:

McGee!
You mustn't call Mr. Gildersleeve a heel!

Fibber:

Wel-l-l . . . maybe not.
But I'll bet he could have a lot of fun
sliding down a shoe horn!
Hey, ain't anybody gonna get me outa here?

Molly:

Now, don't get excited, McGee. . . .
We'll do everything we can to . . .

Old Timer:

(Fade in)

Hello there, daughter.

H'lo, Gildersleeve.

Hiyah, *Johnny* . . . watcha doing?

Fibber:

Whaddye think I'm doin', you old dodo!

Tap dancin'?

Old Timer:

Tap dancing, eh?

(Aside)

You never told me he could tap dance,

daughter!

Lesee you do a off-to-Buffalo, Johnny!

Molly:

For goodness' sakes, stop teasing him. . . .

He's in a terrible predicklement!

Old Timer:

Hey, what's all this about, kids?

What's he doin' out there in the street,

daughter?

Molly:

He's stuck in that fresh pavement,

Mr. Old Timer.

Know any way we can get him out?

Old Timer:

Sure!

Gildersleeve:

How?

Old Timer:

(Excited)

Look! . . .

Git a couple shovels! . . .

See?

Then go down

into the basement of your house . . .

dig a tunnel till you're right under him . . .

then dig up till you reach him

and pull him down through!

Fibber:

(Groans)

Gildersleeve:

Oh, my goodness!

Molly:

That's silly!

Fibber:

It ain't only silly,

it's callous and cruel.

Everybody makin' wisecracks

while I stand here and suffer.

Don't you realize this pavin' material

is gettin' harder every minute?

Call somebody.

Do something!

Molly:

But what will we do?

Fibber:

How should I know?

If you can't think of anything else,

throw me a red and green lantern . . .

and I'll spend the rest of my life here

as a traffic signal!

Old Timer:

Heh-heh-heh . . .

That's pretty good, Johnny,

but that ain't the way I heered it!

The way I heered it,

one feller says t'other feller,

"Sayyyyy," he says—

but hey . . . this ain't any time

for jokes, is it,

with poor little Johnny out there,

stuck in the tar!

Molly:

It certainly isn't!

Gildersleeve:

Of course not!

Old Timer:

Though, on the other hand,

it might cheer him up.

The way I heered it,

one feller says t'other feller,

"Sayyyyy," he says,

"I see where Groucho Marx

is gonna be a professor of humor

at Harvard."

"Zat so?" says t'other feller.

"Where's Harpo goin'? . . .

To Wellesley?"

Hey-heh-heh . . .

Fibber:

(Laughs)

I guess you got somethin' there, Old Timer.

That Harpo is a great guy for blondes,

but . . .

(Laugh stops abruptly)

Hey, what am I laughin' at?

Dad-rat it, get me outa here!

Do something somebody. . . .

Helllp!! Hellp!!

(MUSIC: ORCHESTRA PLAYS "POUPEE VALSANTE, OR BUDDY, YOU WALTZ LIKE A POOP." APPLAUSE.)

(SOUND: CROWD MURMUR . . . LAUGHTER)

Voice 1:

What's that guy doing out there in the street?

Advertising something?

Voice 2:

No, they say he got stuck

in that fresh pavement.

Voice 3:

Well, if he saw they were

going to pave the street,

why didn't he get out of the way?

(SOUND: LAUGHTER)

Voice 4:

They ought to put a rail around him

and use him as a statue of a leading citizen!

(SOUND: LAUGHTER . . . MURMUR OF VOICES)

Fibber:

Hey, Molly!! . . . Molly!!!

Molly:

Yes, dearie . . . here I am!
And here's a little footstool
for you to sit on. . . .
Catch!

(SOUND: WIND WHISTLE . . . THUD)

Fibber:

Much obliged. . . .
Is somebody comin' to get me outa this?
Whoja call?

Molly:

Well, first Mr. Gildersleeve and I
called the Commissioner of Streets.
And he referred us to
the Department of Health.

Fibber:

The Department of Health!

Gildersleeve:

Yes, he said it wasn't healthy
to stand there in the street night and day.
(Laughs)

Fibber:

Well, what did the Health Department say?

Molly:

They referred us to
the License Commissioner . . .
because they said you were
making an exhibition of yourself!

Fibber:

(Groans)

Gildersleeve:

Yes, and the License Commissioner
sent us to the Board of Education.

Fibber:

Dad-rat it,
what's the Board of Education
got to do with it?

Gildersleeve:

They said *they'd* teach you
to stay off freshly paved streets!
(Laughs)

Molly:

But we finally got to the
right people, McGee!! . . .
This is a new type of paving,
and they're sending the inventor of it out!

Fibber:

Well, thank goodness . . . at last!
When will . . .

Voice:

Hey, stick-in-the-mud!! . . .
Can I have your autograph?

Fibber:

Why certainly, bud!
Throw me your death certificate!

(SOUND: LAUGHTER . . . CROWD MURMUR)

Molly:

Oh, dear, Mr. Gildersleeve,
if that man doesn't get here pretty soon,
I don't know. . . .

Oh, how do you do, Mrs. Uppington?

Mrs. Uppington:

How do you do, my deah . . .
and Mr. Gildersleeve.

Gildersleeve:

Ahhh, good day, Abigail!

Mrs. Uppington:

What on earth is the cause
of this boisterous crowd, my deah?

Molly:

It's McGee, Abigail.
He's stuck out there
in the middle of the street. . . .
See?

Mrs. Uppington:

Well . . . *reahhly!*
How . . . er . . . what did . . .
I mean . . . did he step on some chewing
gum?

Gildersleeve:

(Laughs)
Oh, no!
He just started to trot across
a freshly paved street. . . .
The silly asphalt runner!

Molly:

Now, look here, Mr. Gildersleeve . . .

Mrs. Uppington:

But Mrs. McGee . . .

we simply *cawnt* have your husband
making a spectacle of himself. . . .
He is lowering the tone
of the whole neighborhood!

Molly:

Don't give me that Vassar vaseline, dearie!
Next thing you'll get so exclusive
you'll want our fire department
to have an unlisted telephone number!

Mrs. Uppington:

Well, *reahhly*, Mrs. McGee!!
I . . .

Gildersleeve:

(Laughs)
Wait a minute, girls. . . .
Hey, McGee!!!
Here's Mrs. Uppington.
She wants you to get out of there!
(Laughs)
You're lowering real estate values!

Fibber:

Oh, I am, eh?
Uppy, you mean to stand there,
wobbling on your wedgies,
and accuse me o' doin' this on purpose?

Mrs. Uppington:

I reahhly wouldn't know, Mr. McGee. . . .
But if you're posing
as a personal investigator of paving material,
I have a suggestion to make.

Fibber:

Yeah?

What's that?

Mrs. Uppington:

Did you ever hear of a certain place
which is said to be paved with good
intentions?

Fibber:

You mean . . . ?

Mrs. Uppington:

Yes! . . .

And when you get through heah . . .
go *theah!*

Good-bye!

(SOUND: CROWD MURMUR)

Fibber:

Hey, Molly . . .

where's the guy who invented this stuff? . . .
When's he comin'?

Molly:

Just as soon as they can get hold of him,
dearie.

Fibber:

Just wait till *I* get hold of him!
I'll . . .

Wilcox:

(Fade in)

Hey, what is all this? . . .
Come here a minute, Fibber!

Fibber:

No, you come here, Wilcox.

Wilcox:

All right, I'll . . .

Molly:

No! No! No! Mr. Wilcox! . . .
You'll get stuck, too!

Gildersleeve:

McGee is held tight
in that new paving material, Harlow.
Don't set foot on it!

Fibber:

Aw, why didn't you let him come?
He always claimed he was a guy
that would stick by his friends.

Wilcox:

Say . . . you're in a tough spot, pal!
Can't you pull yourself loose?

Fibber:

Who, me?
Why, sure, Wilcox.
I'm just standin' here
till the steamroller comes by.
Then I'll lay down
and get my pants pressed.

Wilcox:

Well, I can really sympathize with you,
Fibber.
Standing in that tar,
you're typical of the stories I hear every day.

Fibber:

Whaddye mean, *I'm* typical!

Wilcox:

You're tarred, aren't you?

Fibber:

Sure, I'm tarred, but . . .

Wilcox:

Well, so is every housewife in the world!
Tarred of the everlasting
scrubbing and cleaning and dusting! . . .
Tarred of trying to keep house
with old-fashioned, inefficient methods!
That's why they all love Johnson's Wax!
Because it cuts housework to a minimum
and keeps floors and furniture
shining and beautiful
and protects them against wear and dirt.
Get some today. . . .
Johnson's Wax for that tarred feeling!!!

Fibber:

Wilcox!

Wilcox:

What?

Fibber:

You're farred!

Wilcox:

I am not!!
You didn't harr me,
and you can't farr . . .
and I can prove it.

Molly:

How, Mr. Wilcox?

Wilcox:

(Fade out)
I'm going to send the sponsor a warrrr!

Fibber:

Send the sponsor a warrr!
If he'd spend more time listening to
Fibber McGee and Molly
and less to Lum and Abner. . .
Hey, when am I gonna get outa here?

Gildersleeve:

Now, now, now . . .
take it easy, little chum . . .
take it easy!
We'll just have to wait
till that paving expert gets here. . . .

Fibber:

Don't "little chum" me, you big chump!
All you've done since I been stuck here
is stand around and crack wise!

Gildersleeve:

Is that so!
Why, you ungrateful little grunion!
You lippy little lizard!
You wait till you get out of there,
and I'll teach you a few manners.

Fibber:

Go on . . .
you couldn't teach a worm to squirm!
You big oaf!
By the time I get loose from here,
I'll be in just the mood
to kick you right in the teeth . . .
and I don't care
if they ain't been paid for yet!

Molly:

Now, now, now, for goodness' sakes, boys!
Stop it!

Fibber:

Let him come out here. . . .
I'll show him.

Molly:

You can't fight here. . . .
And McGee!

Fibber:

Eh?

Molly:

You owe Mr. Gildersleeve an apology.
He's done everything he could
to get the city officials to come out here
and get you loose.

Fibber:

Yeah . . .
and it's like most of his arrangements.
Nothing happens.

Gildersleeve:

Is that so!

Fibber:

Yes, that's so!

Gildersleeve:

Why, you abbreviated anthropological
aberration . . .

Fibber:

Who's an anthropological aberration?

Gildersleeve:

You are!

Molly:

He is not!

Fibber:

I am too!

Gildersleeve:

You are not!

Molly:

Well, make up your mind!
Now stop this bickering, both of you.
Come on, Mr. Gildersleeve . . .
let's go call up the Street Commissioner
again.

Gildersleeve:

All right.
(Sweetly)
Now don't worry, little chum. . . .

Fibber:

Okay, Throcky . . .
and hurry back, Molly. . . .

Molly:

All right, dearie. . . .

(SOUND: CROWD MURMUR)

Voices:

Come on, Joe . . .
let's beat it.

He ain't gonna do nothin'. . . .
Naw, he just stands there like a dope. . . .
Come on . . . Charlie.

(SOUND: CROWD MURMUR . . . FADE OUT)

Fibber:

Hey!!
Don't *everybody* leave!
Somebody stay and talk to me!
Hey!
Aw, dad-rat the dad-ratted luck. . . .
Why does everything have to happen to me!
If I'd of only mailed that letter of Molly's
when I ought to of,
this wouldn't of . . .

Teeny:

Hiyah, mister!

Fibber:

Sorry, sis,
I ain't got time to talk to you now.
I'm in a hurry.

Teeny:

Where you goin'?

Fibber:

I'm goin' down to the . . .
I'm goin' . . .
I'm . . .
Sayyy, come to think of it, I ain't. . . .
Well, whaddye want, sis?

Teeny:

Whatcha doin' out there in the street, mister?

Hmmmmm?
Whatcha doin'?
Hmmmmmm?
Whatcha?

Fibber:

I'm a scare sparrow.

Teeny:

Hmmm?

Fibber:

I says *I'm a scare sparrow.*
That's the same as a scarecrow.
Only, I don't scare crows—
I scare sparrows.

Teeny:

Why?

Fibber:

Well, they make too much noise.
They disturb the frenistans.

Teeny:

What's a frenistan?

Fibber:

That's a kind of a thing
that gets disturbed at sparrows.

Teeny:

Oh . . .
Well, I·betcha you can't scare the widdicums,
I betcha.

Fibber:

What's a widdicum?

Teeny:

It's a little girl
who doesn't believe that frenistan stuff.

Fibber:

(Laughs)
I'm glad you come along, sis.
You cheer me up.

Teeny:

No, you cheer me up.

Fibber:

You cheer me up first.

Teeny:

All righty.
Shall I tell you a story?

Fibber:

Sure, tell me a story.

Teeny:

How about Cinderella?

Fibber:

It ain't riskay, is it?

Teeny:

Well, gee, I . . . hmmmm?

Fibber:

Never mind.
Tell me about Cinderella.
And take your time, sis.
I ain't goin' anywhere for a while.

Teeny:

All righty.

Once upon a time
there was a little girl named Cinderella,
and she had a nasty old stepmother
and she went to a ball and lost her slipper
and the prince found it and he married her
and they lived happily ever after
you wanna hear another one?

Fibber:

No, thanks.
I was gonna ask for the one
about Peter Rabbit,
but the way you boil 'em down,
it'd turn out to be hasenpfeffer.

Teeny:

I can recite pomes, too.

Fibber:

You can?

Teeny:

Hmmm?

Fibber:

I says, you can?

Teeny:

Can what?

Fibber:

Cherries.
And be sure you get all the pits out of 'em.

Teeny:

You're silly, mister.

Fibber:

I guess I am at that, sis.

Go ahead and recite somethin'.

Teeny:

All righty.

This is gonna be a dandy one, I betcha.

The boy stood on the burning deck

Mending a pair of socks.

It roused his ire

When the thread caught fire—

Hot darn!

(Giggles)

Fibber:

If you don't mind, sis,

I think that ought to conclude

your benefit performance.

You wanna earn a nickel

by running an errand for me?

Teeny:

No.

Fibber:

You don't?

Teeny:

No.

I wanna earn a dime.

Fibber:

You're takin' advantage

of my desperation, sis.

I'm gonna report you to the Labor Board.

Okay . . . it's a dime.

Now look.

Teeny:

All righty.

Fibber:

Run down to Kramer's drugstore

and have 'em throw me an evening paper.

Then run over to my house

and tell Mrs. McGee

I want a little table and a deck of cards.

So I can play solitaire.

Oh, yes . . . and a portable radio.

Teeny:

All righty.

Shall I tell her anything else?

Fibber:

Yes.

Teeny:

What?

Fibber:

I'm hungry!

Teeny:

Oh, pshaw!

*(MUSIC: ORCHESTRA. KING'S MEN SING
"LITTLE BROWN JUG." APPLAUSE.)*

(SOUND: CROWD MURMUR)

Molly:

Have you had enough to eat now, McGee?

Fibber:

Not quite. . . .

Toss me one more cookie!

(SOUND: SHORT WIND WHISTLE)

Fibber:

Thanks.

Gildersleeve:

How about coffee, McGee . . . ?
Want some more?

Fibber:

No thanks, Gildersleeve. . . .
You can pull in the hose now.

Gildersleeve:

Okay!

Fibber:

Hey, when is that guy gonna get here?

Molly:

You mean the man
who invented this paving material?
He's due any minute, McGee. . . .
Just be patient.
Are you terribly tired?

Fibber:

I ain't as tired as I am disgusted. . . .
I'm disgusted and humiliated.
And my feet are gettin' numb.
This stuff is gettin' hard.
Hey, did you call the City Hall again?

Molly:

Yes, I did, dearie.

Fibber:

Who'd you get?

Molly:

Myrt.

Fibber:

Myrt!
What'd she have to say?

Molly:

She said her cousin
overturned his canoe yesterday.

Fibber:

Yeah?
Did he get drowned?

Molly:

Oh, no.
He just got tired of paddling
and overturned it to his brother.

Fibber:

Overturned it to his brother!
If that ain't the farthest fetched gag
I ever heard,
and me standing here helpless.

(SOUND: CROWD MURMUR)

Gildersleeve:

By George, here he comes, McGee. . . .
It won't be long now!

Fibber:

What?
Who?

Molly:

It's the inventor of this paving material,

McGee. . . .
He'll know how to get you loose! . . .
Make way there, please, folks. . . .
Let the man through.

(SOUND: CROWD MURMUR)

Molly:

McGee!
Here's the expert!

Fibber:

Hiyah, Bud. . . .
Glad to see you!

Wimple:

Hello.

Gildersleeve:

Oh, my goodness. . .
it's Wallace Wimple!

Molly:

Are *you* really the inventor
of this pavement, Mr. Wimple?

Wimple:

Yes, I am.
And I'm *dreadfully* sorry
that your husband got stuck, Mrs. McGee.
It just makes me miserable to think of it.

Fibber:

Whaddye mean, it makes *you* miserable!
Whaddye think of me?

Wimple:

I'd rather not say—
in front of all these people.

Molly:

Well, how do we get him out of there,
Mr. Wimple?

Wimple:

Well, Mrs. McGee . . .
as I see it, the whole thing depends
on a chemical analysis of the material.
Maybe we can dissolve some of it
around his feet.

Fibber:

That's the first sensible remark
that's been made today.
What's the chemical formula, Wimple?

Wimple:

Oh, that's a secret, Mr. McGee.

Molly:

What do you mean, it's a secret?

Wimple:

That's what I mean. . . .
It's a secret.

Gildersleeve:

Well, you know what the secret is, don't you?

Wimple:

No, but my wife does.

Fibber:

Your wife!
What's she got to do with your invention?

Wimple:

Well, she's really the inventor.
I'm only the one
who saw the possibilities in it
for paving material!

Molly:

What was it in the first place?

Wimple:

Her recipe for chocolate pudding. . . .
The minute I tasted it I said to her,
I said, "Cornelia,"
I said, "this would make *wonderful*
paving material!"

Gildersleeve:

And what did she say?

Wimple:

I don't know. . . .
Everything went black. . . .
But here's what we better do, Mr. McGee.

Fibber:

I don't care *what* we better do . . .
but let's do it!

Wimple:

All righty.
I'll go home and analyze this material
and see how we can dissolve
it around your feet.

Molly:

Will your wife give you the formula?

Wimple:

If she won't, Mrs. McGee . . .

we'll have to use air hammers
and chop him loose.

*(MUSIC: ORCHESTRA BRIDGE. "WILLIAM
TELL" . . . OUT OF MUSIC WITH
CONCRETE BREAKING. AIR HAMMER
EFFECT.)*

Fibber:

Hey, go easy, fellas!
You're gettin' awful close to my feet.

Molly:

Be patient.
You're nearly free, dearie.

*(SOUND: HAMMER SOUND . . . THUDS . . .
CLANKS)*

Man:

Dere you are, buddy!
Sorry you gotta go home
wit' a hunk o' pavement on each foot,
but dat's de best we could do.

Gildersleeve:

I imagine you can soak that off
with turpentine, McGee. . . .

Molly:

Come on, dearie . . .
I'll take one arm
and Mr. Gildersleeve the other . . .

Fibber:

Okay. . . .
Much obliged, fellas. . . .

All right . . .
one side there, everybody.

(SOUND: CROWD MURMUR)

Gildersleeve:

Can you walk, little chum?

Fibber:

I think so. . . . Lemme try. . . .

(SOUND: HEAVY CLUNKS)

Fibber:

Yeah . . . I can manage.

(SOUND: CLUNKING WALK CONTINUES
. . . THEN . . .)

Fibber:

Boy, is this a relief! . . .
I thought I'd *never* get outa there.
You know what the first thing
I'm gonna do is, Molly,
after I get these hunks o' pavement
offa my feet?

Molly:

What, dearie?

Fibber:

I'm gonna run right out
and mail that letter for you!

Molly:

Give it here, McGee.

Fibber:

No, sir . . .

I started out to mail it,
and by the seven sisters of Maud Kelly,
I'm gonna mail it!

(SOUND: FOOTSTEPS OUT)

Molly:

It's no use, dearie.
That letter is no good now.

Fibber:

Whatcha mean?
Who was it to?

Molly:

The Street Commissioner.

Gildersleeve:

My goodness, Mrs. McGee . . .
what did you want him to do?

Molly:

Pave the street in front of our house.

Fibber:

Oh, pshaw!

(SOUND: CLUNKING WALK INTO MUSIC.
ORCHESTRA SELECTION. FADE FOR
CLOSING COMMERCIAL.)

Fibber:

(Mutters)
Of all the dad-ratted . . .
if that wasn't the darndest . . .

Molly:

Who are you talkin' about, McGee? . . .
Egghead Vanderveen?

Fibber:

No, Egghead McGee.
I'm disgusted.
Makin' a spectacle of myself,
everybody jeerin', pointin' at me . . .
and me squawkin' and hollerin' there
like a . . .

Molly:

Oh, stop fussin' about it.
It wasn't that bad.
And anyway,
I'll give you credit for one thing!

Fibber:

What's that?

Molly:

It's the first time you ever put your foot in it
and *then* opened your mouth!

Fibber:

Eh? . . . Oh.
Good night!

Molly:

Good night, all!

(MUSIC: CLOSING SIGNATURE)

FRED ALLEN

Fred Allen made his radio debut with his own series on October 23, 1932. He was already a headliner in vaudeville, having just completed a two-year run in the Broadway review *Three's a Crowd*, but suddenly found himself out of work when the producer of his next show backed out just as rehearsals were about to start. Radio interested Allen because of its promise of a steady job and reasonable working conditions. "In radio, if you were successful, there was an assured season of work," he wrote in his autobiography, *Treadmill to Oblivion*. "The show could not close if there was nobody in the balcony. There was no travel and the actor could enjoy a permanent home. There may have been other advantages but I didn't need to know them."

What began as a marriage of convenience blossomed into a long-term love affair that lasted until June 26, 1949, the night Allen's program signed off for the last time, a victim of his poor health and discouragement at the superior ratings of the competing quiz show *Stop the Music*.

The eighteen years that Allen remained on the air were one of the undisputed high points of American comedy. Allen was a true original, possibly the most creative performer ever to work before a microphone. From the beginning, he disdained the established formats that had already proven successful for other comedians, and throughout his career he had to battle constantly with network officials and advertising agencies to maintain the freedom to do things his own way. Although he started out as a comic juggler in vaudeville, he was more humorist than stand-up comic. He possessed a sophisticated, laconic wit, an unusually inventive imagination and a keen analytic intelligence. Allen was perhaps the most literate of the early radio performers and did most of the writing for his shows. At first this was because his budget was too small to afford outside help, but even after he attained great popularity and financial success, he continued to devote most of his waking hours to searching for new ideas and polishing material for the next week's program. He was also a master of ad lib—to the consternation of the network when his improvisations caused him to run over his allotted time.

Allen hit his comedic stride with the memorable *Town Hall Tonight* series broadcast over NBC between 1934 and 1939. He chose the title himself because he thought it would extend the show's audience to people living outside the big cities. *Town Hall Tonight* presented a full hour of comedy each week. Unlike Rudy Vallee and Kate Smith, who also had sixty-minute programs, Allen could not afford to fill out the hour with high-priced guests, so he had to develop a group of versatile actors and original comedy features. The performers included announcer Harry Von Zell and orchestra leader Peter Van Steeden, as well as Allen's wife Portland Hoffa. Allen and Portland had worked together in vaudeville, but when he turned to radio he found that over the microphone her voice sounded "like two slate pencils mating or a clarinet reed calling for help." To make it work on the air, he developed an appropriately zany characterization for her, then featured her on her own segment of the show.

Other features included Town Hall News, satiric observations on current events, and People You Didn't Expect to Meet, interviews with men and women engaged in such odd occupations as stuffing sausages and selling worms. Perhaps the most popular segment was the closing comedy sketch presented by the Mighty Allen Art Players, Allen's counterpart to the small-town stock company that did repertory at the local theater. The sketches were, as Allen put it, "satires on the fads, foibles and favorites of the day," including the popular Chinese detective Charlie Chan, whom Allen played as One Long Pan. "The Million-Dollar Smile," printed here, is a good example of the Mighty Allen Art Players at work.

During the *Town Hall Tonight* years, Allen was always on the lookout for running gags that would give his show some of the continuity that worked so well in daytime soap operas. By far the most successful was the "feud" with Jack Benny, which began quite by accident in 1936. In the course of praising a child violinist who appeared on the program, Allen remarked that if Benny, "an ancient and rancid violinist who lived out in Hollywood," had heard the youngster, "he should hang his head in symphonic shame and pluck the horsehairs out of his bow and return them to the tail of the stallion from which they had been taken." Benny picked up the challenge the next week on his own program and returned the insults in kind, and the feud was on. The audiences loved it, and the comedians kept it going as long as they both remained on the air. Many listeners took it seriously, but of course it was all in fun. Benny and Allen were the dearest of friends and often performed together on each other's shows. The script I have titled "Reminiscing with Jack Benny" was, according to Allen, one of their favorite encounters.

In 1939 *Town Hall Tonight* changed its name to *The Fred Allen Show*, and that in turn became *The Texaco Star Theater* in 1941. The program vacillated for a while between the old one-hour time span and the more popular thirty-minute format and finally settled into the latter. In 1942 Allen introduced Allen's Alley, the single most acclaimed feature of his radio career. The idea was to bring together the divergent views of a disparate group of comic characters who improbably lived next door to each other. After experimenting on the air for three years with such residents as the amiably cretinous Socrates Mulligan, poet Falstaff Openshaw and a Russian named Sergei Stroganoff, Allen settled on the four figures who made the device work so brilliantly. They were Senator Claghorn, the blowhard Southern chauvinist politician played by Kenny Delmar; Parker Fennelly's New England rube Titus

Moody; Minerva Pious's archetypal Jewish housewife Mrs. Nussbaum and Ajax Cassidy, the Irish drunk acted by Peter Donald. The quartet's diversity was calculated to have regional appeal, and although grounded in ethnic and regional stereotypes, they were written and played so lovingly there was never anything offensive about them.

Allen had been a working performer from the age of sixteen and found it difficult to stay away from the limelight after he closed down his show in 1949. Over the next few years, he made guest appearances on other people's programs, tried out a television special and was about to go into his own television series when he suffered his first heart attack. When he died on March 17, 1956, he was appearing weekly as a panelist on *What's My Line?*

The Mighty Allen Art Players: The Million-Dollar Smile (1936)

Allen:

And now, ladies and gentlemen,

we bring you

those whitecaps on the stormy theatrical sea,

The Mighty Allen Art Players.

These are the first actors

to ever appear in Ibsen's *Doll House*

and have enough room left

to accommodate an audience.

Tonight . . .

with their accident policies paid up . . .

they face you unafraid

to present a Hollywood dilemma.

It's called *The Million Dollar Smile,*

or *The Tooth Will Out. . . .*

Overture, Peter!

(MUSIC: OVERTURE PLAYS, THEN
  FADES)
(SOUND: CURTAIN RISING . . . PHONE
  RINGS)

Secretary:

Titanic Picture Company.

Mr. Allen?

Yes, he's in the filing cabinet.

No, he's not hiding.

He's just absentminded.

He picked up his nail file

and filed himself.

Hold the line.

Telephone, Mr. Allen!

Allen:

Yes, Miss Cast.

What am I doing in this filing cabinet?

Secretary:

What are you doing in the picture business?

Don't ask me.

Answer that phone!

Allen:

Hello.

Technicolor State.

Yes, I know.

You're making *The Last of the Mohicans*

in Technicolor.

What?

Two of the Indians have yellow jaundice.

They're coming out lavender.

No, don't stop.

Go ahead and finish the picture.
Okay.

Secretary:

Who ever heard of a lavender Indian?

Allen:

A despondent Indian is blue, isn't he?

Secretary:

This'll be the last of the
Mohicans . . . positively.

Allen:

Why, the scenery in this picture is beautiful.

Secretary:

So what?

Allen:

If the picture is bad
I'll cut out the actors
and make it a travelogue.

Secretary:

Is your latest Mickey Mouse finished?

Allen:

Yes.
We're having a squeak preview tonight.

Secretary:

What about Bulldog Drummond?

Allen:

The picture's postponed.
Bulldog's got a touch of distemper.

*(SOUND: DOOR OPENS . . . WIND
EFFECT . . .
DOOR SLAMS)*

Allen:

What was that?

Secretary:

Mr. Zanuck just passed through.

Allen:

After this tell him to use the transom.

Picket:

(Off mike)
This joint is unfair to organized—

Allen:

Who is that yelling?
Open that door.

(SOUND: DOOR OPENS)

Picket:

This joint is unfair to organized pickets.

Allen:

Just a minute, fellow.
You sound like a tractor calling its mate.

Picket:

I'm from the pickets' union.

Allen:

Are you picketing me personally?

Picket:

Yes, the boys picketin' theaters
are complainin' about your pictures.

Allen:

Pickets don't go into theaters . . . do they?

Picket:

No, but people comin' out
leave the doors open.
And the boys see bits of your pictures
while they're picketin'.

Secretary:

Is that what they're complaining about?

Picket:

Yes.
The boys want to picket without bein' bored.

Allen:

What's that got to do with me?

Picket:

Either you make better pictures
or the pickets' union wants revolvin' doors
put in all the theaters.

Allen:

Okay, I'll meet you halfway.

Secretary:

Yes, you'll get revolving doors.
Now beat it!

Allen:

Yes.

Picket:

Yes, what?

Allen:

What she said.

118

Picket:

A yellowbelly, hey?
So long!

(SOUND: DOOR SLAMS)

Allen:

What did he mean,
a yellow—ah—er—abdomen?

Secretary:

It must be that egg on your vest.

*(SOUND: DOOR OPENS . . . WIND
EFFECT . . .
DOOR SLAMS)*

Allen:

Good morning, Mr. Zanuck.

Secretary:

You missed him.

Allen:

I wish he'd slow down.
I've been his partner for two years
and I've never even seen him.

Secretary:

That's why you're still his partner.
He's never seen *you.*

Allen:

Never mind that.
Where's the morning mail?

Secretary:

Under your nose.

Allen:

Don't be silly.

That's my moustache.

Where's my personal fan mail?

Secretary:

It's on your desk.

Those three postcards.

Allen:

Ah, a card from Hot Lick, Arkansas.

Secretary:

A fan?

Allen:

Says . . .

"I saw your picture *Love Is a Grunt* last week

and won a set of dishes. . . .

Is there any way I can win

the dishes after this

without seeing your pictures?"

Secretary:

What are the others?

Allen:

Tripod, Texas.

"Saw the trailer on *Weeping Wives*.

If you haven't made the picture, don't!

Business is so bad here,

my Bank Night

is in the hands of the receiver.

Manager, Gem Theatre."

Secretary:

Here's a card from Skolsky.

Allen:

Good old Sid.

Is it a boner?

Secretary:

Read it.

Allen:

"In your picture *Alimony a là Mode* . . .

a close-up shows the hero Fordyce Honeydew

standing at a pool table behind the five ball.

That's a boner.

This perfumed bum

belongs behind the eight ball."

*(SOUND: DOOR OPENS . . . WIND
WHISTLE . . . DOOR CLOSES)*

Allen:

Ah-choo! Ah-choo!

Secretary:

Gesundheit!

Allen:

If Mr. Zanuck doesn't slow down

he'll give me pneumonia.

Secretary:

Mr. Zanuck knows what he's doing.

Allen:

Where did he go?

Secretary:

Even if I knew, he'd be gone by now.

Allen:

Who's in the next office?
Have you looked?

Secretary:

Yes, I looked in before.

Allen:

Well, what did you see?
Where's my memo?

Secretary:

There were eight men dozing around a table.

Allen:

What was it—
a sit-down strike or a conference?

Secretary:

What's the difference?

Allen:

If there's liquor on the table,
it's a conference. . . .
Get my producer Nunnally Johnson
on the phone.

Secretary:

Yes, sir.

Allen:

Ask him why that entire picture
Banjo on My Knee
was made in long shots.

Secretary:

The cameraman couldn't get any closer.

Allen:

Why not?

Secretary:

The actors were eating garlic
all through the picture.

Allen:

What a business.
Get me my toupee.

Secretary:

The pompadour?

Allen:

Any toupee.
I want to pull my hair out.

*(SOUND: DOOR OPENS . . . ARGUMENT
FADES IN)*

Director:

I'm the director, boy.
You'll play the scene the way I say.

Kid:

I'm the star, phony.
I'll play the scene the way I feel it.

Allen:

Boys! Boys!
What is this?
You're a director, Napra.
Why aren't you directing?

Director:

This little punk
is holding up *Hillbilly Heartaches*, F. A.

Allen:

What's the trouble, Rondelay?

Kid:

This hog-caller
is trying to show me how to act.

Director:

You hear that, F. A.?

Allen:

Now . . . see here, boys.
I've got two million dollars tied up
in *Hillbilly Heartaches.*

Kid:

And who's the star?

Allen:

Rondelay Fink,
the boy with the million-dollar smile.

Kid:

Right.
And I'm bigger than Shirley Temple, ain't I?

Director:

Around the ears, yes.

Kid:

Why, I was a star in *Our Gang*
when you were looking at the world
through a buttonhole.

Director:

You'd better watch your tongue, squirt.
My wife's brother-in-law
is related by marriage
to the nephew of a man
who knows Adolph Zukor by sight.

Kid:

I don't care

if you had Donald Duck for dinner.
That doesn't make you a director.

Allen:

Now wait a minute, you two.
I'm the head of this studio.

Kid:

Never mind apologizing.
I want satisfaction.

Allen:

I've spent a fortune making
Rondelay Fink's million-dollar smile
a household word.

Director:

That's what's holding up the picture.
He refuses to smile.

Allen:

Refuses to smile?
Without your smile, Rondelay,
Hillbilly Heartaches is a celluloid tragedy.
It's your trademark.

Kid:

I know, F. A.
I'm doing the best I can.

Director:

I direct him to smile,
what happens?
He pouts.

Allen:

Rondelay!

Kid:

Well . . . I can't smile, chief.

Allen:

Why?

Has your mother told you your salary?

Kid:

No, it ain't money.

Allen:

Come on, Rondelay.

Let's see you smile.

Kid:

If I smile you'll be sorry.

Director:

Come on, Rondelay, smile.

Kid:

All right. . . .

Tee-hee!

Allen:

Your mouth, Rondelay.

What's wrong?

Director:

What's happened to your teeth?

Kid:

I told you I can't smile.

My first teeth are coming out.

Allen:

Shedding your teeth—egad.

How many teeth have you got left?

Kid:

Only one—look.

Director:

One tooth.

Allen:

Your gums look like

an Elk wearing a red vest.

Kid:

You're telling me.

This one tooth is hanging by a thread.

Allen:

This is a dental calamity.

How much of the picture is shot?

Director:

One more scene and it's finished, chief.

Allen:

We've got to make this final scene

immediately, Napra.

What a business—

two million dollars hanging by a tooth.

Kid:

Hollywood can't beat Nature, chief.

Director:

Don't talk.

Allen:

No, Rondelay, don't breathe.

What stage are you working on?

Director:

Stage B.

Allen:

Come, Rondelay, let's go!

(SOUND: DOOR OPENS)

Director:

Hold your lips together, Rondelay.

Allen:

Yes, don't even purse your lips.
A single twitch might be fatal.

Director:

Here we are, Stage B.

(SOUND: DOOR OPENS .. HUM OF VOICES)

Voice:

Hello . . . F. A.

Allen:

I'll say hello later, cast.
We've got to shoot this final scene
with Rondelay Fink right away.
On the set, cast.

Director:

Ready, camera?

Voice:

(Off-mike)
Okay!

Director:

Sound?

Voice:

(Off-mike)
Okay!

Allen:

What is the scene, Napra?

Director:

The boy has a fight with
his hillbilly paw and maw.
He decides to go to the city.
He whistles for his dog.
And we fade as Rondelay
gives his million-dollar smile
and walks down the road
toward Montgomery Ward's.

Allen:

Surefire.
Let's go.

Director:

Okay, everybody.

All:

Yes, Mr. Napra.

Director:

Let's go.
Camera!
Action!

(SOUND: CAMERA SOUND)

Kid:

Good-bye, folks!

Paw:

Where are you goin', son?

Kid:

I'm a-leavin' for the city, pappy.

Maw:

What's got into ye, Luther?

Paw:

Son, you ain't been the same
since you started wearin' garters.

Maw:

Yep, garters led to stockin's.
Fust thing ye know,
he'll be wearin' shoes.

Kid:

I cain't wait fer shoes.
I'm goin' to the city in my stockin' feet.

Paw:

Ye gol-dinged dude.

Kid:

Wal, dude or slob—I'm a-goin'.

Maw:

Y'all packed?

Kid:

You bet.
I got my dog Sampson,
my jackknife
and the catalogue.

Paw:

You ain't a-takin' that catalogue.

Maw:

Not the catalogue, son.

Kid:

Catalogue's mine, ain't it?

Paw:

Catalogue's common property
in the hills, son.
You and Sampson can git
but the catalogue's gotta stay.
Give it cheer.

Kid:

Okay, good-bye, pappy.

Paw:

Good riddance, son.

Kid:

Good-bye, mammy.

Maw:

Tally-ho, son.
You ain't forgettin' nothing?

Kid:

Sure enough.
Where's my dog?
Sampson!
(Whistles)
Thamthon!
Here Thamthon!
Thop the thene!

Director:

Cut!

Allen:

What's wrong?

124

Kid:

My one tooth—
it'th gone.

Allen:

Your tooth is out?

Kid:

Yeth.
When I whithled it blew out—
where ith it?

Director:

There it is on the floor.

Allen:

This is terrible.
The picture's ruined.
Two million dollars wasted.

Director:

Tough luck, F. A.
Two more speeches
and the picture would have been finished.

Allen:

Fate has gone too far this time.

Director:

How long will it take your new tooth
to grow in, Rondelay?

Kid:

Sixth month.

Allen:

I can't hold *Hillbilly Heartaches*
for six months. . . .
I've got it!

Director:

What, F. A.?

Allen:

False teeth!

Director:

What a mind!
False teeth.

Allen:

Colossal!
With false teeth
the million-dollar smile will be saved.

Kid:

Yeth, but I can't wear falth teeth.
My gumth are there.

Director:

You'll only need them two minutes.
We can finish the picture.

Allen:

Yes, Rondelay, you've got to come through.

Kid:

Thure, I'll be a thport.
But where do I get the falth teeth?

Allen:

I'll—take out my uppers.
(Mumble)

(SOUND: TEETH CLICK)

Allen:

Here, Rondelay.

125

Director:

They look wonderful, F. A.
Put them in, Rondelay.
Do they fit?

Kid:

They're a little big.

Director:

Great—look at the smile!

Kid:

I can't close my mouth.

Director:

But as long as you can talk
we can finish the picture.
F. A., you're a genius.
What strategy!

Allen:

(Lisps)
Thrategy will alwayth
thave the thithuation, boyth.
Leth go!

Allen's Alley: Used Cars with Portland Hoffa, Kenny Delmar as   **(c. 1946)**
Senator Claghorn, Parker Fennelly as Titus Moody, Minerva Pious as
Mrs. Nussbaum, and Peter Donald as Ajax Cassidy

Portland:

What is your question tonight?

Allen:

Well,
recently license commissioners
around the country
have been investigating
used-car dealers and others
who have been forcing accessories
on automobile buyers.
And so our question is:
have you had any unusual experiences
trying to buy a used car?

Portland:

Shall we go?

Allen:

As the little boy's lips
said to the bubble gum—
the time has come to blow.

(ALLEN'S ALLEY THEME MUSIC)

Allen:

What a night in Allen's Alley, Portland.
I guess the Senator's cooking dinner.
I can smell the yamburgers from here.
Let's knock.

(SOUND: KNOCK ON DOOR, DOOR OPENS)

Claghorn:

Somebody—
Ah say somebody—
somebody whammed mah what's-this.

Allen:

Yes, I—

Claghorn:

Claghorn's the name.
Senator Claghorn, that is.

126

Allen:

Look—

Claghorn:

Son, why don't you go away?
Go button your nose.
Go hem a hanky, son.

Allen:

I'm sorry, Senator.
If you're busy—

Claghorn:

Ah jest come back
from mah college alma mammy.
They gimme a degree.

Allen:

A degree—
for what?

Claghorn:

Research.
Ah wrote a paper on Horace Greeley.
Ah proved he was cross-eyed.

Allen:

Horace Greeley cross-eyed?

Claghorn:

Ah proved
when Horace Greeley said,
"Go West"—

Allen:

Yes?

Claghorn:

He was lookin' South.

Allen:

You must have had some
commencement day.

Claghorn:

They gimme a muleskin diploma
and mah degree.
What a sight!
The entire faculty of Yazoo Normal
standin' there—
me wearin' mah mortarboard
and seersucker robe.
When Ah finished mah talk on
"Is the Magnolia Doomed?"
the student body rose
and gimme three cheers and a possum.

Allen:

It must have been touching.
But tell me, Senator,
what about this used car business?

Claghorn:

Ah hit the ceilin', son.
But it didn't help.
Ah had to pay over the ceilin'.

Allen:

What happened?

Claghorn:

Ah went to a used-car dealer:
the Chucklin' Confederate.

Allen:

I see.

Claghorn:

Ah had mah name on a list four years.

Finally the Chucklin' Confederate
sent word mah car had come.
He said along with the car
I'd have to take some accessories.

Allen:

Accessories?

Claghorn:

There was linsey-woolsey seat covers,
a weevil spray,
swamp pontoons,
a built-in hall tree,
a canvas hammock,
a sundial,
a melodeon,
two flyswatters
and a set of musical jugs for a horn.

Allen:

I see.

Claghorn:

Ah was willin' to pay the swindler.
Ah had mah shoe off countin' out the money.

Allen:

Uh-huh.

Claghorn:

Somethin' told me to take a gaze
under them accessories.

Allen:

You did?

Claghorn:

Ah folded mah money,
put mah shoe back on.

Ah called the Chucklin' Confederate
a buzzard's whelp
and stalked outta that junkyard.

Allen:

After waiting four years for a car
you didn't take it?
Why not?

Claghorn:

Son, the car was a LINCOLN!
So long, son!
So long, that is!

(SOUND: DOOR SLAMS)

Allen:

Well, the senator solved his problem.
I hope we catch Mr. Moody
before he dozes off.

(SOUND: KNOCK ON DOOR, DOOR OPENS)

Titus:

Howdy, Bub.

Allen:

You look depressed, Mr. Moody.
Is something wrong?

Titus:

My wife lost an ear.

Allen:

Your wife lost an ear?
In an accident?

Titus:

She was carryin' a basket of corn
in from the barn.

Allen:

And?

Titus:

My wife lost an ear.

Allen:

Fine.
Tell me, Mr. Moody,
have you had any experience
buying a car recently?

Titus:

I was rooked to a fare-thee-well.
I was trimmed nearer
than a floorwalker's mustache.

Allen:

No kidding?

Titus:

Effen I ain't a rube,
I'll do till one gits here.

Allen:

What happened?

Titus:

Well, 'bout two months ago
I sold my collection of wishbones.

Allen:

You collected wishbones?

Titus:

I had all kinds of wishbones.
Mouse wishbones,
rabbit wishbones,
ferret wishbones.

I had a horse's wishbone.
'Twas nine feet long.

Allen:

And you sold your wishbone collection?

Titus:

I was plannin' to buy a car.
I sewed my money into one of my mittens
and jumped a Greyhound bus for New York.

Allen:

What about the car?

Titus:

I was winder-shoppin' around,
sizin' things up.
I was lookin' in a winder on Broadway.
Somehow a stranger standin' next to me
got his thumb caught
in the buttonhole of my lapel.

Allen:

I see.

Titus:

Next thing I knowed
he was pullin' me into a doorway.

Allen:

What did this stranger want?

Titus:

At first I thought he was lonesome
and jest wanted company.
Then he says,
"Fixin' to buy a car, Rueben?"

Allen:

Uh-huh.

Titus:

I says, "What's it to ye?"
He says, "Don't git in a pucker.
I'm yer man."

Allen:

The stranger was a car salesman?

Titus:

He took me over to the river.
There was a big yard.
'Twas full of fenders, bumpers,
engines, bodies and all kinds of parts.
I says, "What's this?"
He says, "It's a car cafeteria."

Allen:

A car cafeteria?

Titus:

He says, "Tell me what kind of a car ye want.
I'll go into the yard and assemble the pieces.
But 'fore I start makin' yer car to order,"
he says, "you kin pay me the money."

Allen:

Uh-huh.

Titus:

I shook out my mitten.
He puts the money in his pocket.
He handed me an automobile horn.
He says, "Hold this horn, Hayseed.
I'll git the rest of yer car together."
With that he walked into the yard.

Allen:

What happened?

Titus:

I was there holdin' the horn.
The stranger never come back.

Allen:

Didn't you tell the police?

Titus:

Long 'bout midnight a constable come by.
I told him about the automobile.
I showed him the horn the stranger gimme.
I was wastin' my time.

Allen:

The policeman didn't give you
any satisfaction?

Titus:

He says, "You got the horn, ain't ye?"
I says, "Yes, I got the horn."

Allen:

Uh-huh.

Titus:

He says, "Well, blow, brother!"
So long, Bub!

(SOUND: DOOR SLAMS)

Allen:

Titus is like medicine.
He's always being taken.
Let's try this next door.

(SOUND: DOOR KNOCK, DOOR OPENS)

Mrs. Nussbaum:

Howdy doody!

Allen:

Ah, Mrs. Nussbaum.

That's a pretty gown you have on.

Mrs. Nussbaum:

It is mine cocktail dress.

Allen:

I didn't know you went to cocktail parties.

Mrs. Nussbaum:

We are only living once.

N'est-ce pas?

Allen:

That is true.

Mrs. Nussbaum:

Why not enjoying?

C'est la vie.

Life is a deep breath.

You are exhaling, it is gone.

Allen:

How true.

I didn't know you were given to tippling.

Mrs. Nussbaum:

Tippling?

I am reading everything Tippling is writing.

Boots, Fuzzy Wuzzy, Gunga's Din.

Allen:

No, no.

Tippling is drinking.

Mrs. Nussbaum:

I am drinking only cherry soda—

Dr. Brown's—

with occasionally a Catskill Manhattan.

Allen:

What is a Catskill Manhattan?

Mrs. Nussbaum:

A glass beet soup

with inside floating

a small boiled potato.

Allen:

I hate to break this up, Mrs. Nussbaum,

but have you had any experience

buying a car?

Mrs. Nussbaum:

Pierre, mine husband, is buying secondhand.

Allen:

Really?

What car did you finally buy?

Mrs. Nussbaum:

Pierre, without the glasses,

is going to a friend,

Pincus, a used-car baron.

Allen:

Pierre bought a car without his glasses?

Mrs. Nussbaum:

He is bringing home a limousine.

It is long and black.

Allen:

Fine.

Mrs. Nussbaum:

All around four sides is windows—glass.

Hanging down inside is black drapes

with also tassels.

Allen:

Black drapes?

Mrs. Nussbaum:

On the sides is silver lamps.
It is riding six people.

Allen:

Six people?

Mrs. Nussbaum:

While one is outside driving—

Allen:

Yes?

Mrs. Nussbaum:

Inside, on the floor, is laying five.

Allen:

This isn't a limousine.
It's a hearse.

Mrs. Nussbaum:

This I am telling Pierre.

Allen:

You refused to ride in it?

Mrs. Nussbaum:

I am saying, "Pierre, darling,
foist you are doing one thing
and I am riding!"

Allen:

Before you would ride in the hearse
with Pierre,
what did you tell him to do?

Mrs. Nussbaum:

Drop dead!
Dank you!

(SOUND: DOOR SLAMS)

Allen:

And that brings us to Mr. Cassidy's shanty.
I wonder what is happening
Chez Cassidy tonight?

(SOUND: KNOCK ON DOOR, DOOR OPENS)

Ajax:

What's all the fiddle-faddle?
Who's instigatin' the din?
Oh . . . how do ye do?

Allen:

Well, Mr. Cassidy.
How are you tonight?

Ajax:

Terrible, terrible, terrible.
Me right leg is so heavy
I can't lift it up.

Allen:

Your right leg is heavy?

Ajax:

It's full of iron.
Pig iron.

Allen:

That's silly.
How could your system get full of pig iron?

Ajax:

I've been eatin' pork chops.

(Coughs)

I'm not long for this world.

Allen:

What is that ladder you have there?

Ajax:

I'm going over to Sweeney's for dinner.

Allen:

And you have to carry a ladder?

Ajax:

The dinin' room table is too high.

You can't sit on chairs.

Everybody eats on a ladder.

Allen:

Why is the dining room table so high?

Ajax:

Sweeney is a mounted cop.

He always rides in to dinner on his horse.

Allen:

Oh!

Ajax:

Sweeney never uses a napkin.

He wipes his hands on the back of his horse.

There's so much food

on the back of Sweeney's horse,

he has mice under his saddle.

Allen:

Fine.

Well, tell me, Mr. Cassidy,

what about this used-car dealer business?

Ajax:

We're livin' in an age of high pressure.

People are hounded into buyin' cars

with slogans.

"There's a Ford in Your Future."

Allen:

I see.

Ajax:

Where I'm goin' in the future,

a Ford won't help.

What I'll need is a fire engine.

With an asbestos hose.

Allen:

Uh-huh.

Ajax:

"The Pontiac

Is the Most Beautiful Thing on Wheels!"

Allen:

What's wrong with that?

Ajax:

The most beautiful thing on wheels

is Maureen O'Hara on a bicycle.

Allen:

I see your point.

Ajax:

"Ask the Man Who Owns One."

Allen:

That's Packard.

Ajax:

Have you ever tried
to talk to a man in a Packard?

Allen:

No.

Ajax:

"Ask the Man Who Owns One."
He won't even answer you.

Allen:

Don't you ever use an automobile?

Ajax:

After many years of contemplation,
during which I have studied
the various means of transportation,
and weighed their merits pro and con,
I have arrived at one conclusion.

Allen:

And what is your conclusion?

Ajax:

That it is best for me
to restrict me travel
to one type of vehicle.

Allen:

And that is . . . ?

Ajax:

The station wagon.

Allen:

The station wagon?

Ajax:

Every Saturday night
when they take me away to the station . . .

Allen:

Yes?

Ajax:

They send the wagon.
Good-bye to ye, boy!

(SOUND: DOOR SLAMS)

Reminiscing with Jack Benny   (c. 1946)

Allen:

Well, yesterday afternoon I left home
and started up Third Avenue.
I stopped to read a sign
in a thrift shop window.
Suddenly, from a pawnshop next door,
I heard—

*(MUSIC: JACK PLAYS "LOVE IN BLOOM"
ON THE VIOLIN)*

Allen:

Gad!
There's only one man besides Rubinoff
who can make a violin sound like that.
I've got to see who is in this pawnshop.

(SOUND: DOOR OPENS AND CLOSES)

Jack:

But Mr. Rappaport,
this violin is a simulated Stradivarius.

Allen:

I thought so.
Jack Benny!

(APPLAUSE)

Allen:

Jack, what are you doing here
in a pawnshop?

Jack:

Excuse me just a minute, Fred.

Allen:

Sure.

Jack:

Look, for the last time, Mr. Rappaport,
will you take my violin?

Mr. Rappaport:

If there is anything I hate
it is making decisions.
Let me hear it once again.

Jack:

Okay.

(MUSIC: PLAYS "LOVE IN BLOOM")

Mr. Rappaport:

Something is with the tone.
Let *me* play it.

Jack:

All right.
Here.

Mr. Rappaport:

Now we will see.
Listen.

(MUSIC: ORCHESTRA VIOLINIST PLAYS
"LOVE IN BLOOM" BEAUTIFULLY)

Mr. Rappaport:

That's better.

Jack:

It's strange, Mr. Rappaport.
You're a pawnbroker
and you play my violin better than I do.

Mr. Rappaport:

Why not?
The violin has spent more time with me
than it has with you.

Allen:

Jack, you're not hocking your violin?

Jack:

No, Fred.
I'm just storing it.

Allen:

Storing it?

Jack:

Yes.
I leave my violin with Mr. Rappaport
every summer.
He puts it in a mothproof bag.
It's safe with him.

Allen:

I see.

Jack:

You know how a pawnbroker is—
he takes an interest in things.

Allen:

I know.

Jack:

Then you'll take it again this summer,
Mr. Rappaport?

Mr. Rappaport:

All right, Mr. Benny.
But please, this time just the violin.

Jack:

Just the violin?

Mr. Rappaport:

Yes.
All last summer
I had that Phil Harris and Dennis Day
hanging in my window.

Jack:

Oh, yes!
Yes!
Well, I guess this summer
I can squeeze them into my locker
at Grand Central.
I've got the Quartet in there already.

Mr. Rappaport:

Any place but here, Mr. Benny.
Here's your ticket.
I'll put away your violin.

Jack:

Thanks a lot.
Haven't you forgotten something?
Mr. Rappaport?

Mr. Rappaport:

Oh, yes.
Here's a handful of mothballs for your suit.

Jack:

Thanks.
See you in the fall, Mr. Rappaport.
Let's go, Fred.

Allen:

Okay.

(SOUND: DOOR OPENS AND CLOSES)

Allen:

Gosh, Jack.
You look wonderful.

Jack:

And, Fred, you look wonderful, too.

Allen:

And to think people have been saying
you're a shriveled-up, infirm,
doddering old man.

Jack:

And to think people have been saying
you're a flabby, wrinkled, baggy-eyed
old sourpuss.
They told me you were wearing a veil.

Allen:

People have been saying that's what we are?
Ha! Ha!

Jack:

Yes.

Ha! Ha!

Say, Fred—

Allen:

Yes, Jack.

Jack:

We are, aren't we?

Allen:

I can't get over it, Jack.

I've never seen you looking better.

Jack:

Well, thanks.

Allen:

That beautiful wavy hair—

Jack:

Well—

Allen:

Those sparkling white teeth—

Jack:

Gee—

Allen:

And those long eyelashes—

Jack:

Uh-huh.

What about my nose?

Allen:

Your nose?

Jack:

Yes.

At least that's mine.

Allen:

No, I mean it, Jack.

I don't know how you do it.

You look so young.

Jack:

Really?

Allen:

You don't look a day over—

Jack:

Over what?

Allen:

When I'm your age

I hope I look as good as you do.

Jack:

Now wait a minute, Allen.

If you want—

Allen:

Jack, Jack, what are we arguing for?

We're old friends.

Jack:

You're right, Fred.

Allen:

When I told you you were looking good,

I meant it.

Tell me, Jack,

how do you keep yourself

in such good condition?

Jack:

Well, Fred,
it's the life I've been leading.
I eat the right food,
get plenty of exercise
and keep sensible hours.

Allen:

I see.
What's your average day like, Jack?

Jack:

Well, I get up every morning at seven,
and jump into a cold tub.

Allen:

A cold tub?

Jack:

Yes.
Then I fill the tub with hot water,
and relax for an hour.

Allen:

I see.

Jack:

Then I'm ready for breakfast.
A glass of orange juice
and a long loaf of French bread.

Allen:

A long loaf?

Jack:

Yes.
I lean on the French bread
while I'm drinking the orange juice.

Allen:

Oh, fine.

Jack:

After breakfast I put on a pair of sneakers—

Allen:

And when you have the sneakers on?

Jack:

I sneak back to bed again.

Allen:

How long do you stay in bed?

Jack:

Till lunch.
For lunch I eat a health sandwich.

Allen:

What is a health sandwich?

Jack:

One vitamin pill between two Wheaties.

Allen:

Oh.
And after lunch?

Jack:

I'm off to the golf course.

Allen:

You play golf?

Jack:

If I happen to find a ball, yes.
Otherwise, I caddy.

Allen:

After a hard day of retrieving on the links
you must be ready for dinner.

Jack:

Yes.
For dinner I have two cakes of ironized yeast
and a heaping bowl of spinach.

Allen:

Yeast and spinach.
That must give you plenty of iron.

Jack:

You said it.
I don't know what they do in Rio
on a rainy night,
but at my house
I sit around and get rusty.

Allen:

Well, Jack, that's some day.
No wonder you look in the pink.

Jack:

Tell me, Fred,
how do *you* keep looking so healthy?

Allen:

I hang around the Blood Bank all day.
At night, when they close up,
if they have any blood left over,
they give it to me.
I'm loaded.

Jack:

If I need any plasma
I'll know where to come.

Allen:

You bet.
How do you do it, Jack?
You haven't a wrinkle in your face.

Jack:

Just between you and me, Fred,
I have undergone a little plastic surgery.

Allen:

Plastic surgery?

Jack:

Yes.
Every so often I have this plastic surgeon
take up the slack skin on my face
and tie it at the back of my neck.

Allen:

The back of your neck?
Doesn't it bother you?

Jack:

No.
The only thing is,
now I wear a size twenty-seven collar.

Allen:

I noticed that your Adam's apple
was pulled around under your left ear.
But with it all, Jack,
you still look the same
as the first day I met you.

Jack:

And, Fred, you look the same
as the first day I met you.

Allen:

Remember that first day we met.

*(MUSIC: VIOLINS START TO PLAY
  "MEMORIES")*

Allen:

I was in vaudeville—a star.
I was headlining at the Cecil Theater
in Mason City, Iowa.
After the first show
there was a knock on my dressing room door.

(SOUND: KNOCK ON DOOR)

Allen:

Come in!

(SOUND: DOOR OPENS)

Krakauer:

Mr. Allen,
I'm the manager, Mr. Krakauer.
You've got a great act.
You're a great star.

Allen:

Thank you, Mr. Krakauer.

Krakauer:

With you as the headliner
I've got a great show.
All but one act.

Allen:

Oh.

Krakauer:

I'm canning that guy right now.
He's dressing across the hall.

(SOUND: KNOCK ON DOOR, DOOR OPENS)

Jack:

Yes?

Krakauer:

I'm the manager.
Your act is putrid.
You're canned!

Jack:

Everything went wrong.
When I came on
the orchestra forgot to play "Pony Boy."
When I played "Listen to the Mocking Bird,"
my E-string broke.
At the finish when I play "Glow Worm"
my violin lights up.
The electrician forgot to plug it in.

Krakauer:

My patrons are Iowa farmers.
All week they work in the cornfields.
They come to the theater to forget corn,
not to have it thrown in their faces.
Start packing!

Jack:

But Mr. Krakauer—

Krakauer:

You're through!
Get out!

Jack:

I wish I was dead.

Allen:

What's the matter, son?

Jack:

The manager canned me.

Allen:

Come into my room.

Don't hang back, lad.

Jack:

But—this is the star's dressing room.

Allen:

I know.

Jack:

You mean you're Fred Allen?

Allen:

Yes.

Stop trembling, son.

Sit down.

Jack:

Gosh!

Me in Fred Allen's dressing room.

It's like a dream.

Allen:

What is your act called?

Jack:

Gypsy Jack and his Tziguener Fiddle.

Allen:

Gypsy Jack.

Jack:

This is my first date in vaudeville.

Now I'm canned.

Allen:

Don't give up, Gypsy Jack.

Jack:

But I haven't any money.

I can't get home.

I live in Waukegan.

Allen:

What is the fare to Waukegan?

Jack:

Thirty dollars.

Allen:

Here is thirty dollars, Gypsy Jack.

Go back to Waukegan.

Jack:

Oh, thank you, Mr. Allen.

(MUSIC: VIOLINS PLAY "MEMORIES,"
THEN FADE)

Allen:

Gosh, Jack,

when I saw you leaving the theater that day

in your gypsy suit with the burlap sash,

little did I think I would ever see you again.

What happened?

Jack:

When I finally got home to Waukegan,

I went back to pressing pants

in my Uncle Tyler's tailor shop.

Allen:

Mason City had left no scars?

Jack:

No.

But show business was still in my blood.

141

I used to take my violin around
and play for all of my friends.

Allen:

You were happy.

Jack:

For the nonce.
Then, suddenly I had no friends.

Allen:

And then?

Jack:

One day, I was pressing a pair of pants.
It was a rush job.
The pants belonged to the tenor
in a *Blossom Time* company.
They were leaving that night.

Allen:

I see.

Jack:

I was pressing carefully, avoiding the holes,
when my iron ran into a lump
in one of the pockets.
The lump turned out to be
a ticket to Hollywood.

Allen:

Hollywood!
That was the second time we met.

(MUSIC: VIOLINS PLAY "MEMORIES,"
    THEN FADE)

Allen:

It was on the Twentieth Century Fox lot.

I was starring in my first picture,
Thanks a Million.
I remember that morning
I walked on the set. . . .

1st Voice:

Quiet on the set!
Quiet on the set!
Mr. Allen is ready for this scene!

2nd Voice:

Here's the script, Mr. Allen.

Allen:

Thank you.

3rd Voice:

Chair, Mr. Allen?

Allen:

Thank you.

4th Voice:

Let me touch up your makeup, Mr. Allen.

Allen:

Thank you.

Ratoff:

Mr. Allen,
we are shooting right away
the big comedy scene.

Allen:

Which one, Mr. Ratoff?

Ratoff:

It is the Bowery.
You do a scene with a bum.

Allen:

A scene with a bum?

Ratoff:

Yes.

Joe, bring in the bum.

Joe:

This way, you guys!

Central Casting sent us fifteen

of the seediest extras they could find.

Pick out the crumbiest, Mr. Allen.

Allen:

Hmmm.

How about that one—

in the dirty T-shirt and baggy beret.

Joe:

Okay.

Hey, you—step forward.

Benny:

Yes, *sir!*

Allen:

Just a minute, Beaten One.

I know your face.

Aren't you Gypsy Jack?

Jack:

Yes, Mr. Allen.

But here in Hollywood

my name is Jack Benny.

Allen:

I hardly knew you with that beard.

Jack:

I've been standing in for Gabby Hayes.

This is my big break, Mr. Allen.

Gosh, doing a scene with you . . .

it's like a dream again.

Ratoff:

All right.

Let's get going.

Cameras ready!

Lights!

Joe:

Here's the pie, Mr. Allen.

Jack:

Wait!

A pie?

Ratoff:

Yes.

It's a very short scene.

Mr. Allen hits you in the face with a pie.

Camera!

Lights!

Ready, Mr. Allen.

Allen:

Ready.

Jack:

Wait a minute!

Ratoff:

Hold it!

What is it?

Jack:

What do I do?

Ratoff:

You do nothing.

You just get the pie in the face.

Camera!

Lights!

Get ready to throw, Mr. Allen.

Allen:

I'm ready.

Jack:

One moment, please!

Ratoff:

HOLD IT!

Now what?

Jack:

Don't I duck or anything?

Allen:

No.

You just hold your face still

and *whap*, you get it.

Jack:

It might help if I mug after the *whap*.

Ratoff:

Get another bum!

This bum is a bum!

Allen:

He'll be all right, Gregory.

Now, Jack, pipe down.

Jack:

Sorry, Mr. Allen.

Ratoff:

Camera!

Lights!

Ready, Mr. Allen.

Allen:

All set.

Jack:

Wait a minute!

Allen:

What is it now?

Jack:

What kind of a pie is it, Mr. Allen?

Allen:

Lemon meringue.

Jack:

Couldn't they make it banana cream?

I like banana cream better.

Allen:

It so happens Mr. Zanuck likes

lemon meringue.

Jack:

Oh!

Ratoff:

Camera!

Lights!

Quick, throw it, Mr. Allen!

Jack:

Hold it!

Just one more thing.

Ratoff:

Now what?

Jack:

What part of my face
is Mr. Allen going to hit?
I'd like to get it right
so you won't have to do the scene over.
I'm anxious to make good.

Ratoff:

He will hit you between the eyes,
so the lemon meringue will drip down
on your clothes.

Jack:

On my clothes?

Ratoff:

We will have them cleaned and pressed
for you.

Jack:

The pressing I can do myself.
I don't want to cause trouble.

Ratoff:

(Fast)
Camera!
Lights!
Quick, Fred!

Allen:

Okay.

Jack:

Wait!
Wouldn't it be funnier
if he hit me with a loaf of bread?

Allen:

A loaf of bread?

Jack:

Sliced.

Ratoff:

I've had enough!
You're fired!
Get off the set!

Jack:

But, sir—

Ratoff:

That's all for today, everybody!
This bum has unnerved me.
Put away the pie.
(Fade)
That's all!

Allen:

Well?

Jack:

I wish I was dead.

Allen:

Look, Gypsy.
I told you ten years ago in Mason City—

Jack:

But, Mr. Allen,
I thought the movies—

Allen:

Okay, so you don't need talent in movies.
You still have to have *something*.

Jack:

You're right.
I guess I'm just not meant for show business.

Allen:

Do you still live in Waukegan?

Jack:

Yes, Mr. Allen.
It's thirty dollars by bus.

Allen:

Okay.
Go back to Waukegan.
Here is the thirty dollars.

Jack:

Mr. Allen—
how will I ever be able
to repay your kindness—

(MUSIC: VIOLINS PLAY "MEMORIES")

Allen:

I'll never forget, Jack,
when you left the studio
I gave you the lemon meringue pie.

Jack:

It lasted me all the way to Green Bay.

Allen:

What happened when you got back to
Waukegan this time?

Jack:

I went back to the tailor shop.
But my Uncle Tyler wasn't there any more.

Allen:

There was a new owner?

Jack:

And he made my life miserable.

Allen:

He was mean to you?

Jack:

All day he kept singing those songs of his
from *Blossom Time*.
To this day I hate tenors.
I hate *Blossom Time*.

Allen:

You were unhappy, eh?

Jack:

I was desperate to get away.
Whenever I got a pair of pants to press,
the first thing I did was feel for lumps.
And then one day—

Allen:

Another lump?

Jack:

A big one.

Allen:

A railroad ticket?

Jack:

This time it was money.
I could go where I wanted.
I went to New York.

Allen:

New York.
That was the third time we met.

(MUSIC: VIOLINS PLAY "MEMORIES,"
THEN FADE)

Allen:

New York!
That's where you got your start in radio.

Jack:

Thanks to you, Fred.

Allen:

Oh, it was nothing.
I remember that day I got the call
from a man named Weaver.
A big shot with the
American Tobacco Company.
I entered Mr. Weaver's office—

(SOUND: DOOR OPENS AND CLOSES)

Weaver:

Gad!
Fred Allen!
We've been waiting all afternoon.

Allen:

I got your note, Mr. Weaver.

Weaver:

We've got a big radio program all lined up
for Lucky Strike Cigarettes—
and we want you to be the star.

Allen:

I'm sorry.

Weaver:

Wait till you hear this setup—
we've got Don Wilson to announce;
Rochester, Dennis Day, Phil Harris. . .

Allen:

But I've just signed to do a program
for Tender Leaf Tea and Shefford Cheese.

Weaver:

Well, that does it.
Without Allen we might as well
pull Lucky Strikes off the market.
We'll close the plantations,
put LSMFT back in the alphabet
and send old F. E. Boone back
to Lexington, Kentucky.

Allen:

There must be somebody else you can get.

Weaver:

WHO?
Singin' Sam wants too much money.
The Street Singer went into
the real estate business.
And what a program we had lined up!

Allen:

I'm sorry.

Weaver:

We had this quintet hired
to do the commercials.

Allen:

A quintet?

Weaver:

Yeah.

Show him, boys!

Cast:

HMMMMMMMMMM.

Allen:

Wait!

The guy on the end—

aren't you Gypsy Jack?

Jack:

Yes, Mr. Allen.

Allen:

Jack, you in a quintet?

Weaver:

(Sotto)

His wife Mary is in the show.

We did her a favor.

Allen:

Look, Mr. Weaver,

the star of this Lucky Strike show—

does he have to be funny?

Weaver:

No.

We've got Rochester, Dennis, Phil—

plenty of comedians.

Allen:

Does he have to have any talent?

Weaver:

All we need is a slob

the others can bounce jokes off of.

148

Allen:

Then here's your man—

Jack Benny!

Weaver:

Okay, Benny—you're hired!

Jack:

Fred, I'll never—

never be able to thank you enough.

(MUSIC: VIOLINS PLAY "MEMORIES")

Allen:

So, Jack, that's how you got into radio.

Jack:

Yes, Fred,

and if it wasn't for the thirty dollars

you gave me in Mason City and Hollywood—

Say, funny how things slip your mind.

I never did pay you back that sixty dollars.

(Laugh)

Allen:

No.

Jack:

I lost your address.

And you were traveling around all the time.

I tried to find you through *Billboard*.

Allen:

Forget it, Jack.

Jack:

But it isn't like me.

Allen:

I know.

Forget about it.

Jack:

Gosh, it just happens

I haven't got a cent on me right now

or I'd—

Allen:

Please, Jack.

Don't mention it again.

Jack:

I won't.

Well, Fred,

it's been swell talking over old times.

Allen:

It sure has, Jack.

Tell me, what are you doing now?

Jack:

Nothing.

My program finished last Sunday.

Allen:

You're out of work again, eh?

Jack:

Yes, Fred.

Allen:

What are you going to do?

Jack:

I guess I'll go back to Waukegan.

But, Fred—

Allen:

You don't have to ask me, Jack.

Here's the thirty dollars.

Jack:

But, Fred—

Allen:

And this time stay in Waukegan!

(MUSIC: ORCHESTRA UP, THEN FADE)

(APPLAUSE)

JACK BENNY

Fred Allen called Jack Benny "the best-liked actor in show business," and this affection was shared by the millions of listeners who made *The Jack Benny Program* one of the most popular shows in broadcasting history. Benny's undeniable likability on microphone as well as off seems curiously at odds with the character he portrayed. On the face of it, there would seem to be nothing particularly lovable about a vain, rather pompous and fussy cheapskate so touchy about his age that he could never admit to having reached his fortieth birthday. Yet that is how we felt about him. We loved him. Perhaps it had something to do with the universality of his failings. With any objectivity at all, we would have to recognize them in ourselves. Perhaps it also had something to do with the familiarity they came to have for us over the course of the twenty-three years Benny remained on the air. The merest allusion to his pennypinching or his toupee or the pride he took in his blue eyes and dubious skill on the violin was enough to set all America laughing.

Jack Benny was the master of the running gag, and the best and most durable of those gags was the Benny character itself. It expressed itself in any number of ways: in the predictability of his responses; in such fantastic devices as the underground vault where he hid all his money and the ancient Maxwell automobile he was too cheap to retire; in the catchphrases—"Oh, for heaven's sake!" or "Now cut that out!"—we looked forward to hearing him say every Sunday evening. The fact that we didn't hear them every week but maybe only three or four times a season was a tribute to his perspicacity about what makes a show work and keeps an audience interested. *The Jack Benny Program* was perhaps the most carefully crafted of all comedy shows; John Dunning calls it in *Tune In Yesterday* "one of the best-oiled pieces of precision work on the air." Benny made a particular point of rotating the running gags so they wouldn't be overplayed, and he was always quick to abandon those that didn't really work or had worn out their welcome. He also made a point of backing himself up with an in-depth cast of supporting players so that he would never have to rely on the old standbys to fill up his weekly half-hour.

The front line of support consisted of a quintet of first-rate performers who all had their own carefully defined comic personalities. Mary Livingstone, Benny's wife in real life, was a breezy, ironic deflator of the star's ballooning ego. Orchestra leader Phil Harris played a caricature of the flashy, hard-drinking, woman-chasing, barely literate dance-band musician. Rochester, acted to perfection by Eddie Anderson, was Benny's put-upon chauffeur and housekeeper, who always seemed to get the better of his boss. Tenor Dennis Day was the naive, impressionable kid, a role he continued to fill even after he had eleven kids of his own. Portly announcer Don Wilson was the victim of everyone's fat-man jokes and had his own comedy turn in the humorous commercial at the middle of the program, a Benny innovation designed to keep the comic mood intact while the product was being sold.

All five of these performers joined the show in its early years and remained with it until the end. (Dennis Day was the last to arrive—in 1939, when he replaced Kenny Baker, who had signed with Fred Allen.) They were an important part of the show's success, and Benny generously allowed them a large share of the laughs. Irving Fein, Benny's producer, tells us in his biography of the comedian that on one program Benny went so far as to let them take over the entire half-hour, limiting himself to a single line at the end. He regularly let himself be the butt of their humor, an unusual reversal of the standard relation between star and hired help.

Benny's second line of support was just as strong. There was the versatile Mel Blanc, the voice of Bugs Bunny and the other Warner Brothers cartoon characters, who impersonated everything from Professor LeBlanc, Benny's frustrated violin teacher, to his parrot and wheezing Maxwell. There was Artie Auerbach, who played Mr. Kitzel ("Peek-le in the mee-dle and the mustard on top!"). There were Sheldon Leonard, the racetrack tout ("Psst! Hey, buddy!") and Frank Nelson, the epicene floorwalker ("Ye-ess?"). There was gravel-voiced Andy Devine ("Hiyah, Buck!"), who came in for the Buck Benny sketches that became so popular that Paramount pictures developed them into a feature film. With all this talent, there was somehow even room for the Sportsmen Quartet and visiting stars like Ronald Colman and Danny Kaye. It had to be the fullest, most richly textured thirty minutes in radio.

Benny made his first radio appearance in 1932 on an interview show hosted by Ed Sullivan, then a columnist for the New York *Daily News*. His oft quoted opening lines were, "This is Jack Benny. . . . There will now be a slight pause while everybody says, 'Who cares?'"—a bit of self-deprecation that seems to contradict the egotism of the Benny character that developed later but which is actually very much at the heart of it. Benny was already a twenty-year veteran of vaudeville and was currently starring on Broadway in *Earl Carroll's Vanities*. But he had become fascinated with the potential of radio, and when he was offered his own series as a result of the Sullivan appearance, he left the security of a high salary to try his luck in the new medium.

Irving Fein writes that, having spent years developing a seventeen-minute act, Benny was terrified by the prospect of having to come up with new material every week. His close friend George Burns solved the problem by lending him his writer, Harry Conn. Conn stayed with Benny for four years, and when he left he was replaced by a series of other top comedy writers. Unlike Fred Allen, Benny was not a writer himself. His great talents were his timing and delivery and his skill as an editor and idea man. In his first series he introduced a number of innovations that were to become mainstays of radio comedy: the comic commercial, satires of current movies and the extensive use of sound effects.

The Jack Benny Program began broadcasting over NBC on May 2, 1932, and was an immediate hit. In 1934 Benny moved to the seven o'clock Sunday evening time spot he would occupy the rest of his radio career and began being sponsored by General Foods' Jello, a relationship that lasted until 1942. In later years sponsorship was taken over by Grape Nuts Flakes and then Lucky Strike Cigarettes. In 1949 he was paid two million dollars to come to CBS, where he remained until 1955, when he switched over to television.

Buck Benny Rides Again with Phil Harris, Mary Livingstone, Kenny Baker, Don Wilson and Andy Devine (c. 1946)

Jack:

That was Kenny Baker
singing "Night and Day"
from *The Gay Divorcee*,
assisted by the orchestra.
And a very good orchestra, too.
In fact, they can play anything by request.
Last week they were requested
to play hockey.

Phil:

And we won, too.

Jack:

Oh, you did?

Phil:

What's the matter with my orchestra?

Jack:

Oh, nothing, Phil, nothing.
I heard they're very conscientious.
I understand they go
to the pawnshop every day
and practice for hours.

Phil:

Is that so!
What about that violin of *yours?*

Jack:

Well, my violin was never in pawn.

Mary:

It was never in *tune.*

Jack:

Now listen, Mary, who are you with . . .
Phil or me?

Mary:

Me.

Jack:

Well, I'm glad that's settled. . . .
And now, ladies and gentlemen,
Kenny Baker will sing—

Kenny:

I sang already.

Jack:

Oh! . . .
Well, tonight, ladies and gentlemen,
as our feature attraction,
we will continue with our Western drama,
Buck Benny Rides Again,
or *Is His Saddle Red!* . . .
I will again play the part
of Sheriff Buck Benny,

as tough an hombre as ever
talked back to an orchestra leader . . .
a rip-snortin', rortin', cavortin'
Charles Lorton and Edward Everett Horton.

Crowd:
Wow!

Jack:
You ain't heard nortin'. . . .
This will go on immediately
after the next number,
which will be played by a man
who doesn't seem to worry much
whether he's going to stay
with this organization or not . . .
and his orchestra.
(Loud cough)

(MUSIC: ORCHESTRA PLAYS)

Jack:
That was "It's De-Lovely"
from the Broadway production
Red Hot and Blue. . . .
And now for the next installment
of our serial,
Buck Benny Rides Again.
The opening scene is the office
of the sheriff of Cactus County,
where we find the sheriff and his deputies
waiting for news as to the whereabouts
of Cactus-Face Elmer. . . .
Curtain . . .
Music . . .

(MUSIC: ORCHESTRA PLAYS LAST
   STRAIN OF "I'M AN OLD COWHAND")

Jack, Kenny & Wilson:
"I'm an old cowhand
From the Rio Grande,
But my legs ain't bowed
And my cheeks ain't tanned—"

Wilson:
"I'm a guy who
Never saw a cow—"

Kenny:
"Never rode a steer
'Cause I don't know how—"

Jack:
"And I sure ain't fixin'
To start in now—"

Jack, Kenny & Wilson:
"Yippey-i-oh ki-yay . . .
Wheeeeee! . . .
Yippy-i-oh ki-yay."

*(SOUND: PHONE RINGS DURING
   LAST LINE)*

Jack:
Hold it a second, boys.
There's the phone.

(SOUND: RECEIVER BEING PICKED UP)

Jack:
Hello . . .
Yes, this is the sheriff's office. . . .
What's that, madam? . . .
You say there's a gang of rowdies
disturbing the peace? . . .

We'll be right over
and put an end to that immediately. . . .
Where do you live, madam? . . .
Oh, right upstairs? . . .
Hmm!

(SOUND: CLICK OF PHONE)

Jack:

Boys, we gotta stop singin'.

Wilson & Kenny:

Shucks!

Jack:

I feel like swearin' myself. . . .
We never have any fun.

(SOUND: KNOCK ON DOOR)

Jack:

Come in!

(SOUND: DOOR OPENS)

Cowboy:

Oh, sheriff!

Jack:

Hello, Deadeye. . . . What's up?

Cowboy:

Someone stole my horse.

Jack:

Hmm, someone stole your horse, eh?
Why don't you lock your barn?

Cowboy:

They stole that, too!

154

(SOUND: DOOR SLAMS)

Jack:

Dawgone it, he got away
before I could think of an answer. . . .
Boys, there's been too much
shootin' and thievin'
goin' on around these hyah parts.
It's gettin' so those outlaws
are takin' everything
that ain't nailed down.

Wilson:

That's right, sheriff.

Jack:

Well, what are we gonna do?

Kenny:

Nail everything down.

Jack:

You got something there, deputy. . . .
This sure is a tough town. . . .
Well, we ought to be gettin' some news
about Cactus-Face pretty soon.
I wonder what time it is.

(SOUND: THREE GUNSHOTS AND
A "CUCKOO")

Jack:

Hmm, didn't know it was that late.

(SOUND: KNOCK ON DOOR)

Jack:

Must be Daisy, my fiancée.
(That's Western for sweetheart, folks.) . . .
Come in.

(SOUND: DOOR OPENS)

Jack:

Hullo, Daisy.

Mary:

Hullo, Horse-Face.

Jack:

Well, gal,
a feed bag hangin' from *your* ears
wouldn't look exactly out of place.

Mary:

Shut your trap, Buck.
Every time you open it, you whinny.

Jack:

Whatcha doin' in town, gal . . .
Christmas shoppin'?

Mary:

Yeah, I just bought a case of brandy
and some peanuts. . . .
The brandy's for pappy.

Jack:

Who's the peanuts for?

Mary:

His pink elephants.

Jack:

Your pappy sure is a drinkin' man.
What makes him that way, Daisy?

Mary:

He was weaned on herring
and he's been thirsty ever since.

Jack:

Hmm! . . .
If he keeps it up,
he'll be able to rent his nose
for a stoplight.

Mary:

Say, Buck, have you got any news
about our stolen cows?

Jack:

Nope,
and no news as to the whereabouts
of Cactus-Face Elmer. . . .
I gotta speak to your pappy about that.
Where is he now?

Mary:

He's gone down to Ike Muller's Saloon
for the weekend.

Jack:

Well, it's nice there.

*(SOUND: APPROACHING HEAVY
 FOOTSTEPS)*

Mary:

Here comes pappy now!

Jack:

He sure walks heavy, don't he?

Mary:

That's the fellow that's carrying him.

Jack:

Oh!

(SOUND: DOOR OPENS)

Phil:

Hullo, Buck.

Hullo, Buck.

Jack:

Hmm, seein' double again, eh? . . .

What are you so happy about, Frank?

Phil:

Well, Buck, I'm celebratin'

'cause you got my cows back.

Jack:

Hold on.

I didn't get your cows back yet.

Phil:

It's too late now,

the celebratin's under way.

Jack:

Why, I don't even know

where Cactus-Face Elmer is.

Phil:

You don't?

Why, Ike Muller tells me that Cactus-Face

just walked into the Gem Theater

to see a movin' picture.

Jack:

He did?

Phil:

Yeah.

And the sheriff of the next county

is waiting outside the theater

till you gets there.

Jack:

The sheriff of the next county, eh?

What's his name?

Phil:

Puddin' and Tame,

Puddin' and Tame,

Ask me again

And I'll tell you the same.

Jack:

Hmm! . . .

One more crack like that

and I'll play Ring-around-Your Eyesie. . . .

Well, now that we got Cactus-Face cornered,

I'd better rush right over there.

Kenny:

Can we go with you, Buck?

Jack:

Nope, it might be dangerous.

I'm a-goin' alone! . . .

Where's my horse?

Mary:

You're sittin' on him.

Jack:

Oh! . . .

Well, then I better get goin'.

I'm gonna get Cactus-Face this time,

dead or alive! . . .

Good-bye, folks, and a Merry Christmas.

BUCK BENNY RIDES AGAIN!

*(SOUND: FOUR HEAVY HORSE'S HOOFS
ON WOOD)*

Jack:

Open the door, Frank.

(SOUND: DOOR OPENS . . . THEN HORSE'S HOOFS ON GRAVEL, GALLOPING AWAY, AND AS THEY FADE, CUT—)

Wilson:

Scene Two. . . .
We now take you
to the front of the Gem Theater,
where we find Buck Benny just arriving.

(SOUND: HORSE'S HOOFS VERY FAST)

Jack:

Whoa!

(SOUND: HOOFS COME TO A DEAD STOP)

Jack:

Hm, them four-wheel brakes
sure are sumthin'.

Kenny:

(Does a whinny)

Ike:

Hey, Buck!

Jack:

Hullo, Ike.
I hear that Cactus-Face
just walked into this theater.

Ike:

Yes sir, not more than ten minutes ago. . . .

Buck, I want you to meet
the representative of the law
from the next county. . . .
This is Sheriff Andy Devine!

Crowd:

(Applause)

Jack:

Hmm, Main Street
sure is crowded tonight. . . .
Sheriff, I'm sure glad to know ya.

Andy:

Glad to know ya too, Buck.

Jack:

It was darn nice of Universal Studios
to let you come over here
and help me out in this case.

Andy:

Cain't stay with you long.
I'm startin' on a new picture tomorrow.

Jack:

Is that so?
What's the name of it?

Andy:

It's called *The Road Back*.

Jack:

Well, whatcha cryin' about?

Andy:

I ain't cryin'.
That's the way I talk.

Jack:

By the way, Andy,
did you see me in *my* latest picture,
The Big Broadcast?

Andy:

Yup.

Jack:

How did you like *me* in it?

Andy:

I thought you were right lousy.

Jack:

The word is "lovely."

Andy:

Oh!

Jack:

Well, reckon we done enough advertising
about our pictures.

Andy:

Well, ain't nobody gonna say that
Jello is the most tempting dessert
in these hyar parts
and every day millions of cowboys
keep eatin' it?

Jack:

Thanks, Andy, that was Devine. . . .
Now listen, sheriff,
I heard that Cactus-Face Elmer
is inside this theater.

Andy:

That's right,
and I'm hot on his trail.

158

Jack:

Well, what are you doin' *out*side?

Andy:

I *saw* the picture.

Jack:

Well, we gotta get Cactus-Face dead or alive!
What's playin' here anyway?

Andy:

William S. Hart.

Jack:

Oh, Bill Hart, eh.
Well, come along, I'll buy the tickets.
We can kill two birds with one stone. . . .
Stoop down, Andy,
and I'll getcha in for half-price.

Andy:

All right, but I feel kinda silly.

Jack:

Two tickets, miss . . .
one child and one adult.

Woman:

Here you are, sonny.

Jack:

He's the child.

Woman:

Oh! . . .
Tell him to trade that pipe in for a lollipop.

Jack:

Hmm! . . . Come on, Andy.

(SOUND: COUPLE OF FOOTSTEPS)

Man:

Tickets, please.
Keep your stubs for Bank Night.

(SOUND: MORE FOOTSTEPS)

Jack:

Hmm, it's awfully dark in here.
I wonder where the usher is.

Andy:

There he is—
up in front with a gun.

Jack:

That's William S. Hart.

Andy:

Oh, he cain't find a seat either.

Jack:

Hmm, sure is dark. . . .
Oh, here's a couple of empty seats.
Let's sit down.

Lady:

Sir!

Jack:

Oh, pardon me, lady. . . .
Move over one seat, Andy.

Lady:

S-s-s-s . . . s-s-s-s-s.

Jack:

Why, lady, are you hissin' the picture?

Lady:

No, I'm fryin' an egg.
I've been in here a month.

Jack:

Hmm! . . .
Hey, Andy, my seat's movin'!

Andy:

That's funny, mine's movin' too.

Jack:

It is?

Kenny & Wilson:

Moo-o-o-o-o!

Jack:

Dawgone it, we're sittin' on a couple of cows!
Wait a minute, are you Frank Carson's cows?

Kenny & Wilson:

No-o-o-o!

Jack:

That's a lie! . . .
Come on, sheriff,
Cactus-Face must be right close-by.

Andy:

There he goes now,
out that side door!

Jack:

I'll get him!

*(SOUND: TWO GUNSHOTS . . .
SCREAMING AND EXCITEMENT . . .
CHAIRS BEING TURNED OVER, ETC.)*

Andy:

Look out, Buck, he's shootin' back!

(SOUND: TWO MORE GUNSHOTS)

Jack:

Ooooh, he got me.

Andy:

He did, eh?
Are you hurt bad?

Jack:

Ooooh, reckon I'm done for.

Andy:

Don't give up, Buck.
You'll be all right.

Jack:

(Groans again)

Andy:

Come on, Buck . . .
Buck, say sumthin'! . . .
SAY SUMTHIN'!

Jack:

(Very weakly)
This will be continued next Sunday night—
Was I killed? . . .
Will we get Cactus-Face? . . .
Will Buck Benny ride again? . . .
Tune in next Sunday and find out. . . .
Play, boys.

*(MUSIC SEGUE INTO
ORCHESTRA NUMBER)*

Two Scenes with Rochester   (1945)

1

Rochester:

Hello, Mr. Benny,
this is Rochester.

Jack:

I know, I know. . . .
What do you want, Rochester?

Rochester:

I called to tell you
there's been a little excitement here.

Jack:

Excitement? . . .
What happened?

Rochester:

Well, the milkman turned his truck
in our driveway
and it got loose from him
and ran all over the front yard.

Jack:

Did he hit anything?

Rochester:

You know that big willow tree
by the house?

Jack:

Yes.

Rochester:

Well, it's really got something
to *weep* about now!

Jack:

Oh, my goodness.

Rochester:

Then he bounced off the tree
and knocked over the birdbath.

Jack:

The birdbath?

Rochester:

Yeah . . .
and I just hung up clean guest towels!

Jack:

Never mind that. . . .
What else happened?

Rochester:

Then he crashed into the front of the house
and broke milk bottles all over the place.

Jack:

You mean my front lawn is covered
with broken milk bottles?

Rochester:

Milk bottles, policemen and CATS!

Jack:

Holy smoke!
I can imagine what my lawn looks like.

Rochester:

Yeah . . .
you oughta see those cats lappin' up the milk
and spittin' out the grass.

Jack:

Oh, for heaven's sake.

Rochester:

Not only that. . . .
A cocker spaniel ran up on the lawn
and jumped right into the middle
of everything.

Jack:

Good. . . .
Did the cocker spaniel chase the cats off?

Rochester:

Chase 'em off?
They're using his ears for napkins!

Jack:

Rochester, stop being funny.

Rochester:

Do you really want me to?

Jack:

No, no, go on. . . .
Anyway, I don't believe a word of this.

Rochester:

It's true, boss.
It happened about two hours ago.

Jack:

Well, what's on the lawn now?

Rochester:

Broken bottles and *fat cats!*

Jack:

Well, roll 'em off,

and I'll be home right after the broadcast. . . .

Good-bye.

Rochester:

Good-bye. . . .

Good-bye, that is.

(SOUND: CLICK OF RECEIVER)

Jack:

I never saw anything like it. . . .

Every time I leave the house

something happens.

Mary:

What happened now?

Jack:

A delivery truck got loose on my front lawn

and broke about a hundred quart bottles.

Phil:

(Crying)

Oh no, Jackson, no, no, no!

Jack:

Phil, it was milk.

Phil:

Oh.

Jack:

I knew it wouldn't worry you too much. . . .

2

Don:

Ladies and gentlemen, about three hours ago

Jack Benny left home for the studio. . . .

Rochester was driving him,

and on the way they had a little tire trouble.

So let's go back and find out what happened.

(MUSIC BRIDGE)

*(SOUND: HAMMER POUNDING ON
TIRE RIM)*

Jack:

How much longer before

you have the spare on, Rochester?

Rochester:

Just a couple of minutes.

Jack:

Couple of minutes. . . .

It would have been fixed long ago

if I'd done it myself.

Rochester:

Hand me the wrench, will you, boss?

Jack:

Okay . . . here.

Rochester:

That's the screwdriver.

Jack:

Oh, the wrench. . . .

Here.

Rochester:

That's the pump.

Jack:

Oh . . . here.

Rochester:

That's the hubcap!

Jack:

Oh, you want the wrench. . . .

Here.

Rochester:

You're back to the screwdriver again!

Jack:

Oh.

Rochester:

You know, boss,

you sure ain't mechanically minded.

Jack:

I am, too.

Rochester:

Then why do you call me every morning

to screw the cap back on your toothpaste?

Jack:

Look, just hurry with the tire.

Rochester:

I'm almost finished.

Jack:

Good. . . .

I just can't understand having a blowout. . . .

It's a *very* good tire. . . .

It's a General.

Rochester:

I know . . .

but you've run that General down

to a buck private!

Jack:

Stop being silly. . . .

That tire hasn't got so many holes in it.

Rochester:

It hasn't?

Boss, the inner tube could be arrested

for indecent exposure!

Jack:

What?

Rochester:

Even the wheel is ashamed

to go around with it!

Jack:

Rochester, that's a terrible joke . . . awful.

Rochester:

Hee-hee-hee.

Jack:

What are you laughing at?

Rochester:

You always say that,

and two weeks later

it shows up on your program.

Jack:

It does not. . . .
Now come on, you're all through.
Let's get going.

*(SOUND: CAR DOOR OPENS AND CLOSES
. . .
MOTOR STARTS UP, FADES DOWN AND
OUT)*

Jack:

You know, Rochester,
one of the reasons I haven't fixed this car up
is that I've been thinking of
getting a new one.

Rochester:

Really, boss?

Jack:

Yes . . .
I think this car has just about
seen its best days.

Rochester:

I told you that before you bought it!

Jack:

I know, I know.

Rochester:

Do you really think you'll buy a new car,
boss?

Jack:

Well, it all depends on what they'll allow me
for a trade-in on this car. . . .
How much do you think
they'll appraise it for?

Rochester:

*Boss, when a car gets this old
they don't appraise it,
THEY WEIGH IT!*

Jack:

Well, they have to give me a good price
or I won't trade. . . .
We're pretty close to NBC
so you'd better start looking
for a parking place.

Rochester:

Why don't we go into a parking lot?

Jack:

Rochester!

Rochester:

Sorry, boss. . . .
I was lettin' my postwar plans
get the best of me.

Jack:

Hmmm . . .
here's a parking place
right in front of the studio.

Rochester:

Okay.

*(SOUND: CAR STOPS . . . DOOR OPENS
AND CLOSES)*

Jack:

I'm going in,
and you stay here and watch the car.

Rochester:

Yes sir. . . .

Hee-hee-hee . . .

what an automobile. . . .

This is the car

that made the Irishman stop smiling!

Jack:

Rochester!

Rochester:

And drove Muntz mad!

Jack:

Never mind, just stay here and wait for me.

The Life of Jack Benny with Don Wilson, Mary Livingstone, Phil Harris, (c. 1944) Eddie Anderson as Rochester and Danny Kaye

Don:

Ladies and gentlemen,

it has been said that Jack Benny

has brought more laughter to more people

than any man who ever lived.

And now I bring you the man who said it—

Jack Benny!

(APPLAUSE)

Mary:

Don—

Don, you wasted that introduction,

because Jack isn't here yet.

Don:

He isn't?

Where is he?

Phil:

Maybe he followed some babe

down Vine Street

and forgot to look up when he passed NBC.

Don:

Don't be silly, Phil.

Jack doesn't follow girls.

Mary:

He doesn't, eh?

How do you think he met me?

Phil:

No kiddin', Mary,

is that the way you met Jackson?

Mary:

Yeah.

If I didn't have to stop for that traffic light,

I'd still be working at the May Company.

But I'm not sorry.

I'm making just as much working for Jack.

Phil:

Gee, you're lucky.

But where is Jackson anyway?

Mary:

Oh, he'll show up in a minute.

And fellas, wait'll you see him.
Oh, brother!

Don:

Why, what's the matter, Mary?

Mary:

Well, Warner Brothers called him up
and told him they want to make a big feature
called *The Life of Jack Benny.*

Phil & Don:

The Life of Jack Benny?

Mary:

Yeah,
and you know, fellas,
since Jack found out about it,
he's absolutely unbearable.
I never saw such conceit in all my life.

Phil:

Well, if that's the case,
when Jackson gets here,
I'm leavin'.

Mary:

Leaving?
Why?

Phil:

If he's gettin' to be anything like me,
there'll be no standin' the guy.

Mary:

You said it, Phil.

(SOUND: DOOR OPENS)

Mary:

Oh-oh, here he comes now.

Jack:

(Very ritzy)
Well, hello, everybody.
Hello, Donald.

Don:

Hello, Jack.

Jack:

Philip.

Phil:

Hello.

Jack:

How do you do, Miss Livingstone?

Mary:

Jack Benny,
take off that monocle.

Jack:

That's not a monocle.
I broke my bifocals
and managed to save one focal.
Here, Donald,
take my gloves and cane.
Thank you.
There.

Phil:

Gloves and cane.
Oh boy, are you snooty!

Mary:

Phil, the gloves are snooty.
The cane is necessary.

Jack:

That I shall ignore entirely.

Mary:

(Mocking)

That I shall ignore entirely,

pip-pip.

Jack:

Go ahead, go ahead,

have your little fun,

but you'll all apologize

when you know what's happened to me.

Phil:

We know, we know.

Don:

Yes, Jack,

Mary told us that Warner Brothers

were going to make a picture

about your life.

Jack:

Yes sir,

the same studio that made

the life of Emile Zola,

the life of Louis Pasteur,

the life of Mark Twain.

And now,

the life of Jack Benny.

(FANFARE OF TWO TRUMPETS)

Jack:

Now cut that out!

Smart-aleck musicians.

Phil:

You know, Jackson,

I can't understand any studio

wanting to make a picture of your life.

Jack:

What do you mean?

Phil:

I'm the guy.

Color, glamor, excitement!

That's what they should make—

The Life of Phil Harris.

Jack:

The Life of Phil Harris!

Phil:

Sure!

Jack:

Phil, the story of your life

wouldn't pass the Hays Office.

So don't be ridiculous.

Phil:

All right,

so what's so interesting about your life?

Jack:

Mine is a story of adventure and courage.

The real true life of Jack Benny.

(FANFARE OF TWO TRUMPETS)

Jack:

Now stop with that!

Enough's enough. . . .

Listen, Phil, you may not believe this,

but my life has been

one adventure after another.

It started when I ran away from home
to face the world all by myself.

Phil:

How old were you?

Mary:

Thirty-two.

Jack:

I was twenty-seven!
I remember because I didn't want to leave
until I finished high school.
Thirty-two!
And look what happened to me after that.
Broadway, vaudeville,
musical comedy, radio!
Why, when they make the picture of my life
it'll be as long as *Gone With the Wind*.

Mary:

It should be;
they both started in the same period.

Jack:

Miss Livingstone,
your adolescent attempts at levity
fail to amuse me.
Well, fellows, I have to leave you now.
Rochester is waiting in the car
to take me to Warner Brothers.

Phil:

Hey, wait a minute, Jackson,
we got a radio program to do.

Jack:

(Sarcastic)
Radio—

hmmm—
radio!

~~**Phil:**~~

~~Yeah, radio.~~
~~R-a-rad-r-a.~~

~~**Jack:**~~

~~Oh, brother,~~
~~is he gonna have trouble~~
~~when television comes in.~~
~~Anyway—~~

~~**Phil:**~~

~~Television.~~
~~T-e-l-u-~~

Jack:

~~Never mind.~~
Come on, Mary,
you can go with me.

Mary:

Okay.

(MUSIC BRIDGE)

Jack:

Gee, Mary,
just to think of it
gives me a thrill.
Imagine on the marquees of theaters
all over the country,
in the big bright lights,
The Life of Jack Benny!

(FANFARE OF TWO TRUMPETS)

Jack:

Oh, shut up!
Come on, Mary.

168

(SOUND: AUTO MOTOR AND HORN)

Jack:

Take it easy, Rochester.
Watch where you're going.

Mary:

Oh, Jack, don't be so nervous.

Jack:

I'm not nervous.

Rochester:

You must be, boss.
You're tellin' me to take it easy
and you're drivin'.

Jack:

What?
Wait a minute, Rochester.
When we started out
you were driving.
What happened?

Rochester:

Remember that big bump
we hit back there?

Jack:

Yes.

Rochester:

Well, when the people put us back in the car,
they put us in wrong.

Jack:

Oh—oh—oh.
Well, you take the wheel now.
And hurry up.
I want to get to the studio.

Say, Mary, I just thought of something.
If they're going to make the story of my life,
I shouldn't only be acting in it,
I should direct it.

Mary:

Jack—

Jack:

And not only that.
Who knows my life better than I do?
I should write it, too.

Mary:

Well, if you do all that,
you might as well produce it.

Jack:

Yeah.

Mary:

That'll look fine on the screen.
The Life of Jack Benny,
starring Jack Benny,
directed by Jack Benny,
written by Jack Benny
and produced by Jack Benny.

Jack:

Won't that look swell?

Rochester:

Swell and monotonous!

Mary:

(Laughs)

Jack:

What are you laughing at?

Mary:

I'll lend you my girdle
and you can be your own leading lady.

Jack:

Oh, that'd be going too far....
Gosh, imagine.
The story of my life.
Rochester, let's put the top down
so people can see me.

Mary:

So people can see you!
Oh, Jack!

Rochester:

That's nothin', Miss Livingstone.
This morning he wanted to ride down
Hollywood Boulevard
on a white horse like Lady Godiva.

Mary:

Lady Godiva?

Rochester:

Yeah,
but his toupee wasn't long enough.

Jack:

Rochester,
I was just going to do that to save gas,
that's all.

Rochester:

Hee-hee-hee.
I wonder how I'd look on a white horse?

Jack:

Say, here we are at the studio.
Stop right at the main gate.

Rochester:

Okay, boss.

* * *

Jack:

Now let's see.
Where's Jerry Wald's office?
He's in charge of production for my picture.

Mary:

Maybe it's down this corridor.

Jack:

Yeah, here are some offices.
Let's see—
Waterman, Silverman, Overman, Gentleman,
Kern, Kertchalk, Wald.
Here it is.

(SOUND: DOOR OPENS)

Receptionist:

Yes?

Jack:

I'm Jack Benny.
Mr. Wald is expecting me.

Receptionist:

Mr. Wald's in conference.
Would you mind waiting?

Jack:

Not at all.
Come on, Mary,
let's sit down over there.
(Hums "Love in Bloom.")

Mary:

Say, Jack,

170

look at the fellow
sitting on the other side of the room.
Isn't that Danny Kaye?

Jack:

Danny Kaye?
Where?

Mary:

Reading that newspaper.

Jack:

Oh yeah.
And he used to be such a nice kid.

Mary:

Used to be?
What did he ever do to you?

Jack:

What did he do to me?
Did you see that picture he made,
Up in Arms?

Mary:

Yes, he was a big hit in it.
He was sensational.
What about it?

Jack:

What about it?
I'm having enough trouble with Paul Lukas.

Mary:

Oh, Jack!

Jack:

And now Danny Kaye.
Get that nonchalant manner?

Sitting there reading that newspaper.
And look at that expression on his face.
Loaded with confidence.
That Danny Kaye burns me up.

Mary:

You know, Jack,
I can't understand it.
Every time somebody makes a little progress,
you get sore at 'em.

Jack:

I do not.

Mary:

You do, too.
When Mickey Rooney put on long pants,
you stopped talking to him.

Jack:

I did not.

Mary:

Why, you even bit Lassie.

Jack:

Well, she bit me first!
Anyway, this is different.
I practically gave Danny Kaye his start.
Why, I remember the day
he came to me for advice
and I was fool enough to—

Mary:

Oh-oh!
Jack, Danny sees you
and he's coming over.

Jack:

Oh well,

I'll just have to hide my feelings.

(*Hums one strain of "Love in Bloom"*)

Kaye:

Hello, Jack.

Jack:

Hello, Danny.

Kaye:

How are you, Jack?

Jack:

I'm fine, fine.

How's your mother, Danny?

Kaye:

She's fine.

Jack:

And your father?

Kaye:

He's fine, too.

Jack:

Well, the next time you see them

tell 'em they certainly have a louse for a son.

Mary:

Jack!

Jack:

Well—

Kaye:

Jack, what's the matter?

What happened?

I thought we were friends.

Jack:

Friends!

A lot you know about friendship.

I heard about that rumor

you're spreading around

that you're the new comedy sensation.

Kaye:

But Jack,

I didn't spread that rumor.

And I'm sorry my picture was a big hit.

Jack:

Oh, sure, sure.

Kaye:

And if it'll make you feel any better,

I'm sorry that I came to Hollywood.

Jack:

Being sorry doesn't help.

You made the picture.

You were a hit,

and the damage is done.

It's too late to apologize.

Mary:

Oh, Danny,

don't pay any attention to him.

Kaye:

Mary, what's the matter with Jack?

Mary:

He's jealous of any newcomer

that's a big success.

Kaye:

Gosh, Jack,

I wouldn't hurt you for the world.

I know how you love show business.

I wouldn't do anything

to take the bread out of your mouth.

Jack:

Go ahead, go ahead,

keep talking.

I know what you're thinking.

Kaye:

No, Jack, you've got me all wrong.

I've always been your fan.

Why, I've followed your career for years.

Jack:

Really?

Well!

Kaye:

Sure, Jack,

and I could never hope to become as popular

as you used to be.

Jack:

Used to be?

Kaye:

(Excited and fast)

I mean I used to was—

I mean—

Jack:

That's better.

Kaye:

Honestly, Jack,

I think you're great.

In fact, every time I pass a theater

where your picture is playing

I go in to see it.

I could see your pictures every night.

I think you're the

greatest comedian in the world.

Jack:

You do?

Kaye:

Yeah, I think you're swell.

Jack:

Oh. . . .

Well, then I'm sorry I acted the way I did,

Danny.

I—I think you're pretty swell, too.

Kaye:

But you're sweller than I am.

Jack:

No, no, Danny,

you're the swellest.

Kaye:

No, Jack, you're the swellest.

Jack:

Well—

Mary:

As soon as the swelling goes down,

can I get a word in here?

Jack:

Oh, I'm sorry, Mary.

Danny and I were just

complimenting each other.

Oh, say, Danny.
You know Jerry Wald sent for me
because Warner Brothers are going to make
a picture of my life.
And to show you how much I really like you,
I'm going to ask them
if they can't find something
for you to do in my picture.

Kaye:
Thanks, Jack,
I hope you can fix it.

Receptionist:
Oh, Mr. Benny,
Mr. Wald will see you now.

Jack:
Thank you.
Come on, Mary.
You too, Danny.

* * *

Jack:
Hello, Mr. Wald.

Kaye:
Hello, Mr. Wald.

Mary:
Hello, Mr. Wald.

Wald:
Hello, Jack,
hiya, Danny,
hello, Mary.
Sit down.

Kaye:
Thank you.

Jack:
Thank you.

Mary:
I'll go out
and get a chair for myself.

Jack:
Oh, excuse me, Mary.
Sit here.

Wald:
Well, Jack,
I'll bet you're pretty excited
now that Warner Brothers are going to make
the story of your life.

Jack:
Yes, I'm quite thrilled.

Wald:
We've got the whole thing laid out, Jack.
We're going to make your entire life story
from the day you were born
to the day you died.

Jack:
Died?
How can that be?

Mary:
When you start acting
and the director says shoot,
he won't be kidding.

174

Jack:

Mary, don't be so funny.
Anyway, that picture's
going to be directed by me.

Wald:

You?
You're going to direct the picture?

Jack:

I'm going to write it, too.

Wald:

Oh, direct it and write it, eh?

Jack:

Yes sir!

Wald:

Who's going to supervise it?

Jack:

I am.

Wald:

Who's going to produce it?

Jack:

I am.

Wald:

Who's going to finance it?

(LONG PAUSE)

Kaye:

May I have the next dance with you,
Miss Livingstone?

Jack:

Danny, please.

Wald:

Now, look, Jack,
we've been making pictures for a long time,
and you're not going to tell us
how to run our business.

Jack:

Well—

Wald:

Now get this.
We're going to make a picture called
The Life of Jack Benny,
and you're not going to direct it.

Jack:

I'm not?

Wald:

No,
and you're not going to write it,
supervise it
or produce it.

Jack:

Well, I guess you're right.
I should be satisfied just starring in it. . . .
I am going to star in it, ain't I?

Wald:

(Slowly)
Well, Jack,
that's what I wanted to talk to you about.

Jack:

  Mary, get me a chair.

  What did you want

  to talk to me about, Mr. Wald?

Wald:

  Well, we feel that somebody else

  ought to play the part of Jack Benny.

Jack:

  Somebody else?

  For heaven's sake,

  what's the matter with me?

Wald:

  Well, you've been Jack Benny too long.

Jack:

  What?

Wald:

  We feel that we ought to

  inject some new blood.

Mary:

  New blood!

  Any blood will help.

Jack:

  Mary, you keep out of this.

  Well, look, Mr. Wald,

  if you don't think I'm capable

  of playing myself in my own picture,

  who did you have in mind?

Wald:

  Danny Kaye.

Jack:

  Danny Kaye!

176

Wald:

  Yes,

  that's why I sent for him.

Jack:

  You sent for Danny!

  Danny, don't just sit there.

  Say something.

  Danny Kaye, you knew about this all the time.

Kaye:

  No, I didn't, Jack,

  really I didn't.

  This is all a surprise to me.

Jack:

  Imagine even thinking

  of making a picture of my life

  without me being in it.

Wald:

  Jack, I didn't say

  you weren't going to be in it.

  I have something very important for you.

Jack:

  You have?

Wald:

  Yes!

  You're going to play the part of your father.

Jack:

  My father?

Wald:

  Yes.

  Danny Kaye will be your son.

  And I think Mary will be excellent

  in the part of Jack's childhood sweetheart.

Kaye:

So do I.

Jack:

You keep out of this.

Kaye:

Yes, father.

Jack:

Don't father me, you traitor.

Wald:

Now, Mary,
you'll be Jack's boyhood sweetheart,
Millicent Fairchild.

Jack:

Millicent Fairchild?
What are you talking about?
The name of my girlfriend in Waukegan
was Gussie Baglequist.
Baglequist—not Fairchild.

Wald:

We can't use Gussie Baglequist.
The name doesn't sound romantic.

Jack:

Well, she was a darn pretty girl.
It so happens I have a snapshot of her
right here in my pocket.
Take a look at that.

Wald:

Say, she is pretty.
But what's that thing ˙
she's holding in her right arm?

Jack:

That's a horse's hind leg.
Gussie was a blacksmith
and a darn good one.

Kaye:

A blacksmith?
What's that?

Jack:

For your information, city boy,
blacksmiths put shoes on horses. . . .
And if you ask me if they need a ration stamp,
I'll punch you in the nose.
What a guy to play my life.

Kaye:

I don't know why you're mad at me, Jack.
It wasn't my idea.

Jack:

Hmmm.
And to think, Mr. Kaye,
that I loaned you the money
to come out to Hollywood.
It's the last time
I'll ever do you a favor.

Kaye:

A fine favor,
twenty-two percent interest.
I coulda done better at a bank.

Jack:

What do you think
the Benny Trust Company is—
a chili bowl?

Wald:

All right, boys,

let's cut out this arguing.

Now here's a scene

I want you to try, Danny.

It's where you come in and

ask your father

for money to buy a violin.

You read the father's part, Jack.

Jack:

Okay,

but why I'll never know.

Wald:

Stop mumbling.

Go ahead, Danny.

Remember, you're asking

your father for money,

and you're Jack Benny at the age of nine.

Kaye:

Yes, sir.

(Clears throat)

Papa—

Jack:

Wait a minute.

When I was nine years old, I could talk.

Now read it right.

Wald:

Go ahead, Danny.

Ask the old man again.

Jack:

Hmm.

Kaye:

Okay.

(Clears throat, then in Russian dialect)

Poppa, poppa,

could I have it four dollars

for to buying a wiolin?

Jack:

Just a minute there.

What's the idea of doing Russian?

Kaye:

Well, isn't Waukegan in Russia?

Jack:

No, it's in Illinois.

Jeepers!

Wald:

Try it again, Danny.

Remember, you're a little country boy.

Kaye:

Okay.

(As a goofy rube)

Hey, Paw, Paw—huh.

Can I have four uh dollars

to buy a violin?

Huh, Paw, huh?

Jack:

Now stop it, stop it.

What do you think I was

when I was a kid—

a moron?

Mary:

And besides,

he outgrew it.

Jack:

Yes, heavens to Betsy!

Wald:

Danny, you better try it as a city boy.

Kaye:

A city boy?
Okay.
(Brooklyn dialect)
Hey, Pop, Pop,
kin I put da bite on yuz
fer four frogskins
tuy buy a fiddle?
Come on, Pop, whatcha say?
Whatcha say?

Jack:

Now cut that out! . . .
Look here, Mr. Wald,
if this is the way you're going to do
the story of my life,
you can drop the whole thing.

Wald:

All right,
then we won't make the picture.

Jack:

Now let's not be hasty, Mr. Wald.
What's bothering you?

Wald:

You're bothering me,
and I'm sick of it.
We're not going to make
The Life of Jack Benny.

Jack:

Well, that's okay with me.

Good-bye!
Come on, Mary.
Come on, Danny.

Jack:

Pulling that stuff on us.

* * *

Kaye:

But Jack,
this was a great opportunity for me.
I don't know when
I'll ever get another chance like that.

Jack:

Look, Danny,
let me give you a little piece of advice.
You're a very clever kid,
you're very talented
and you've got a lot of charm,
but take it easy.
Climb the ladder of success slowly,
one rung at a time.

Kaye:

Yes, Jack.

Jack:

And when you get to the top,
don't let it go to your head.
Don't ever be hammy.

Kaye:

I won't Jack.

Jack:

Come on, kid,
let's go see
George Washington Slept Here.

EDDIE CANTOR

Eddie Cantor was the first of the big vaudeville headliners to establish himself on radio. When he began his own series for Chase and Sanborn Coffee in 1931, he was thirty-nine years old and already had behind him a full career that had taken him from singing on street corners for nickels and dimes as a kid to starring on Broadway in the *Ziegfeld Follies*. Although Cantor had made some occasional radio broadcasts as early as 1921, he first became seriously involved with the medium after a successful guest appearance with Rudy Vallee early in 1931. This led to his own series for Chase and Sanborn later that year, which achieved enormous popularity within weeks after it went on the air. Cantor's success was not unnoticed by fellow vaudevillians like Ed Wynn, Fred Allen and Jack Benny, who soon launched programs of their own.

Cantor had a particularly good feel for what would make comedy work on the radio. He was the first performer to give his audience the freedom to laugh out loud whenever they wished. He also introduced full-scale dress rehearsals before a live audience to test the effectiveness of his shows. Always popular, Cantor remained on the air practically without a break until 1950, when he made the transition to television. The only years he couldn't be heard were 1935, when he was touring Europe, and 1939, when his forthright criticism of

American isolationism in a speech at the New York World's Fair resulted in his being temporarily blacklisted.

Cantor's shows employed a comedy-variety format and used a relatively small cast of supporting players. The earlier programs featured the violinist Rubinoff (whose lines were read by Alan Reed or Lionel Stander) and Parkyakarkas, the comic Greek cook played by Harry Einstein, father of present-day comedian Albert Brooks. In 1935 Bert Gordon joined the cast as the irrepressibly silly Mad Russian. Gordon had worked with Cantor when they were both members of Gus Edwards's troupe of child performers, and he remained an important part of the Cantor show for many years. His standard opening line, "How do you do?," delivered with manic high spirits in a guttural Russian-Jewish accent, became one of the country's most quoted catchphrases. At various times the singers on the show included such Cantor discoveries as Bobby Breen, Deanna Durbin and Dinah Shore. His announcer, who doubled as straight man, was first Jimmy Wallington and then Harry Von Zell. The regular cast was usually filled out by guest stars like Al Jolson, W. C. Fields, Cary Grant or Caesar Romero, who appeared in the 1947 sketch printed here.

On the stage the Cantor trademarks had been his banjo eyes, horn-rimmed glasses, straw hat and minstrel blackface. On radio they became his wife Ida, their five daughters and the ongoing jokes about his inability to produce a son. Another memorable running gag was his candidacy for the presidency in the 1940s, with its mock-urgent campaign chant, "We want Can-tor!" Cantor had an unusual sense of social responsibility, and he used his huge national exposure to promote various worthy causes. As he finished singing his closing theme, "I Love to Spend One Hour with You," he would turn serious and use the last few moments of air time to ask his audience to help support the March of Dimes, defense bonds or some other good works.

California and New York with Harry Von Zell (1945)

Von Zell:

You're foolish, Eddie,

going to New York

and leaving this beautiful weather behind.

Cantor:

Are you kidding, Harry?

I have much more pep in New York. . . .

Most people do. . . .

Now take California—

they're so slow out here.

The sun kinda slows 'em down.

I saw two fellas

waiting to cross Hollywood Boulevard,

and they talked it over very casually:

(Slowly)

"Is the light red?"

"Is it green?"

And finally they lay down in the gutter

to continue the conversation.

But in New York the people have *pep!*

Two fellows waiting to cross the street—

the first one says,

"Come on, Joe, let's go—

the lights are *against* us!"

They start across the street—

a cab hits them—

and they're lying in the gutter, too . . .

but no conversation!

You see the difference?

In California

the guy hasn't crossed the street yet,
but in New York
he's already getting out of the hospital.

Von Zell:

Eddie, you're right.
People do take life easier in California.

Cantor:

Sure. . . .
In New York
a fellow gets up at seven in the morning,
jumps into his clothes,

swallows a cup of coffee,
nibbles on a piece of toast,
looks for a bus—
(Ha! ha! ha!)—
jumps into the subway . . .
he's in his office at eight o'clock.
But . . . in California
a man gets up at nine o'clock . . .
goes back home and eats a hearty breakfast,
plays nine holes of golf,
gets to the office at two-thirty,
and at two-forty-five—
he's fired!

The Bullfight with Caesar Romero and Bert Gordon as the Mad Russian (1947)

Cantor:

Well, Caesar Romero,
I see you're all packed
and ready to shove off to Mexico
to make a new picture.

Romero:

Yes, Eddie.
You know, I wish you were coming with me.
Mexico is so colorful and so relaxing.
Every afternoon you can see the laborers
taking their siesta.
There they are,
lying flat on their backs in the streets.
You know, in Mexico we call them peons.

Cantor:

In California, we call them pedestrians!

Romero:

Well, the first thing I'm going to do

is watch the bullfight.
In the picture I'm making
I play the matador,
so I've got to fight a bull.

Cantor:

A ladies' man like you fighting a bull?

Romero:

Why not?
I've been practicing for three months.

Cantor:

With a real bull?

Romero:

No . . .
with Elsie the Cow.

182

Cantor:

How do you like that?
Can't get him away from the girls. . . .
Caesar, I can't understand
why Daryl Zanuck cast you as a bullfighter
when he could have had me.

Romero:

I don't understand.

Cantor:

Well, I think I'm more the type
for these swashbuckling roles.
You know, only last night
I had a dream that I was the star
of that picture *The Three Musketeers*.
There I was alone on a desert island
with my other two musketeers,
Betty Grable and Virginia Mayo.

Romero:

Now wait à minute.
The three musketeers are all men.

Cantor:

Listen, when I dream,
I do my own casting! . . .
You take care of Ida.

Romero:

Eddie, you shouldn't envy me.
You know, playing a bullfighter
can be dangerous.
Frankly, I'm a little worried
about fighting a real bull.

Cantor:

Then you'll never make a good toreador.

A brave bullfighter
likes to hear the roar of the bull.
He doesn't run away.
He steps right up to the bull,
grabs it by the horn,
squeezes it,
and you hear:

Mad Russian:

HOW DO YOU DO!

Cantor:

Imagine that face on television! . . .
Russian, this is Caesar Romero.
In his next picture he's going to fight a bull.

Mad Russian:

Hmmm, I can help him.
I been fighting since I been knee-high
to a grasshopper.

Cantor:

You've been fighting bulls?

Mad Russian:

No . . . grasshoppers!

Cantor:

Grasshoppers?

Romero:

Eddie, this man is silly.

Mad Russian:

Mine dear Sneezer.
I will teach you all I know
about bullfighting.
And then after you fight the bull,
I will come into the arena to see you.

Cantor:

And tell Caesar how good he was?

Mad Russian:

No . . .

I come to bury Caesar,

not to praise him!

Cantor:

Aw, Russian, I think you're a fake.

Mad Russian:

Sir, I will have you know

I was the best bullfighter in all Mexico.

Romero:

No, not Mexico.

It's Me-*hico*.

Hico, hico.

Mad Russian:

Wanna little bicarbonate? . . .

That was very fun-yah!

That was *very* fun-yah!

Cantor:

Say, Russian?

Mad Russian:

Ye-ess?

Cantor:

I'll bet you were never inside a bull arena.

Mad Russian:

That, sir, is a barefaced truth! . . .

The date: July 10, 1940.

The place: Barcelona.

The arena is packed.

I walk to the royal box and make mine bow.

Ten thousand people

raises their voices in a shout:

"BOOLA BOOLA!

LOPA LOOLA!"

Cantor:

What does that mean?

Mad Russian:

They want me thrown out!

Romero:

So what happened in the bullfight, Russian?

Mad Russian:

I was fascinated by a beautiful senorita.

She threw me a rose.

Just then the bull came rushing at me.

I made a grab with my bare hands.

Romero:

You grabbed the bull?

Mad Russian:

No . . . the senorita!

Cantor:

What about the bull?

Mad Russian:

Let him get his own senorita!

Cantor:

So what happened?

Mad Russian:

The bull ran towards me.

Romero:

He lunged?

Mad Russian:

Lunged?
He looked like he didn't even have breakfast!

Cantor:

Were you frightened?

Mad Russian:

Not. for long. . . .
About three years.

Cantor:

Yes, yes, go on.

Mad Russian:

Suddenly I stopped in mine tracks,
and the bull hit me a telling blow.

Romero:

Where did he hit you?

Mad Russian:

I ain't telling!

Cantor:

What finally happened?

Mad Russian:

The bull snorted.
Time to pull out mine sword.
The bull charged at me.
Time to pull out mine bugle.

Romero:

Now wait a minute.
If the bull charged at you,
why did you pick up your bugle?

Mad Russian:

Time to blow!

Cantor:

My dear Russian,
with only a trumpet in your hand
and the bull charging you,
it's a wonder you were not killed.

Mad Russian:

Impossible, yes?
You see . . .

Cantor & Romero:

Ye-ess?

Mad Russian:

To fool the bull I was dressed as a cow.
And when the bull cornered me . . .

Cantor & Romero:

Ye-ess?

Mad Russian:

I whispered . . .
"Moo-oo!
Moo-oo!"

Cantor:

So?

Mad Russian:

So we've been going steady
for the last six years!

Cantor:

Russian, get out of here!

(MUSIC CUE UP)

EDGAR BERGEN AND CHARLIE McCARTHY

What can a ventriloquist possibly do on radio? The lack of direct visual contact with his audience makes his skill at throwing his voice and speaking without seeming to move his lips utterly beside the point. All voices are equally authentic over the air. But there are compensations. The fact that we are cut off from the mechanics of his performance allows us to focus in on a much more consequential part of his act—his ability to create an independent character out of some unseen part of his own inner nature, then engage this alter ego in a dialectic that, in a truly creative performer, exposes the ever-shifting multiple perspectives of a mind in motion. In this respect, our not being able to see the ventriloquist actually works to his advantage. At least that's how it seemed to work for Edgar Bergen, who after a decade of only limited success in vaudeville with his dummy Charlie McCarthy, achieved national popularity almost as soon as he made his first radio appearance.

Bergen created such a well-defined, fully realized character with his dummy that Charlie seemed to take on a life of his own that posed a constant challenge to the relatively pallid personality of his creator. Charlie was the irrepressible, sassy kid in even the best behaved of us, always failing in school and running through his allowance, with a precocious interest in girls that (like the top hat, monocle and evening dress he wore in publicity stills and movies) indicated a bon vivant in the making. Bergen was the well-intended but overly circumspect father figure who skulks about watchfully in even the most carefree of spirits. Together, they played out the ongoing argument between youth and age, id and superego, freedom and responsibility, untrammeled imagination and solemn common sense. The differences extended even to the voices with which they delivered the repartee of the particularly well-written dialogue. Bergen's was soft and gentle if a bit pompous in its didacticism. Charlie's was energetic and loud, full of the high energy self-confidence of the very young.

The plot thickened even further when Bergen introduced a second dummy in 1939. Mortimer Snerd, the slow-talking, buck-toothed country bumpkin, expressed yet another dimension of the Bergen personality and contrasted with Charlie to present an opposing view of childhood. Where Charlie was assertive, combative, schoolyard smart and never at a loss for words, Mortimer was shy, wistful, good-natured and accepting, even of his own naivete and ignorance. If the child in us identified with Charlie's untamed spunkiness and rejection of all authority, the adult in us felt a loving protectiveness for Mortimer's sweetness and vulnerability.

Edgar Bergen was born in 1903 and developed an interest in magic and ventriloquism while he was still in grammar school. Significantly, perhaps, Jim Harmon tells us in *The Great Radio Comedians* that he first sketched Charlie's face on the flyleaf of his history book when he was a senior in high school. To help pay his way through premedical studies at Northwestern University, Bergen entertained with Charlie at parties and semiprofessional shows, but the brash, cheeky kid inside finally got the better of him, and he dropped out to become a full-time vaudevillian.

Following ten years of hand-to-mouth life on the road, Bergen made his radio debut in 1936 as a guest on Rudy Vallee's *Royal Gelatin Hour*. The response was so strong that the next year he began his own series on NBC for Chase and Sanborn Coffee, which remained his sponsor until 1948. With an unusually strong cast that included W. C. Fields, Don Ameche, Nelson Eddy, Dorothy Lamour, bandleader Ray Noble and announcer Bill Goodwin, the show soon became one of the top-rated programs on the air. One of the weekly high points was Charlie's running "feud" with Fields, a self-declared hater of children, especially those who were smart-mouthed scene stealers. *The Chase and Sanborn Hour* maintained its popularity even after the supporting stars were dropped and the format was shortened to thirty minutes from the original hour. In the early 1940s Abbott and Costello joined the show for a while, and Don Ameche returned to play the Bickerson sketches of marital discord with Frances Langford. Bergen moved to CBS in 1949, where he continued under various sponsors until 1956.

The Grasshopper and the Ant   (1945)

Charlie:

My, Mr. Bergen,

how *nice* you look today.

Charlie:

You look so well groomed,

so . . . shall we say . . . *prosperous.*

Bergen:

Well, thank you, Charlie.

Bergen:

(Hammy)

I believe I *do* have an air of distinction. . . .
(Suspiciously)
Wait a minute! . . .
What are you after? . . .
Money, I'll bet!

Charlie:

Weelll . . .
as a matter of fact,
I *am* in an embarrassing position. . . .
I got caught with my finances down.

Bergen:

But, why tell *me* about it?

Charlie:

Well, I thought you might . . .
leave me the lend of a mild loan. . . .
(Aside)
Dreamer that I am! . . .

Bergen:

So, you're over a barrel again?

Charlie:

Over it? . . .
This time I'm *wearing* it.

Bergen:

Instead of hounding me,
why don't you borrow a little
from your piggy bank
to tide you over?

Charlie:

Because . . . that little piggy has none.

Bergen:

Oh, I see.

Charlie:

Not a sou.

Bergen:

Then you should *earn* some money. . . .
Don't you think you're old enough
to go to work?

Charlie:

I suppose you *know*
I could ask *you* that same question? . . .
(Aside)
That burns him up!

Bergen:

Charlie, you should make a practice
of saving twenty percent of your allowance.

Charlie:

I don't make that much!

Bergen:

Well, perhaps I can illustrate my point better
by telling you an Aesop's Fable.

Charlie:

Oh, let's not do it the hard way!

Bergen:

It's the fable of the Grasshopper and the Ant.
Tell me, what do you know
about the habits of the ants?

Charlie:

Not much. . . .
I haven't been in touch
with the underground lately.

Bergen:

Well, this particular ant was very industrious.
He worked hard all the time. . . .

Charlie:

I hate him already.

Bergen:

You see, ants never waste a minute.

Charlie:

Oh no? . . .
How about all the time they spend at picnics?

Bergen:

All summer long this ant gathered food
and hid it away for the future.

Charlie:

Why, the little sneak! . . .
That's *hoarding!*

Bergen:

The grasshopper just took it easy . . .
chirping and hopping around . . .
while the ant . . .

Charlie:

I'll string along with the grasshopper. . . .
He's got personality . . .
and, besides, he can spit tobacco juice—
(Spits)
Ping!

Bergen:

Not only did the grasshopper
loaf all the time,
but he made fun of the ant for working . . .
so the ant said,

(Ant voice breaks)
"Beware—"

Charlie:

Easy does it, Bergen. . . .
Don't strain your voice.

Bergen:

The ant said to the grasshopper . . .
(Overly dramatic)
"Beware . . .
Winter will come
and you'll be sorry you didn't prepare. . . .
I have spoken!"

Charlie:

(Aside to audience)
Ladies and gentlemen,
you see before you
the remains of a frustrated actor.

Bergen:

And true enough, winter came. . . .

Charlie:

It usually does.

Bergen:

Then it was a different story. . . .

Charlie:

Oh, good. . . .
I was getting awfully tired
of *this* one.

Bergen:

Stop interrupting! . . .

Snow covered the ground . . .
and the grasshopper was without food . . .
and being without food,
he had nothing to eat.

Charlie:

NO! . . .
Now there's a sloppy hunk of logic for you.

Bergen:

There wasn't a leaf . . .
not a blade of grass to eat. . . .

Charlie:

The poor grasshopper! . . .
Couldn't we drop him something by
parachute?

Bergen:

(Dramatically)
The Ant refused him food
and he was starving! . . .

Charlie:

Oh, no, no . . .

Bergen:

Yes, slowly, slowly starving . . .

Charlie:

(Almost crying)
Is there a crust of bread in the house?

Bergen:

It was the grasshopper's own fault. . . .
You shouldn't feel sorry for *him*.

Charlie:

I can't help it. . . .
We were getting to be such friends,
the little chisler.

Bergen:

Now Charlie, I hope you will be wiser
than the grasshopper in the future. . . .
This fable teaches us a lesson.

Charlie:

It do?

Bergen:

Yes . . .
the lesson is this. . . .
The ant works very hard,
perseveres and saves . . .
and as a reward—

Charlie:

Somebody steps on him!

Bergen:

No.

Charlie:

All right then,
DDT gets him!

Goodwin:

Say, Edgar,

what about that golf tournament

that you and W.C. Fields

were supposed to play off yesterday?

Who won?

Bergen:

We didn't get very far, Bill.

Goodwin:

You didn't, Edgar?

What was the matter?

Bergen:

Well, I should have known better than to let

Charlie caddy for us, of course.

Goodwin:

Do you mean there was trouble?

Bergen:

Well, I'll tell you what happened, Bill.

Charlie and I got there first—

it was a beautiful morning—

it was a great day for golf. . . .

(MUSIC BRIDGE)

Charlie:

Did we have to get out here so early, Bergen?

It's awful cold this time of day.

You know, I just bet you anything

Mr. Fields doesn't even show up.

Bergen:

Oh, he promised to be here at six-thirty.

Fields:

(Singing)

"Give me my boots

and my bottle . . ."

Charlie:

Here comes W.C.!

You're a walking ad for black coffee, Bill.

Hello, Mr. Fields, hello.

Fields:

Hello, my little chum.

I was thinking of you only yesterday.

Charlie:

No!

You were!

Fields:

Yes.

I was cleaning out the woodshed at the time.

Reminded me of you.

Charlie:

Mr. Fields,

is that your nose

or a new kind of flame thrower?

Fields:

Very funny, Charles, very funny.

What's this kid doing around here anyway,

Edgar?

Charlie:

Well, I'm going to be your caddy, Mr. Fields, and I'm going to keep score, too.

Fields:

Oh-oh!

Charlie:

He suspects.

Bergen:

Would you rather I kept score, Bill?

Fields:

To be perfectly frank with you, Edgar, I've never trusted either one of you.

Charlie:

What do you mean by that crack?
I want you to know
that Bergen is just as honest as you are, you crook, you.

Fields:

That tips off the whole thing.
You'd better come out of the sun, Charles, before you get unglued.

Charlie:

Do you mind if I stand
in the shade of your nose?

Bergen:

Let's not start that now, fellows, please.
I'm sure Charlie
will be a fair scorekeeper
for both of us.

Fields:

Tell me, Charles,
if I take three drives and three putts,
what's my score?

Charlie:

Let's see—
three and three?
That's four, Mr. Fields, four.

Fields:

Oh, very good, very good, Charles.
How do you arrive at four?

Charlie:

Well, I'll tell you.
You see, when you were putting,
a quarter fell out of your pocket, you see.

Fields:

Oh, yes, yes.
Well, that sounds like
a workable arrangement.

Bergen:

Oh, isn't this a lovely day, Bill?
Lovely.
You know,
the air is so intoxicating.

Fields:

Intoxicating, is it, eh?
Stand back and let me take a deep breath.

Bergen:

Now I want you to be quiet, Charlie.
Mr. Fields is going to tee off.

Charlie:

Oh, yes, yes.

Fields:

Yes, quiet, please.

I shall now take my usual stance.

Charlie:

I wouldn't do that.

The ground is a little too wet.

Fields:

Quiet, you termite's flophouse.

Bergen:

Now, Charlie,

I want you to keep quiet.

He's getting ready to drive.

Charlie:

Oh, yes, yes,

I'm sorry.

Bergen:

If you don't mind a suggestion, Bill,

you're not holding your club right.

Bend your elbow a little more.

Charlie:

Pssh!

That's pretty good—

telling Fields how to bend his elbow!

That's like carrying coals to Newcastle.

Fields:

Charles, my little pal?

Charlie:

Yes, Mr. Fields?

Fields:

Do you know the meaning of *rigor mortis?*

Charlie:

No, sir.

Fields:

Well, you will in a minute.

Bergen:

Now let's try and avoid that sort of thing.

And, Charlie, I want you to stop it.

You have Mr. Fields all unstrung.

Fields:

Somebody get me a sedative—

with an olive in it.

Noble:

Pardon me, gentlemen,

but could I play through?

Bergen:

Well, we'd rather you didn't.

You see, we'll be getting along

in a minute now.

Noble:

Oh, I'm sorry,

but there's no harm in asking.

Fields:

I wouldn't be so sure.

Bergen:

All right, Bill.

Hadn't we better get on with the game?

Fields:

Of course, Edgar, half a tick.

Did I ever tell you of the time
I was caddy master
at the Bunkferheiden Country Club?

Bergen:

No!

Charlie:

Bunkferheiden.
I didn't know he could say it.

Fields:

It was a tough one to say, too.
It was at the top of Mount Jungfrau
in Switzerland.

Bergen:

All right, Bill.
Now there are people waiting
to play through.

Fields:

Oh, I have lots of time left, Edgar.
I hit a ball nine and three-quarter miles.
It rolled into an open manhole
in front of Mr. Swobenhalica's rathskeller.

Bergen:

I don't believe I've heard of the place.
I don't know where it is.

Fields:

It's but a stone's throw
from Folfinger J. Undercuffler's.

Bergen:

Well, I don't know where that is, either.

Fields:

Oh, you don't get around much, do you?

Noble:

I say, old chaps,
would you mind awfully?

Charlie:

Yes, we would.

Noble:

Oh!
Sorry.

Fields:

By the way, caddy,
what's the score?
How do I stand?

Charlie:

I often wonder.

Bergen:

But there is no score, Bill.
We haven't started playing yet.

Fields:

Oh, so we haven't.
Caddy, you'd better give me my ball
out of my golf bag.

Charlie:

Is it in this compartment, sir?

Fields:

No.
That's where I keep my olives.

Charlie:

You know,
this is the first golf bag I ever saw

with a faucet on it.
What's in there?

Fields:

Oh, a little snakebite remedy.

Goodwin:

Excuse me, gentlemen,
but I'm the president of
the Greens Committee.

Charlie:

I'll take spinach.

Bergen:

Just what do you want?

Goodwin:

Well, I'm afraid you're being
a little too turf on the tough. . . .
I mean too rough on the truff.
I don't know what I mean.

Fields:

What's the matter with that guy?
Has he got DT's?

Goodwin:

You see before you
the shattered wreck of a man—
an unhappy creature who has ceased to know
the joys of human existence.

Fields:

Oh!
A teetotaler, eh?

Goodwin:

Sir.

I have no sympathy for a man
who is intoxicated all the time.

Fields:

You don't, eh?

Bergen:

You have no sympathy for him?

Charlie:

A man who's intoxicated all the time
doesn't need sympathy.

Fields:

That was my line
and I forgot it.
It was a good one, too.

Charlie:

You don't know how I enjoyed taking it.
(To Goodwin)
What *are* you so sad about?

Goodwin:

Six months ago my wife left me
and went back to her mother.

Bergen:

That's too bad,
but why are you still crying?

Goodwin:

Tomorrow she's coming back—
and bringing her mother with her.

Bergen:

Let's get on with the game, Bill.
What do you say?

Noble:

Oh, I say, chaps,
could I please play through?

Bergen:

What are you in such a rush about?

Noble:

Well, I really should get home—
You see, my house is on fire.

Fields:

There's nothing nicer
than coming home to a warm house.
Where was I?

Bergen:

You were teeing off.

Fields:

Oh, yes,
I was teeing off.

Bergen:

Now this time keep your eye on the ball.

Charlie:

If you can get your eye
to detour around your nose.

Fields:

Tell me, Charles,
is it true when you slide down a banister,
the banister gets more splinters
than you do?

Charlie:

Why, you bugle-beak!
Why don't you fill your nose with helium
and rent it out for a barrage balloon?

Fields:

Listen, you animated hitching post,
or I'll sic a beaver on you.

Bergen:

You'll do no such thing!
You will not harm a hair
on this boy's head.

Fields:

That's not the end
I'm going to work on. . . .

The Physiology Lesson   (1945)

Charlie:

Hello, Mr. Bergen. . . .
How are you getting along . . .
besides in *years*, I mean.

Bergen:

I'm doing very well . . .

but how are *you* getting along . . .
principally in school, I mean.

Charlie:

Ai-yiyi! . . .
Not so good.
I got a test coming up.

Bergen:

How do you think you'll come out?

Charlie:

I doubt if I'll even place or show.

Bergen:

I hope you'll do better than that.

Charlie:

Me, too. . . .
The teacher's beginning to suspect
my IQ is PU.

Bergen:

Charlie, it will soon be graduation time again.
Do you think *perhaps this year*
you'll get out of the eighth grade?

Charlie:

From what I hear,
I'll be held over again
by popular demand.

Bergen:

You better *not* be. . . .
Now what is the exam on?

Charlie:

Fizzle-ology.

Bergen:

Physiology?
Well, that's *one* subject
I'm sure I can help you with. . . .
I'll be glad to share my knowledge with you.

Charlie:

That's like sharing the hole in the doughnut.

Bergen:

Now you take the word *physiology* itself. . . .
Let's break it down.

Charlie:

Okay.
Let's pull the legs off first.

Bergen:

The human body—
it's a wonderful thing.

Charlie:

Yeah . . .
we couldn't live without it. . . .
I've got a list of questions we may be asked.
They're mostly on anatomy.

Bergen:

Oh, you ought to *like* anatomy.

Charlie:

Well, on *some* people it looks good . . .
especially girls. . . .
Now take that blonde in the first row. . . .
Hiya, beautiful . . .
hubba hubba!!

Bergen:

Oh, stop it. . . .
I really know anatomy. . . .
You remember, I studied to be a doctor. . . .
Sometimes I'm very sorry
I gave up medicine.

Charlie:

Oh, but think of all the lives you saved
by doing it.

Bergen:

Give me that list of questions
and I'll quiz you
to see how many you get right. . . .
Let's see now, first question:
name the parts of the head.

Charlie:

The face . . . and hair . . .
except in *your* case.

Bergen:

Never mind that. . . .
Next question:
now, Charlie,
where are your vocal cords?

Charlie:

In *your* throat . . .
heh-heh-heh. . . .
(Aside)
Ain't that just too subtle.

Bergen:

See if you can answer this one:
what is the location of the lungs?

Charlie:

The lungs are bounded on the north
by your neck . . .
on the east and west by your elbows . . .
on the south by your gizzard—
carburetor?

Bergen:

That's pretty good. . . .
Now what are the muscles for?

Charlie:

To keep your bones from rattling.

Bergen:

Wrong.
Where do you find the liver?

Charlie:

Under the onions?

Bergen:

Wrong, Charlie.

Charlie:

It *must* be next to the bacon.

Bergen:

Wrong again. . . .

Charlie:

Well, at least I'm consistent.

Bergen:

Perhaps you can at least answer this:
what is the function of the heart?

Charlie:

To fall in love with. . . .
Some function, eh kid?

Bergen:

Never mind the question. . . .
I'll try to explain
the heart and circulation to you
my own way. . . .
Now, the heart pumps the blood,
which is red in color
due to hemoglobin. . . .

Charlie:

The hemo-whoma?

Bergen:

Remember when I took you to the doctor,
Charlie,
and he said your hemoglobin was only sixty?

Charlie:

Well, that's pretty good.

Bergen:

No, that's bad.

Charlie:

Well, that's the best I could do.

Bergen:

Your hemoglobin count should be
from ninety to one hundred.

Charlie:

I wouldn't know where to keep them.

Bergen:

Keep what?

Charlie:

All those homely goblins. . . .

Bergen:

No, Charlie . . .

Charlie:

Heebie-jeebies?

Hoblin geemers? . . .

Bergen:

No.

Charlie:

By golly, I'm warm.

Bergen:

I give up, you're hopeless. . . .
How in the world do you expect
to pass that examination?

Charlie:

Well, the smartest kid in our class
has a nervous habit
of tapping his pencil during examinations.

Bergen:

What about it?

Charlie:

Well, it just *so happens* that he accidentally
taps out the answers to the questions
in Morse code.

Bergen:

Why, Charlie!
Do you expect to pass the test *that* way?

Charlie:

Yeah, if the teacher doesn't start
jamming our wave length!

Bergen:

I'd like to buy some of these magazines
to read on the train. . . .
Well, if it isn't Mortimer Snerd.

(APPLAUSE)

Mortimer:

Hullo, Mr. Bergen.

Bergen:

So you're running the magazine stand here?
Well, well, you're quite an enterprising
young man.

Mortimer:

Yup, yup! . . .
Shows I got something in my head
besides brains.

Bergen:

Well, I'm glad to do business with you. . . .
Let me see, what shall I get?

Mortimer:

We got the latest *Good Housebreaking*
magazine.

Bergen:

No thank you.

Mortimer:

How about this? . . .
Reader's Indigestion. . . .
It's the September issue too.

Bergen:

What issue did you say?

Mortimer:

September . . . September. . . .
That's the name of
quite a well-known month.

Bergen:

I want something to read on the train.

Mortimer:

What train you goin' on?

Bergen:

The Chief.

Mortimer:

Then how about some Indian stories?

Bergen:

(Laughs)
You amuse me . . .
after all, there is only one Mortimer Snerd.

Mortimer:

Yup, yup! . . .
I'm pretty scarce, I guess.

Bergen:

I think I'd like this detective story. . . .

Mortimer:

That's a good story.

Bergen:

Oh, you've read it?

Mortimer:

Most of it . . .

I'm almost up to the beginning.

Bergen:

That's a silly way to read a story.

Mortimer:

Wull . . .

I may be silly . . .

but when I *set* my mind to something . . .

it . . . er . . .

it just *sits* there.

Bergen:

Okay, Mortimer . . .

these are the ones I want. . . .

Here's the money.

Mortimer:

Okey-dokey . . .

here's your change.

Bergen:

Wait a minute. . . .

You didn't give me the right change.

Mortimer:

Sorry . . .

but I can't correct mistakes

after you leave the counter.

Bergen:

But you gave me a quarter too much.

Mortimer:

Too bad. . . .

It'll learn you to be more careful.

Bergen:

Mortimer, how can you be so stupid?

Mortimer:

Well, it ain't something

you just get out of books!

The Visit with Mortimer Snerd   (1955)

Mortimer:

(Singing)

"I'll never smile again

Like I smole before."

Bergen:

Why such a sad song, Mortimer?

Mortimer:

Oh, I got the dismals.

Bergen:

The dismals?

Mortimer:

Yah, I'm sorta down in the humpty-dumps.

Bergen:

Why?

Mortimer:

Well, I'm worried.

Bergen:

Worried about what?

Mortimer:

Wull, let me see now. . . .
How many guesses do I get?

Bergen:

Surely you must know
what you're worried about?

Mortimer:

I'm worried about things
back home on the farm.
Everything is all topsy-turtle.
We got sixteen new mouths to feed.

Bergen:

Well, are they pigs or chickens?

Mortimer:

No, my Uncle Sorghum and Aunt Busillas
and their kids.

Bergen:

Uncle Sorghum and his family.

Mortimer:

I didn't even know I had an Uncle Sorghum
and they're all moved in

and living with me now—
if you can call that living.

Bergen:

Are you sure they have that many children?

Mortimer:

Wull, let me see now—
There is Vestibula, Twitchy,
Narrowhead, Fungus
and Grunion, Quagmire, Putrid and Slurp
and the triplets Myrt, Burt and Squirt. . . .
Oh, yah, and then there's the older sister
Groucho.

Bergen:

A sister named Groucho?

Mortimer:

Yah, they call her that because
she has a mustache and smokes cigars.

Bergen:

Well, that must make things pretty crowded
around your house.

Mortimer:

Yah, they sleep all over the place—
in the kitchen too.

Bergen:

And they don't mind that?

Mortimer:

Well, no . . .
except Cousin Twitchy.
He ain't used to sleeping in a strange sink.

Bergen:

Well, they've made themselves at home,
haven't they?

Mortimer:

Yah, they're even wearing my clothes. . . .
Jerkimer got up this morning
and got right into my best suit.

Bergen:

Well, now that is annoying.

Mortimer:

Yah . . . .
What's more, he didn't even give me time
to get out of it first.

Bergen:

They don't sound like very attractive people.

Mortimer:

No.
They sure made a mess of the house.

Bergen:

I can imagine that.

Mortimer:

I didn't realize how dirty the house was
until the dog came in
and tried to bury a bone in the living room.
We got wall-to-wall dirt now.

Bergen:

Well, how could they drag
so much dirt into the house?

Mortimer:

Well, you know,
when the little kids go to sleep,
you know, they play
"this little piggy went to market."

Bergen:

That's nice.

Mortimer:

Yah, with real pigs they play it.

Bergen:

I know it must annoy you,
but remember, Mortimer,
˙blood is thicker than water.

Mortimer:

Oh, yah.
And then again, what isn't?

Bergen:

Relatives certainly can be a problem.
Do you know what Hubbard said
about relatives?

Mortimer:

No, and I don't care to listen to
that kind of language.

Bergen:

Oh, you've heard
the saying of Elbert Hubbard:
"The devil gives us our relatives.
Thank God we can choose our friends."

Mortimer:

No, how does it go?

Bergen:

It just went.

Mortimer:

I must have been lookin' the other way.

Bergen:

Mortimer, how do you handle
the food situation?
The meals must be a problem for so many.

Mortimer:

Oh, it's a regular madhouse at mealtime.
They go at it like they wuz mad at it.

Bergen:

You mean they all stab for the food at once?

Mortimer:

Yah, this morning I reached for a pork chop
and I got my arm so full of forks
it looked like a porcupine.

Bergen:

Well, with so many around a table
I guess they have to eat fast
in order to get anything.

Mortimer:

You never saw such fast eaters.
Why, they're eatin' their dessert
before the echo of their soup has died away.

Bergen:

Mortimer, why on earth
don't you get rid of that mob?

Mortimer:

Wull, it's kind of flatterin'
havin' them around.
They think I'm awful smart.

Bergen:

They do?

Mortimer:

Yah.
They think I'm a regular Albert Epstein.

Bergen:

Oh, I see.

Mortimer:

Kinda a nice change to hear somebody
say to me,
"How can you be so smart?"
Ho! Ho!

Bergen:

So they think you're hot stuff.
They really must come from the hills.

Mortimer:

Yah, they can't get over
the new fandanglements in my house.

Bergen:

You mean your modern improvements?

Mortimer:

Yah, they can't get over the idea
of having a water pump right in the kitchen.

Bergen:

Well, Mortimer, that's very nice,

but if they're going to stay
I think they should work and earn their keep,
and also be a little neater around the house.

Mortimer:

Yah.
I asked them why they didn't wear shoes,
and they says,
"What do you think we are—horses?"

Bergen:

Well, maybe they'll get tired of you
in a few days.

Mortimer:

I don't think they're ever going to leave.

Bergen:

What makes you say that?

Mortimer:

I happened to overhear Uncle Sorghum say,
"We'll stay until he gets wise."

Bergen:

Mortimer, I'm beginning to see the light.

Mortimer:

Wull, turn it up a little brighter
so I can see it too.

Bergen:

He's not your uncle.
They're not your relatives.
I think they're a bunch of impostors.

Mortimer:

Yuh?

Bergen:

Well, of course.
How can you be so stupid?

Mortimer:

Wull, it comes easy
after you reach the first plateau.

BOB HOPE

Bob Hope's talents were so well suited to radio and he eventually achieved such great success over the air that it is surprising how long it took him to make an impact on the medium. Hope made his first radio appearance in 1932 on *The Capitol Family Hour*, a Sunday-morning series broadcast live from the Capitol Theatre in New York, where he was part of the vaudeville bill. It wasn't until 1938 that he began his own long-running show for Pepsodent Toothpaste that established him in the first rank of radio entertainers. In the intervening years he appeared from time to time on such programs as Rudy Vallee's *Fleischmann Hour*, the strangely titled *Bromo Seltzer Intimate Hour* and *The RKO Theater of the Air*. In the middle '30s he even had several short-lived series of his own, including *The Woodbury Soap Hour* and bandleader Shep Field's *Rippling Rhythm Review*, which also featured announcer Ben Grauer and singer Del Casino. But he was far more successful on the stage, where his Broadway appearance in Jerome Kern's *Roberta* made him a musical-comedy star in 1936. Hope's radio breakthrough didn't come until early 1938 with *Your Hollywood Parade*. The series, hosted by Dick Powell, was a failure, but Hope's weekly monologues on the events of the day were a hit and led to his own show for Pepsodent later that year.

Hope's skill as a monologuist was perhaps his greatest asset as an entertainer, something he came to realize in his early years in vaudeville, where after a false start dancing and playing blackface comedy, he finally hit his stride as a stand-up comedian. "The Dude Ranch" monologue included here from the *Rippling Rhythm* show makes it clear that, he had certainly mastered the form by 1937. Most of the special characteristics that came to define the Hope style are already apparent: the breezy, irreverent tone, the high-energy pacing and delivery, the rather aggressive attack saved from offensiveness by the way it turns inward upon itself and makes Hope a target as well as the perpetrator of the humor. The one thing missing, which would come the next year and finally put him over in radio, was the humorous treatment of topical events.

The monologue was the perfect vehicle for the brash, self-confident wise guy of the Hope persona, and it remained a high point of his shows throughout his career. Particularly memorable are those delivered from the military bases he started playing even before World War II. Hope cannily filled them with local references and, to the delight of his GI audiences, used his apparent familiarity with their lives to give voice to the unarticulated grievances of the enlisted underclass.

The monologues set the tone and style for the comedy sketches that were also a regular feature of his shows. Hope used the skit less as a dramatic rendering of situation and character than as a vehicle for freewheeling gags. He was aided on this portion of the program by a relatively small group of supporting players. Chief among them was Jerry Colonna, the delightfully fantastical subverter of logic and sanity, who joined Hope in 1938 and remained with him for ten years. Others included Barbara Jo Allen ("Vera Vague"), bandleader Skinnay Ennis (the recipient of Hope's skinny jokes until he was replaced by Les Brown in 1947), singer Frances Langford and announcer Wendell Niles. There were also frequent guest stars like Judy Garland, Red Skelton and Bing Crosby, with whom Hope conducted a popular running "feud," in the manner of Jack Benny and Fred Allen. Curiously, in the sketches Hope was more the butt of the comic ridicule than its agent. Everyone had something funny to say about his ski-jump nose, conceit, envy, spreading middle and lack of physical bravery and athletic skill.

The rapid barrage of gags that was the Hope show required a tremendous amount of material. To keep up the pace and quality week after week, Hope hired a large number of writers—as many as twelve at one time—and developed an unusual way of working. The authors of *The Amazing Careers of Bob Hope* tell us that he would assign a subject for the next week's show and then send each writer off to prepare an entire script by himself. When they all reconvened at the script conference, the jokes that got the best response were put into a master script which was ninety minutes long, triple the length that could be used. After two days of rehearsal, Hope and his cast would play the full ninety minutes before a live audience while the engineers recorded the show; then the best thirty minutes would be broadcast that Tuesday night.

The Bob Hope Show maintained its high ratings throughout the 1940s and began to lose its popularity only when radio was superseded by television. In 1953 Hope added a daily fifteen-minute morning show to his weekly evening program, but he gradually phased himself out of radio and by the late '50s was devoting himself to television, films and personal appearances.

The Dude Ranch with Ben Grauer (1937)

Grauer:

And now, ladies and gentlemen,

as I read over this script

I come to a line that says . . .

presenting BOB HOPE!

(APPLAUSE)

Hope:

Thank you, folks.

Nice reading, Ben.

Just sit down on that semicolon
till your next announcement.

I feel great tonight, ladies and gentlemen.
I was out on a dude ranch last week.
You know, that's where
tenderfeet from the city
go to get into the real Western atmosphere.
Soon as they arrive
they get on horseback.
Then they ride and ride,
and by evening
they're not tender *feet* anymore!

But it was a wonderful ranch.
Ultramodern in every respect.
The cowboys don't even have to
round up cattle.
They have a public address system.
The foreman grabs a microphone and says,
"Calling all cows, calling all cows!"
(Laughs)
I milked that one nicely.

I flew out to the ranch in a plane.
Ben Grauer followed by carrier pigeon.
I slept right out in the bunkhouse
with the cowboys.
What a swell bunch of fellows they were—
Except one new hand.
He was a real braggart.
But they fixed him.
Every time he shot off his mouth
they put a notch in his lip.

There was another cowboy there
that I liked—
a little Mexican.
He had just come up from the Rio Grande.
Out of a drain pipe.

The next day
I was strolling around the ranch,
and Del Casino came running along hollerin',
"Yippee, yippee, yippee!"
I stopped him and said,
"You're really into the spirit of things,
aren't you, Del?"
And he said,
"Spirit of things, my eye.
I lost my spurs this morning,
and I just put my pants on and found them.
"Yippee, yippee, yippee!"

At nights we had impromptu entertainment.
Everybody gathered around the campfire
and sang songs or told stories.
I was a big hit.
In fact, they wanted to hold me over—
over the camp fire!

But as we were sitting there,
I heard a long-drawn-out wail.
Everyone got quiet,
and I said to the foreman,
"What is that, a wolf?"
And he said, "Nah. . . .
That's the owner going over the books!"

When we got back to the ranch house
there was a buffalo stampede.
Del hit the jackpot on the nickel machine.

Shep Fields was with us.
There is a cowboy. . . .
He even wears a sombrero and chaps
when he eats a Western sandwich.
The only Easterner I know
who's got a ten-gallon hat
and a stomach to match!

One day they held a rodeo on the ranch.
The way the cowboys wrestled
those wild steers
really inspired me.
I tried the same thing. . . .
They let the ornery critter out of the chute.
I raced after him,
jumped off my horse

and grabbed him by the head.
First I wrestled him to the left.
Then I yanked him over to the right.
Twenty seconds went by . . .
a minute . . .
two minutes. . . .
Boy, I thought I'd never
get that rabbit on his back!

At the Naval Air Station at Los Alamitos   (1943)

Hope:

How do you do, ladies and gentlemen?
This is Bob
"Broadcasting from the Naval Air Station
at Los Alamitos"
Hope,
telling you naval aviators
that whether you're just an ordinary student
or at the head of your class,
be sure to use Pepsodent
and your teeth will never be washed out
in a glass.

Well, here I am at Los Alamitos,
a nice quiet little town. . . .
I wouldn't say that Los Alamitos is small,
but it looks like something
Henry J. Kaiser built
during his lunch hour.
Los Alamitos is so small
it's the only place in America
where the draft board had to draft
the draft board.

I got a wonderful reception
when I arrived here.
Every naval flier in the place
made a rush for me as I walked in . . .

wearing a heavy veil
and a low-cut evening gown.
The naval cadets seldom see girls here.
In fact, this is one of the few places
where your copy of *Esquire*
comes with an interpreter.

But I'm happy to be among you
men of the navy.
You know, my family goes back
to John Paul Jones.
In fact, they went back
to John Paul Jones so often,
the bottle was empty before I got there.

But you all know Thursday's
April Fool's Day,
and the youngsters are beginning
to play pranks already.
I reached down for a wallet
in the middle of the street in Los Alamitos,
and some kid with a string pulled it away.
He didn't fool me long, though. . . .
And it was only a short bus trip
back from San Diego.

Just to see if the government's got

a sense of humor,
my brother sent back his income tax signed
"April Fool."
They've got a sense of humor.
My brother is now at Leavenworth
till next April, the fool. . . .

This year in Hollywood,
I saw a crowd of civilians going crazy.
They were gathered outside of the post office,
and the president of the ration board
was leaning out of the window
with a T-bone steak on a yo-yo.

And you know how kids in the neighborhood
always put a brick under an old derby
so when you kick it you'll break your toes?
I'm too smart to be fooled
by that old derby gag,
so when I stepped outside my house
yesterday and saw one,
I just heaved a rock at it. . . .
As soon as I get my house built again,
I'm gonna find out where those kids
got that land mine.

But isn't this a beautiful auditorium?
We're thrilled to be the first show
to come out of this recreation hall,
which was just built.
Well, it wasn't exactly built.
They just turned on the garden hose
and waited for a sandstorm.
In fact, the building is so new,
the paint still smells.
They say no,
but I still insist it's the paint.

But everything is clean and fresh.
I've been giving my house
a little spring cleaning this week.
I wanted to clean out my Frigidaire,
but my relatives beat me to it.
What a cleaning job I did.
My doorbell rang and I answered it
in my apron and old dust cap.
Some woman looked me over
and shoved a paper in my hand.
I thought she wanted my autograph,
so I signed it. . . .
How do you resign from the WACs?

On the Atcheson, Topeka and the Santa Fe (1945)
with Ken Niles, Frances Langford and Jerry Colonna

Niles:
All aboard! . . .
All aboard!

(SOUND: TRAIN PULLING OUT AND FADE)

Hope:
Well, here I am

on the good old Atcheson, Topeka and
the Santa Fe.
Wonder how I'll do this trip?
Say, there's a cute gal—
I'll walk by and drop my handkerchief. . . .

(SOUND: FOOTSTEPS AND LOUD THUD)

Hope:
. . . Oops—

Guess I shoulda taken my lunch money
out of it! . . .
Gee, there's an empty seat
right next to that beautiful doll.
Ahem—may I take this seat?

Frances:

Yes—

if you take it far enough.

Hope:

Well, in that case
I'll sit right down.
Thanks.
(Creak of seat)
Gee, just made it!

Frances:

You just made it?

Hope:

Yeah, we're coming to a tunnel! . . .
Don't wanna appear rude, ma'am,
but where you headed for, ma'am?

Frances:

I'm just passing through the Middle West.

Hope:

I knew you weren't from these parts.

Frances:

How could you tell?

Hope:

. . . From *those* parts!

Frances:

Where are *you* headed for?

Hope:

For the city—
Sort of outgrew the farm.

Frances:

I thought farm boys were tan—
Your face is white.

Hope:

Yeah,
I was in a hurry
with the milkin' this morning!

Frances:

Say, if you're going to the city
you better set your watch back an hour.

Hope:

Okay, guess I will.

*(SOUND: RATCHET, CLASHING OF
GEARS, SQUEAK OF PULLEYS . . .
HAMMERING, RING OF BELL, HISSING
OF STEAM)*

Hope:

Needs a new crystal, doesn't it? . . .
Come on, honey,
let's get chummy.
You better make hay while I'm shinin'. . . .
You know you don't run across my kind
very often.

Frances:

No, I spend most of my time
above the ground!

(SOUND: TRAIN WHISTLE)

Colonna:

Peanuts . . . popcorn . . .

get your racing forms. . . .

Frances:

What?

Colonna:

Oops!

I'm on the wrong track.

Hope:

Don't mind me—

I'm gonna put my feet up on that seat

and make myself comfortable.

(Series of giggles)

Frances:

Well, what are you laughing at?

Hope:

Plush tickles m'toes! . . .

Say, I recognize you now.

You're an actress, ain't ya?

Frances:

Yes, I've starred in several cinemas.

Hope:

Yeh—

and ya been in some movies, too! . . .

But no kiddin',

the minute I seen you

I knew you were in pictures.

Frances:

How'd you know I was in pictures?

Hope:

I could tell by the *frame!* . . .

Haw! Haw!

Great company, ain't I?

Frances:

Yes, now that you're here,

the train doesn't seem half so *jerky!* . . .

I suppose you're the traveling salesman!

Hope:

Nope, I'm the farmer's son. . . .

Heh-heh—

Missed out all around, didn't I? . . .

(Sniffs)

Say, you got perfume on.

Why do you wear that stuff?

Frances:

In your case, *for self-defense!* . . .

I bet you've led a wild life in your time.

Hope:

Have I!

Why, before I was ten

I was chewin' licorice! . . .

Excuse me for a minute, ma'am. . . .

(SOUND: ORANGE CRATES BEING DEMOLISHED . . . CONTINUES FOR A WHILE)

Frances:

. . . Well . . .

aren't you going to offer me

some of your cracker jack?

Hope:

Nope.
The last girl I gave some to
stole the prize!

Frances:

You mean you go out with girls?

Hope:

Oh, I've done my share of livin'.

Frances:

Well, what do you do for excitement
when you're with a girl?

Hope:

Wiggle my ears.

Frances:

Wiggle your ears?
That's not exciting.

Hope:

It is when you got four of 'em! . . .
Say, how about a kiss?

Frances:

Be careful—
The conductor's looking.

Colonna:

All right, I been watchin' you, bud—
Don't you know the rules
about passengers annoyin' the ladies?

Hope:

Yes, I know the rules.

Colonna:

Well—
Then get behind me
and wait your turn!

Frances:

Where are we, conductor?

Colonna:

We'll be in Santa Fe in half an hour.

Hope:

We'll be in Santa Fe in half an hour?
What makes it so bumpy?

Colonna:

The track ended in Topeka!

(SOUND: TRAIN STOPS . . . COW MOOS . . .
TRAIN STARTS AGAIN)

Colonna:

Victorville!

Hope:

Wait a minute—
I thought we were due in Kansas City
in four hours.

Colonna:

Oh, don't worry—
We take a short cut to the right
and make it in fifteen minutes.

Hope:

But there's a big mountain on the right.

Colonna:

Don't worry.

I have a guy named Mohammed

who moves the mountain

so the train can get past.

Watch, the train is turning off now.

(SOUND: BIG CRASH . . . SMASH . . .
CRUNCH . . . CLANKETY BANG!)

Colonna:

Egad!

IF THIS HAPPENS *ONE MORE TIME,*

THAT MOHAMMED IS *THROUGH!*

The Big Game with Ken Niles, Jerry Colonna, Frances Langford, Skinnay Ennis and Red Skelton   (1945)

Niles:

Excitement here on the

Southern California campus

is building to a tense peak

as Homecoming Week and the football season

race toward Saturday's climax.

The excitement has spread to Bob. . . .

He has decided to join

the Southern California squad.

Upon hearing that Bob is to play football

for Southern California,

the president of the university is *aghast.*

He says . . .

Colonna:

Extractum ghast ex bellum . . .

or, in English . . .

get that spook outta here!

Niles:

When Frances Langford

was asked to comment

on Bob playing football for USC . . .

she said:

Frances:

I'm very proud.

And, after all, why shouldn't I be? . . .

He borrowed my bloomers!

Niles:

A professor of social science

summed up the situation as follows:

Voice:

This is no doubt one

of the most flagrant examples

of the recent tendency for women

to take over men's occupations!

Niles:

We take you now to the USC locker room,

where the coach, Rufus Von Colonna,

is giving the team a pep talk

before the game.

The coach is speaking:

Colonna:

All right, men, quiet! . . .

Quiet! . . .

QUIET!—

WHO'S THE JACKASS DOING ALL THAT

BRAYING? . . .

Ha-ha—silly me—

QUITE AN ECHO IN HERE,

ISN'T THERE! . . .

Attention, men!

We're going out there to play football today.

We're going to play hard. . . .
We're going to play for all we're worth . . .
but above all, we're going to play fair!

(SOUND: APPLAUSE)

Colonna:

NO, NO, DON'T APPLAUD. . . .
GIVE THE CEMENT
A CHANCE TO HARDEN
AROUND YOUR BRASS KNUCKLES!!!

Hope:

Colonna, are you the football coach here?

Colonna:

That's right, Hope. . . .
J. Crossbar Colonna,
football coach,
lover of clean sport
and champion of fair play . . .
also *answers to all examinations sold cheap!*

Hope:

Professor . . . you're non compos mentis!!

Colonna:

I know . . . *they just pledged me yesterday!!*
Now, before we go over today's plays,
let's see if all the players are here. . . .
Left end?

Hope:

Here.

Colonna:

Left tackle.

Ennis:

Here.

Colonna:

Left guard.

Girl:

Here.

Colonna:

Egad . . .
I told 'em not to hold
those sorority dances
in this locker room.
Now, men, we're going
to use strategy on 'em today—
You're facing a tough team,
so do exactly as I tell you.
When your opponents have the ball—
tackle 'em hard, stop 'em!!
When *you* have the ball . . .
when *you* have the ball . . .
ha, ha, ha, *silly me*!!
That's all, men, now get in there
and win for dear old UCLA.

Hope:

UCLA?
Colonna, this is USC!

Colonna:

It is?

Hope:

Of course!

Colonna:

Ha-ha . . . silly me . . .
must've got on the wrong bus this morning!!
All right now, men . . . get dressed. . . .
It's almost game time.

Ennis:

Say, Bob, I lost my shoulder pads. . . .
Help me find my shoulder pads.

Hope:

Let's take these things one at a time. . . .
Let's find your shoulders first.
Well, look at you!
The last time I saw you undressed,
you were just skin and bone.

Ennis:

Was I?

Hope:

Yeah . . .
what happened to the skin???!!

Ennis:

Stop kibitzin', Bob,
I gotta strap on this chest protector.

Hope:

Where? . . .
Skinnay Ennis wearing a chest protector—
that's funny.

Ennis:

What's so funny about it? . . .
You wear a helmet!

Hope:

Have you got the band
writing material for you now?
But let's get ready for the game. . . .
The football needs a little more air in it. . . .
Blow it up, will you, Skin?

Ennis:

Sure.

*(SOUND: SHORT BLAST OF AIR . . . SLIDE
WHISTLE UP . . . THUMP)*

Ennis:

Well, don't stand there. . . .
Pull me down off this ceiling.

Hope:

I wanna make a hit with the girls
when we trot out on the field, Skin. . . .
Is my nose guard on straight?

Ennis:

Yeah, it's on straight, Bob . . .
but before the game starts
you better *shift it over*
so it will protect your nose!

Colonna:

All right, men,
we're about to go out on the field—
Now here are my final plans—
Niles, you play left tackle . . .
Ennis, you play center . . .
and Hope . . .
you stay in the car
and keep the motor running. . . .
Ooops, wrong plans!

Hope:

We're ready, coach!

Colonna:

Fine, and remember, men . . .
I've got it all fixed. . . .

No matter what you do
the referee won't stop the play.

Hope:

The referee won't stop the play?
How come?

Colonna:

. . . I just stole the pea outta his whistle! . . .
And for my final surprise
I've got a new player here for the backfield.
Say something, Flash!

(SOUND: COW MOOOOOOOOO)

Hope:

Colonna . . . a cow!
You're gonna put a cow in our backfield?

Colonna:

Sure. . . .
Think how confused they'll get
tryin' to figure out
whether she's carrying the ball or not!!

Hope:

Look, coach, could we kind of hurry
out on the field?
I might have a chance to speak to my girl,
Frances.

Ennis:

Oh, is she here?

Hope:

Yeah, I gave her a couple of tickets
so she could bring her little nephew, Junior.

(SOUND: CROWD NOISE)

Frances:

Come on, Junior, hurry up.
Wasn't it nice of Bob to give us the tickets?

Skelton:

I don't know, Aunt Frances. . . .
Goodness, I can't stand this height.
I think I is getting dizzy.
I is going to black out.

Frances:

Now Junior, we aren't that high.

(SOUND: AIRPLANE ZOOMS QUICK AND
OUT)

Skelton:

(Pause)
We aren't, huh? . . .
A P-38 just passed us . . .
underneath!

(SOUND: CROWD CHEERS)

Frances:

There's the team coming out on the field.
There's Bob—
Gee, he must be
the most important player on the team—
He's the only one that's got a bucket!

Skelton:

Which one is he?

Frances:

The one I'm pointing at.

Skelton:

Ohhhhhh, what a cute liddle face . . .
and handy, too—

he can point without using his finger! . . .
(Yells) . . .
Hey, Hope—wear a nose guard. . . .
Without it you is off-sides!

Frances:

Junior! . . .
Oh, Robert, yoo-hoo . . .

Skelton:

Wait, auntie—
I whistle loud and let him know we is here.
(Whistles)

(SOUND: IRON BALLS ON FLOOR)

Skelton:

Ohhhhh, there goes the last of me baby teeth.
Now I won't have no use
for that tube of Pepsodent he promised me.

Frances:

Here he comes. . . .
Up here, Robert.

Hope:

Hello, Frances,
your face looks very pretty today.

Skelton:

Ain't she pretty?
You'd never know her face
was warmed over from last night, would you?

Frances:

How are you, Bob? . . .
Oh, Bob, this is my little nephew, Junior.
I had to bring him to the game with me.

Hope:

What's the matter?
Haven't you got a deep-freeze locker?
Well, hello, hello, hello.

Skelton:

Oh, shut-up!

Frances:

Junior, now you say hello to Robert!

Skelton:

I don't want to.

Frances:

I said, say hello.

Skelton:

Now, you let me ignore him
or I will bang me little head
against this cement wall.

(SOUND: POUNDING ON CEMENT)

Hope:

Stop banging your head on that wall.
Do you want to chip the cement?
Come here, I want to talk to you.
I'd like to dump you in DDT.

Skelton:

Let go of me arm! . . .
Let go of me arm!!

Frances:

Robert, stop pulling his arm.

Hope:

I'm not pulling his arm. . . .
I'm just holding on;
he's doing the pulling!

Skelton:

Don't you hit me.

Hope:

I'm not going to hit you.
I think that was a very clever trick,
and I want to pat you on the back for it.

(SOUND: SLAP)

Skelton:

Oh, you hit me! . . .
You bwoke me widdle back!
You bwoke me widdle back—

Hope:

I didn't touch your back,
I tapped you on the shoulder blades.

Skelton:

You bwoke—
You didn't cut yourself, did you?

Colonna:

Hurry, Hope—
Get out on that field—
The game is about to start.

(SOUND: CROWD CHEER)

Skelton:

I want to play!
(Starts crying)
I want to play football!

Colonna:

Oh, all right.
Hey, Hope, to pacify this pest,
let him kick the ball.

Hope:

All right. . . .
Now here, I'll hold the ball for you
and you kick it.

Skelton:

Oh-tay.
Weady?
Here I come!

(SOUND: LITTLE FEET RUNNING AND A
LOUD BASS DRUM)

Hope:

(Pause)
Little nearsighted, ain't you, kid?

(APPLAUSE)

JIMMY DURANTE AND GARRY MOORE

O n the face of it, it would seem the most improbable of partnerships. Jimmy Durante was born in 1893, the son of an immigrant barber on New York's Lower East Side. He had spent most of his career in vaudeville and nightclubs, first as a ragtime piano player and bandleader, then as part of the song-and-dance comedy team of Clayton, Jackson and Durante, then finally as a solo entertainer. In the late '20s and early '30s he had made a number of films and done some radio, including Billy Rose's short-lived *Jumbo* series in 1935, but he was essentially a stage performer. Garry Moore was born two decades later in 1915, the son of a Baltimore attorney, and had spent most of his professional life in radio, first as a news announcer and sports commentator, then as a comedy writer and finally as a performer on such shows as *Club Matinee, Beat the Band* and the early morning six-day-a-week *Everything Goes*. The differences in their ages and backgrounds were reflected in their humor and the characters they projected. Durante was "hot": full of knockabout ebullience and battered bewilderment, especially when confronted with the intractable complexities of the English language. Moore was "cool": self-contained, witty, literate, well educated.

The pair was brought together by producer Phil Cohan in 1943, when a quick replacement was needed for the popular Abbott and Costello show. Costello had suffered a heart attack and Abbott refused to perform without him, leaving NBC with an open half-hour that had to be filled immediately. Cohan, who had been thinking about pairing Durante and Moore on their own series, rushed the show into production in only three weeks, and although the first program was a little shaky, Durante and Moore worked together beautifully and soon attracted their own enthusiastic following. When they finished substituting for Abbott and Costello, they began their own thirty-minute comedy-variety program, *The Camel Caravan*, for Camel Cigarettes. In 1945 they changed their sponsor to Rexall Drugstores and continued the series for another two years.

Perhaps the key to the success of the Durante-Moore combination was that it played up the differences between the performers rather than trying to minimize or obscure them. Durante emphasized the twenty-two-year gap in their ages by addressing Moore as "Junior" and taking a father's pride whenever his partner got off a good one ("Dat's my boy dat said dat!") The real-life affection that existed between them came through so strongly over the air that, according to John Dunning's *Tune In Yesterday*, many listeners thought they actually were father and son. The show also played up the differences in their ability at handling language. In a regular weekly feature, Moore would tell Durante about one of his previous occupations, faultlessly getting his mouth around such tongue-twisting dialogue as, "I used to work in Wauwatosa, Wisconsin, in the water works, as a reasonably reliable referee for the refrigerator repair wreckers, recluses and renegade rumrunners, Jimmy." Then Durante would try to say it back to him, to the audience's delight, mangling the words almost beyond recognition.

The partnership ended amicably in 1947, when Moore decided to go out on his own to reaffirm his individual identity as a comedian. His contributions to the show as writer and performer were great, but in truth it was dominated by the elemental natural force of the Durante personality. What we remember best are his running gags about his outsized nose and his unseen friend Umbriago, his patter songs ("Ink-a Dink-a Doo" and "You've Gotta Start Off Each Day Wid a Song"), his expressions of exasperation ("Everybody wants ta get inta da act!" and "It's da condishuns dat prevail!") and, of course, his inexplicably poignant sign-off, "Goodnight, Mrs. Calabash, wherever you are."

Durante continued for Rexall for three years with his own *Jimmy Durante Show*, while pursuing his newly energized career in nightclubs and film. He left radio for television in 1950. Moore went on to host *Take It or Leave It* and *Breakfast in Hollywood* and began his own *Garry Moore Show* in 1949. He too turned to television in the 1950s, where he continues to this day.

The Hunting Trip

Moore:

And now, America's favorite pinup boy!

It's Jimmy Durante—

in person!

(MUSIC: ORCHESTRA BEGINS PLAYING "YOU'VE GOT TO START OFF EACH DAY WITH A SONG")

Durante:

(Singing)

"Ya gotta start off each day wid a song.

Even when things go wrong.

You'll feel betta.

You'll even look betta—"

(SOUND: DOGS BARKING AND HOWLING)

Durante:

Waita minute!

Waita minute!

(MUSIC STOPS)

Durante:

Who gave Lassie a ticket? . . .

I don't mind Lassie bein' here,

but she got the foist four rows

filled with puppies! . . .

Hey, Garry.

Right after the program tonight

I gotta surprise for you.

Moore:

What is it, Jim?

Durante:

I wantcha to come over t'my house

for a wild duck dinner!

Moore:

Oh, I'm crazy about wild duck.

Is it going to be a formal dinner?

I mean, would it be appropriate

to wear a black tie?

Durante:

Indeed it will.

The duck is *dead!* . . .

After I shot five times and missed,

it died laughin'.

Moore:

Practicing in your backyard, were you?

Durante:

Are you joshin', Junior?

Why, I just got back

from a four-day huntin' trip . . .

through the wilds of Pismo Beach!

I was really roughin' it.

I carried a huntin' knife, a shotgun,

a vacuum cleaner,

a waffle baker, a Moiphy bed

and a set of hair coilers. . . .

Moiphy is very fussy about his hair.

Moore:

You were really roughing it, eh?

Durante:

You said it.

For three days I lived on nuthin' but

milk from a Persian cat!

Moore:

Wait a minute, Jimmy.

How do you get milk from a Persian cat?

Durante:

You take away th' saucer!

(Breaks up)

Ah, Durante, you should be on the radio! . . .

But believe me, Junior,

I was desperate.

Why, if I hadn'ta shot a beaver,

I'd have starved t' death!

Moore:

A beaver?

But, Jimmy, they're no good for food.

Hunters make hats out of beavers.

Durante:

Make hats outta beavers?

That's amazing!

Moore:

What's amazing?

Durante:

How do they train 'em

to stop growin'

at six an' seven-eighths?

Moore:

Weak Ovaltine! . . .

But the most amazing—

Durante:

Wait a minute!

That's my line!

He not only gets the laugh—

he takes the straight line, too!

Moore:

What were you saying?

Durante:

I said the most amazin' experience

of my entire huntin' trip

occurred on the fourth day. . . .

I found the loveliest little babblin' brook

and in no time at all

there was two salmon

fryin' over an open fire.

Just then I heard a footstep behind me

and a voice said:

Game Warden:

Just a minute, bud.

Can't you see that sign:

No fishing allowed?

Durante:

I wasn't fishin', Mr. Game Warden.

Game Warden:

Oh, no?

Then how did those two salmon

get into your frying pan?

Durante:

Suicide pact! . . .

They'll do anything

to get away from Del Monte!

Game Warden:

Well, them salmon are under fourteen inches.

Throw 'em back, wise guy.

And the next time I catch you

pulling 'em in under fourteen inches,

I'll give you a summons!

Durante:

Well, Garry—

(Where did he go?

He musta fell in a crack!)

Well, Garry,

I threw the salmon back

and then a strange thing happened. . . .

The most beautiful creature I ever saw

stepped outta the river,

brushin' the water outta her golden tresses

and her fig leaf!

She looked at me and said:

Nymph:

Hel-lo!

Where have you been all my life?

Durante:

Wait a minute. . . .
How tall are you?

Nymph:

Five-feet-four and a half.

Durante:

Thank goodness! . . .
For a minute I thought
I'd haveta throw you back!

Nymph:

You're a man, aren't you?

Durante:

If I'm not,
I'm sure foolin' my scoutmaster! . . .
Pardon me for mentionin' this,
but you need a new dress.
That one you got on
is worn down to the shoulders!

Nymph:

I've never seen a man before.
Look into my eyes.
Deep into my eyes.

Durante:

Which part?
The whites or the yolks? . . .
(She got me under her spell.)

Nymph:

I'm mad about you.
I love your hair.
I love your eyes.
I love your cute little button nose.

Durante:

Button nose!
Aren't you makin' a molehill
out of a mountain?

Nymph:

Oh, you do like me, don't you?

Durante:

Like ya?
You're the best thing I ever caught
with th' bait *I* got!

Nymph:

I want you to love me.

Durante:

What can I do?
I'm under her spell.

Nymph:

I feel as though I want to be kissed.

Durante:

This kid must be sufferin'
from an overdose of Sen Sen! . . .
But let's talk about you,
my little wood nymph.
Tell me about yourself.
Your dreams.
Your struggles.
Your telephone numba!

Nymph:

Oh, I have no telephone.
I'm a creature of nature.

The forest is my home.
The wooded valleys are my dining room.
The weeping willows are my boudoir.

Durante:

Have ya got a vacancy downstairs?
Oh, just a little place t' hang my hat.

Nymph:

Oh, you must forgive me if I seem impetuous.
No man has ever been
in these mountains before.

And when I see you like that
I can't fight it any longer.
Kiss me!

*(SOUND: LONG NOISY KISS ENDING
WITH A LOUD POP)*

Nymph:

What are you thinking?

Durante:

Somebody's been in these mountains before!

225

EASY ACES

Easy Aces traced the day-to-day domestic lives of Goodman and Jane Ace, who were husband and wife off-microphone as well as on. Written and supervised by Goodman Ace, it was probably the most literate, urbane comedy series of its time. Its sophistication resided less in its plotting and characters than in Ace's distinctive dialogue. As with George Burns and Gracie Allen, who made their radio debut the same year *Easy Aces* went on the air, the basic joke was the wife's comical denseness and the violations of language and logic it gave rise to. But where Gracie's malapropisms and non sequiturs led to vaudeville-inspired gags and routines, Jane's took the form of witty language play that disclosed unintended dimensions of meaning. In a whiny nasal twang that also contrasted with the peppy enthusiasm of Gracie's delivery, Jane would come up with such lines as "I want your candied opinion," "We were insufferable friends together" and "Time wounds all heals." Mr. Ace—as he was always called on the show, even by his wife—was less the straight man setting up the jokes than their long-suffering victim. His characteristic response to Jane's outrages was the lament, asked of no one in particular, "Isn't that awful?"

The greater sophistication of the show's humor was of a piece with its urban setting. As its theme "Manhattan Serenade" announced, it took place specifically in New York City rather than the usual unnamed or fictional small town somewhere in Middle America. Mr. Ace pursued a successful career in a Manhattan advertising agency, while Jane dabbled in such big-city pastimes as psychiatry, astrology and shopping for a mink coat. Jim Harmon observes in *The Great Radio Comedians* that the Aces always gave the impression that they had plenty of money, certainly much more than their listeners.

According to John Dunning's *Tune In Yesterday*, *Easy Aces* was created quite by accident one evening in 1930 while Goodman Ace, a movie and play reviewer for a Kansas City newspaper, was doing his local *Movie Man* show. As he came to the end of the broadcast, the program director motioned him to stay on the air because the performers for the next show had failed to show up. Ace had nothing prepared, so his wife jumped in to help him improvise a sketch about the previous evening's bridge game, and thus the series was born. In 1931 *Easy Aces* moved to Chicago and the CBS network. Two years later it moved on to NBC in New York, where it acquired the long-term sponsorship of Anacin. It was heard Monday, Friday and Saturday evenings, sharing the time spot with the very different *Mr. Keen, Tracer of Lost Persons*. The show continued until 1945, usually in a fifteen-minute format but sometimes for a half-hour. In 1948 it was revived for a while as a thirty-minute show under the title *Mr. Ace and Jane*.

Goodman Ace also worked as a writer on various radio and television shows. His credits include *The Danny Kaye Show*, *CBS Is There* and Perry Como's television series. For a number of years he produced a memorable column for *The Saturday Review*. In 1970 Doubleday published a collection of his scripts with the title *Ladies and Gentlemen—Easy Aces*, which were the words of the show's familiar sign-on.

Jane Goes to a Psychiatrist

Ace:

Well, this is Friday,

the day Jane hurried down

to the psychoanalyst's office

to continue telling him the story of her life—

only she noticed he yawned through

most of the story she told him yesterday,

so today she has made up

a lot of exciting things that didn't happen

to hold his interest.

This is the day which will

set back psychoanalysis

twenty-five years,

one which became known in medical circles

As Black Freudday.

Montel:

That's it, Mrs. Ace . . .

just lie back and relax

and we'll take up where we left off yesterday.

I hope we can do as well today

as we did during our first hour.

Jane:

Oh, this is gonna be a thriller-diller, doctor.

Montel:

Yes.

Let's take it from after

your high school graduation.

Jane:

Yes.

Well, sir, doctor—

oh, you're gonna like this—

it was the summer I graduated.

The heat was on.
And we were driving home from a party.
Sally Anderson and I—and two fellows.
The fellow she was with later left town,
the fellow I was with later became Mr. Ace,
my husband. . . .
You see, Sally and I always double-dated.
We've been insufferable friends for years.

Montel:

Insufferable—ah-ha!

Jane:

Oh yes, always together
like a couple of simonized twins.

Montel:

Simonized—yes, go on.

Jane:

Yes, sir.
Well, we were in the car
and one of the boys was driving.
The one in front.
I was in front with him.
Sally was in back with the other one.
We were singing and laughing—
"Shine On, Harvest Moon"—
you know how schoolkids are—
foolface and fancy free.

Montel:

Foolface—ah-ha.

Jane:

Yes, you know—
just out for a good time—

not wild or anything like that. . . .
Or would you *prefer* wild?

Montel:

What's that?

Jane:

No, I guess you wouldn't.
Well, we were driving along,
when alongside our car came another car—
and in that car was another boy
I used to go with
and he was jealous
that I was out with Mr. Ace
who later became my husband.
So I leaned over to Sally in the front seat
and I said, "Isn't that Roy?"
And she said—

Montel:

Just a moment, Mrs. Ace—
you said before *you* were in the front seat.

Jane:

Oh did I?
Well, Sally leaned over to *me*
in the front seat,
and *I* said, "Isn't that Roy?"
Is that better?

Montel:

Yes, I believe it is.

Jane:

And Sally said, "Yes, I believe it is."
Well, Roy was so mad
I was out with Mr. Ace
who later became my husband
that he wasn't watching

where he was driving
and he almost bumped into us—
he looked kinda wild—
almost besmerk, you might say.

Montel:

Ah-ha.

Jane:

Ah-ha.
So Mr. Ace,
the one who later became my husband,
started to drive faster to get away from him.
And pretty soon we were both going so fast—
Well, I'll tell you how fast we were going—
We were twelve miles from town—
and would you believe
we made it in eight miles?

Montel:

You—made—it—in eight—miles—

Jane:

Eight miles if I'm a day.
And then to clap the climax—
we suddenly heard the whistle
of a train coming around the hill.
Oh, I forgot to tell you there was a hill—
around the bend—
and we had to cross the tracks—
but there we were,
going like bats out of a bellfry. . . .

Montel:

Bellfry—yes.

Jane:

And we were going so fast we couldn't stop—

and the train was going even faster—
we couldn't hear the train whistle—
whoo whoo—
and we were going Oh Oh—
We all knew that if something didn't happen
this was the end. . . .
Well, good-bye, doctor,
I'll see you tomorrow.

Montel:

Wait a minute—
what *happened*?

Jane:

My hour is up, doctor—
to be continued tomorrow.

(MUSIC BRIDGE)

Ace:

Well, the story Jane made up
out of whole wheat
turned out to be a serial.
While Dr. Montel was hurrying over to see
his psychoanalyst,
Jane rushed home to tell her mother and me
what had happened on her second visit
to the good doctor's office.

Jane:

Well, sir, dear, he didn't yawn today.
I told him a story about
being in a car with you,
who later became Mr. Ace, husband,
and a train was coming around the hill
and it looked like it was gonna hit the car—

and then I stopped.
Well, you could have knocked him over
with a fender.

Ace:

You mean to say
you told him the story up to that point
and walked out?

Jane:

Well, I haven't figured up a finish yet.

Ace:

Isn't that awful.

Mother:

But Janie, I don't understand—
didn't the doctor even examine
for bruises
you might have gotten
in the accident with the train?

Jane:

Oh no, mother—
you don't understand—
he isn't that kind of a doctor.
He's a doctor for mental conflicts.

Mother:

Mental conflicts?
I never had those, Janie—
is it anything like dizzy spells?

Jane:

Oh no—mental conflicts.
It's for people who worry.

Mother:

Worry.
Who doesn't worry?
Except my sister, your Aunt Wilma.
She used to worry all the time.
And then one day she decided
to stop worrying,
and overnight her hair turned brown.

Jane:

Mother,
maybe you better come with me
to see Dr. Montel.

Ace:

I lost track here.
Jane, you're not going back there tomorrow.

Jane:

Oh, I have to go back—
I have to figure out a finish for that story
and tell it to him.
Wait a minute—
tomorrow I can't go.
I took some material to the dressmaker
the other day—
I have to go for a fitting.
Dear?

Ace:

What?

Jane:

You'll go in my place.

Ace:

You want me to go be psychoanalyzed
in your place?

Jane:

Unless you wanta go in my place
to the dressmaker for a fitting.

Ace:

Yes, I will go, Jane.
I want to visit that doctor.
Maybe I can help him.

(MUSIC BRIDGE)

Ace:

The next morning I went to see Dr. Montel.
His office was just as Jane had described it,
tall, dark, brown,
and I was greeted
by a short nurse with a leather seat,
at a desk.

Nurse:

Good morning.
May I help you?

Ace:

I want to see Dr. Montel.

Nurse:

Do you have an appointment?

Ace:

Yes—eleven o'clock.

Nurse:

What's the name?

Ace:

Mrs. Ace.

Nurse:

Oh yes—
I have it in my book right here.
(Pause)
Mrs. Ace?

Ace:

Yes, Jane Ace.

Nurse:

Oh, to be sure.
Well—
well, the doctor will see you in a minute.
Won't you have a chair, MRS. Ace?

Ace:

No, no, you don't understand—
you see . . .
oh well—yes, thank you.
I'll sit right here.

Nurse:

No, no, not here.
Over there against the wall.
That's it, Mrs. Ace—just relax—
the doctor will be with you in a moment.
Don't get excited—don't be nervous.
Everything's going to be all right.

Ace:

I'm not excited—
I'm not nervous.

Nurse:

That's right—just relax.
The doctor will buzz when he's ready for you.

Ace:

Thank you.

Nurse:

Ha-ha yes.

Ace:

Ha-ha yes.

(SILENCE)

Nurse:

Well, you're looking well today, Mrs. Ace.

Ace:

It's just this makeup.

Nurse:

Pancake?

Ace:

Well, no, thank you.

I just had breadfast.

Nurse:

Uh . . .

the doctor will see you in just a moment,

Mrs. Ace.

Would you like to look at this magazine?

Ace:

Well, yes, I don't mind—

Nurse:

No, no, don't get up—

I'll slide it over to you across the floor.

Ace:

Oh, thank you.

Oh, the *Ladies' Home Journal*, yes.

Nurse:

Yes.

There are lovely new dress designs

in this month's issue.

Ace:

That reminds me—

I wonder how I'm making out with that dress

I'm having fitted over at the dressmaker's.

Nurse:

You're having a fitting at the dressmaker's

later on, Mrs. Ace?

Ace:

No, I'm over there being fitted now.

Nurse:

The doctor will see you

in just a moment, Mrs. Ace.

Ace:

Thank you.

Yes, I have to go to the dressmaker

for everything.

I just simply can't find my size

in ready-mades.

Even hose, I have to have 'em made special.

Nurse:

Me too, Mrs. Ace.

And the nylons they sell you these days.

This morning I put on

a brand-new pair of nylons

and no sooner did I get here

when I got a run in 'em.
All the way up to here.

Ace:

Really?
Up to where?

Nurse:

Look, Mrs. Ace—
all the way up to—

(SOUND: BUZZER RINGS)

Nurse:

Oh, the doctor will see you right now,
Mrs. Ace.

Ace:

Now he sees me.
This is psychoanalysis?

Nurse:

Go right in.

Ace:

Thank you.
It's been nice almost seeing you.

Nurse:

Remember me to Mr. Ace.

Montel:

Come, come in, Mrs. Ace.

(SOUND: DOOR CLOSES)

Montel:

Well, I'm happy to—
who are *you?*

Ace:

I'm Mr. Ace.

Montel:

Oh, you're the one who later became Mr. Ace.

Ace:

What goes on here?
Yes, I'm Mr. Ace—
she couldn't make it today.

Montel:

Oh no, oh no.
I was hoping she would come.
I've been on pins and cushions
since she left here.
I've been going besmerk.

Ace:

Besmerk.

Montel:

I've been trying to write a paper
on her history—
but my bearings are all bawled up.

Ace:

Oh, brother.

Montel:

Even my wife can't understand
what's happened to me—
and we've been insufferable companions
for years.

Ace:

Murder.

Montel:

I've always been so foolface and fancy free—

Ace:

Look, Ja—doctor.
I don't want my wife coming here anymore.
Will you please tell—

Montel:

Not come here anymore?
She built the story up to
the psychopathic moment
and then she walked out.
She's got to tell me what happened—
you were in the car—
you can tell me—
you were speeding along in your car—
brbrbrbr—
the train was coming around the hill—
whoo whoo—
you couldn't stop—
the train couldn't stop—
what happened?

Ace:

We were killed.

Montel:

Oh, *thank* you, Mr. Ace.
Thank goodness.
You took a load off my—
you were killed?

Ace:

Look, doctor—

Montel:

Interesting case.
Lie down, Mr. Ace.

Ace:

Me?

Montel:

Very interesting.
Now I want you to tell me
the story of your life
from as far back as you can remember.

Ace:

Well, I was born in a Wild West show
at the age of three—

Montel:

Ah-ha.

(MUSIC BRIDGE)

Ace:

That doctor will never forget that hour,
if he lives to be twelve years old.
I fixed his wagon—
because the very next day in his office—
(Fade)

Montel:

That's right—
just lie back comfortably and relax.
Now I want you to continue the story
from where we left off.

*(THE NEXT TWO SPEECHES ARE READ
TOGETHER)*

234

Jane:

Well, after we got out of the train wreck,
the boy who later became
Mr. Ace, my husband . . .

Ace:

Well, doc, after I got out of
the Wild West show,
I decided to become an Indian—

Jane:

Dear, please—
you're pushing me off the couch.

Ace:

Well, move over, Jane—
I gotta have some room.

Jane:

Move up a little—

the palms of your feet
are hanging over the end of the couch.

Ace:

I can't move over—
you push over a little.

Jane:

I can't—
there's no room.

Ace:

Well, somebody's gotta move.

Mother:

All right, children,
if it makes you happy for me to move,
I'll move.

(MUSIC PLAYOFF)

HENRY MORGAN

The ironic tone was set at the very beginning with the playing of the opening theme, "For He's a Jolly Good Fellow." Henry Morgan was many things, but jolly was never one of them. He was quizzical and sardonic, at times maybe even cranky, but the closest he came to jollity was the relish he took in turning the cutting edge of his wit against the victims of his outrage. Morgan never suffered fools gladly, and the pompous fools with pretensions were the ones he loved to give it to the most. His own opening line—"Hello, anyone. Here's Morgan," delivered in a low-key, offhand manner—was an implicit rebuke to the high-pressure bombast of the standard announcer's introduction, with its fiction that everyone in the country, if not the planet at large, had been sitting tensed in front of the Philco waiting impatiently for whatever wonderful program they had in store for us.

Morgan was radio's sharpest-tongued, most combative satirist. Throughout the 1940s, not a decade notable for its candor, he took upon himself the job of exposing the frailties of some of America's most complacent entrenched institutions, from the telephone company to the corporate sponsors of his own show. The attacks on the latter were a particular delight to his fans. This was before the time the humorous soft sell came into fashion, and the man who paid the bills demanded reverence and solemn superlatives for his product. Morgan's refusal to play the game kept him in constant trouble. When he accused Life Savers of "mulcting the public" for putting holes in the center of their candy, the company canceled its advertising the next day. Schick Injector Razor's slogan "Push-pull, click-click; change blades that quick" became "Push-pull, nick-nick," and when the company threatened to pull out of the show because of low ratings, Morgan confided to his audience, "Frankly, I don't think it's my show. I think it's their razor."

Morgan began in radio in 1931 as a pageboy at New York's WMCA, where for his eight dollars a week he would occasionally get to go on the air when an extra voice was needed. Within two years he had become a full-time staff announcer, the youngest in the country, but he was eventually fired for being, as he put it, "too fresh." Moving on to an announcer's job in Philadelphia, he was fired again, this time for, among other offenses, laughing on the air during the Missing Persons report. After jobs in Duluth and Boston, he returned to New York in 1938 as staff announcer on WOR. Two years later he got the first of his own shows, *Meet Mr. Morgan*. As he tells it, the management felt he had been doing too much kidding around on the air and thought maybe his own show would allow him to get it out of his system.

Meet Mr. Morgan eventually became *Here's Morgan*, the classic quarter-hour aired six times a week over WOR. In 1946, Morgan switched over to ABC, which gave him national exposure and much more elaborate production. *The Henry Morgan Show*, as it was now known, had an orchestra that played Bernie Green's appropriately witty arrangements and a full cast that included Arnold Stang (Morgan's perfect foil) as well as Art Carney, Alice Pearce, Durwood Kirby, Betty Garde, Minerva Pious and Maurice Gosfield. When Schick dropped its sponsorship in 1947, it was taken over by Bristol Myers and then by Rayve Creme Shampoo. Neither of them was spared Morgan's barbs. The show went off the air in 1950.

A Commercial (1946)

Morgan:

On behalf of
the Eversharp Schick Injector Razor,
which changes blades automatically,
I would like to bid you a fond nothing. . . .

The Eversharp Schick Razor
comes complete with twenty blades,
and that's all the company
can afford to give you
for a dollar and a quarter.

They have no time for good wishes.
They want you to know that
the Eversharp Schick Injector Razor

changes blades automatically
and the company itself gives you
an excellent value.
And from there on, they quit.

They don't bring you the correct time
through their courtesy.
They don't particularly hope
that you have a happy weekend.
They don't wish you a cheery good evening.
I don't think they even like you.
They don't like *me*.

But I figure this way:
I bought a Buick last month,

and they didn't say
they were madly in love with me.
Why should Eversharp be so crazy about you
for a dollar and a quarter?
You get your money's worth.
You get a fine shave.

What more do you want?

Never mind if they don't like you.
I like you. . . .
Don't like *them* much.

Long Distance   (1946)

Morgan:
  You know, years ago
  people used to make jokes
  about how hard it was
  to get a number on the telephone.
  Nowadays there aren't any jokes
  because there's no trouble.
  The phone works fine.
  This summer,
  when I was up in Cape Cod in Massachusetts,
  I was living near the town of Truro.
  T-R-U-R-O, a town.
  And I had to call Los Angeles from there.
  And so first I asked myself the big question:
  will my alarm clock go off
  when the three minutes are up?
  And then I placed the call:

(SOUND: LIFTS RECEIVER, DROPS COIN,
  DIALS OPERATOR)

Operator 1:
  Operator.

Morgan:
  I want to call Los Angeles.
  The number is Westwood 8927.

Operator 1:
  (Excited)
  You want to call *Los Angeles!*

Morgan:
  Yeah.

Operator 1:
  Oh, what number?

Morgan:
  Westwood 8927.

Operator 1:
  Los Angeles!

Morgan:
  Yeah.

Operator 1:
  California?

Morgan:
  That's the one.

Operator 1:
  Thank you!
  Just a minute now.

(SOUND: CIRCUIT RINGS)

Operator 2:
This is Hyannis, operator.

Operator 1:
Hello, this is Truro.
I have a call for Los Angeles.
Westwood 8927.

Operator 2:
Los Angeles?

Operator 1:
Yes!

Operator 2:
What number?

Operator 1:
Westwood 8927.

Operator 2:
Is that *in* Los Angeles?

Operator 1:
Just a minute. . . .
Is that in Los Angeles, sir?

Morgan:
Mm-mm.

Operator 1:
Yes, that's in Los Angeles, Hyannis.

Operator 2:
Well, one moment, please.

(SOUND: CIRCUIT RINGS)

Operator 3:
This is the Wellfleet operator.

Operator 2:
This is Hyannis, Wellfleet.
I have a call from Truro to Los Angeles.

Operator 3:
What number?

Operator 2:
Westwood 2897.

Operator 1:
Westwood 8297.

Morgan:
Westwood 8927!

Operator 1:
I'm sorry, sir.

Operator 2:
I'm sorry, Truro.

Operator 3:
I'm sorry, Hyannis. . . .
What is that number?

Operator 2:
Uh, Westwood 8927, Wellfleet.

Operator 3:
How do you spell the exchange?

Operator 2:
W for Walter,
E for Edward,
S for Samuel,
T for Thomas,
W for Walter,
double O as in Oscar-Oscar
and D for David.

Operator 3:
One moment, Truro.

Operator 1:
One moment, sir.

Morgan:
Are we still in Massachusetts?

Operator 1:
Oh, sure! . . .
Just a minute now.
Wellfleet is calling Boston.

Morgan:
Swell.

(SOUND: CIRCUIT RINGS)

Operator 4:
Boston.

Operator 3:
This is Wellfleet, Boston.

Operator 4:
What is that again?

Operator 3:
Wellfleet:
W for William,
E for—

Morgan:
W for *Walter!*

Operator 3:
Wellfleet, Boston:
W-E-double L-F-L-double E-T.

Operator 4:
Where are you calling, Wellfleet?

Operator 3:
Los Angeles, California.
The exchange is Westwood.

Operator 4:
What is that exchange?

Operator:
W-E-S-T-W-double O-D.
Westwood 2897.

Operator 1:
Westwood 8927.

Operator 4:
Who was that, Wellfleet?

Operator 3:
That was Hyannis.

Operator 1:
No, Wellfleet.
This is Truro.

Operator 3:

Where is Hyannis?

Operator 2:

I'm on the *line*, Wellfleet!

Morgan:

Westwood 8927, please.

Operator 4:

What is that?

Morgan:

Westwood 8927, Truro. . . .
Uh, Wellfleet . . .
Boston? . . .

Operator 4:

Just a moment, please.
I'll call the New York operator.

(SOUND: CIRCUIT RINGS)

Operator 5:

Yeah?

Operator 4:

This is Boston, New York.
Calling Los Angeles.
Westwood 8927.

Operator 5:

Callin' what?

Operator 4:

Westwood.
W-E-S-T-W-double O-D.

Operator 5:

D for David
or T for Thomas?

Operator 3:

D for David, New York.

Operator 5:

Who th' heck was that?

Operator 3:

This is Wellfleet, New York.

Operator 5:

Who?

Operator 3:

W-E-double L—

Operator 5:

Awright, awright, awright! . . .
Who's makin' dis call?

Morgan:

Me.

Operator 5:

Who's zat?

Morgan:

Me:
M-E.

Operator 5:

Awright, I'll call Los Angeles.

241

Morgan:

It's up to you.

(SOUND: CIRCUIT RINGS)

Operator 6:

This is Los Angeles.

Operator 5:

This is New Yawk, Los Angeles.
I want Westwood 8927.

Operator 6:

Westwood 8927.
Do you want the charges?

Operator 5:

Do yah want de charges, Boston?

Operator 4:

Do you want the charges, Wellfleet?

Operator 3:

Do you want the charges, Hyannis?

Operator 2:

Do you want the charges, Truro?

Operator 1:

Do you want the charges, sir?

Morgan:

Nah.

Operator 6:

I will ring the number.

Operator 1:

Just a minute.
Please deposit
two dollars and twenty-five cents.

Morgan:

Okay.

(SOUND: DROPS NINE QUARTERS INTO THE PHONE)

Operator 1:

That was only two dollars.

Morgan:

That was two dollars and a quarter!

Operator 1:

Well, I'll return the money
and you can drop it in again.

(SOUND: COINS RETURNED, THEN DROPPED BACK INTO THE PHONE)

Operator 1:

Thanks a lot.
We're ready, Hyannis.

Operator 2:

We're ready, Wellfleet.

Operator 3:

We're ready, Boston.

Operator 4:

We're ready, New York.

Operator 5:

Okay, L.A.

Operator 6:

Ringing your party, sir.

(SOUND: PHONE BUZZING)

Housekeeper:

Hello.

Morgan:

This is Mr. Morgan.

May I talk to Mrs. Morgan?

Housekeeper:

I'm sorry.

Mr. Morgan is not here.

Morgan:

This is Mr. Morgan.

Housekeeper:

Mr. Morgan is *not here!* . . .

He's in Truro, Massachusetts.

Morgan:

Thanks.

(SOUND: HANGS UP THE PHONE . . .
TELEPHONE RINGS, RECEIVER
PICKED UP)

Morgan:

Yeah?

Operator 1:

This is Truro operator.

Did you get your party?

Morgan:

No.

Operator 1:

Why not?

Morgan:

He's in Truro.

(MUSIC CUE UP . . . APPLAUSE)

BOB AND RAY

Most of the earlier generation of radio comedians came from vaudeville. Bob Elliott and Ray Goulding started out in radio, and radio itself was their subject, the prime metaphor in their comic critique of the dull, fatuous, inept and smug.

The short sketches that made up their shows took off on the inanities of virtually every type of broadcast that filled the airways during the years their careers were formed. Playing all the voices themselves and working together with extraordinary empathy, they peopled their programs with bumbling announcers, drunken sportscasters, dippy quiz-show contestants, long-suffering soap-opera heroines and all the other untenable characters who were radio at its sappiest. As Kurt Vonnegut puts it, their shows "feature Americans who are almost always fourth-rate or below, engaged in enterprises which, if not contemptible, are at least insane."

The passage of time and the transforming power of nostalgia (as well as the selectivity practiced in such backward glances as this book) make us tend to forget what an arid wasteland radio must largely have been during its so-called Golden Age. But Bob and Ray give the permanence of art to the abiding mediocrity that was, one suspects, the broadcasting norm.

In caricaturing the programs and performers that were all too typical of the medium, Bob and Ray also satirize the audiences who listen to them. We are what we tune in on. Yet their humor is so accepting and they take such obvious delight in their surreal creations that there is a pervasive geniality in their satire. One also senses an underlying fondness for the medium they parody so knowingly. Parody is imitation at the remove of irony, and imitation is the sincerest form of flattery. Significantly, they perfected their comic mythologizing of radio during the 1950s, just when it was being supplanted by television and the kind of shows they lampooned were fading from the air.

Ray Goulding was born in 1922 and Bob Elliott a year later. They met in 1946 when they were both working as staff announcers at Boston's WHDH. During their years together at the local Boston station, they developed their special brand of off-center humor improvising skits on the air after the news and before the baseball games. In 1951 they moved to New York and received their first national exposure with an early evening fifteen-minute show on NBC. They have worked for one network or another in one format or another ever since.

Person-of-the-Month Club

Bob:

Friends,
are you bored stiff
because you have to go through life
always being the same person?

Ray:

Haven't you often thought
that you could make the grade
if you could just start over again
as somebody else?

Bob:

Well, now you can start over again
as somebody else—
not just once, but many times,
thanks to an amazing offer being made
by Bob and Ray Enterprises.

Ray:

Yes, friends.
Your dream of assuming a new identity
can come true each and every month

when you're a member of
the Bob and Ray Person-of-the-Month Club.

Bob:

It sounds incredible,
but it's true, neighbors.
Once you're enrolled as a member
of the Bob and Ray Person-of-the-Month Club,
the postman will bring right to your door
every thirty days
all of the documents you need
to assume a new and fascinating identity.

Ray:

You'll get phony credit cards,
a bogus driver's licence,
new laundry marks for your clothes,
family photos of people you don't know
to put around your house.

Bob:

You'll even receive
one hundred sheets of stationery
complete with envelopes

handsomely embossed
with somebody else's name.
In a matter of minutes,
you'll be ready to start writing letters
and signing them with a name
your friends and loved ones never heard of.

Ray:

Now, naturally,
we don't expect you to take our word
for the many advantages of membership in
the Bob and Ray Person-of-the-Month Club.
Let us read to you from just a few of the
thousands of unsolicited testimonial letters
that have come pouring into
our lavish New York post office box.

Bob:

A gentleman in Ohio writes:
"For years, I have wanted
to shed my old identity
and become the Shah of Iran.
Now my dream has come true
thanks to the amazing benefits
of your organization."

Ray:

From Arizona, a lady writes:
"I was thrilled to pieces
when I got your July club selection.
Imagine a simple housewife like me
suddenly becoming Vaughn Monroe."

Bob:

From Indiana, we received
this heartwarming note:
"I had virtually given up hope of
becoming Theodore Roosevelt
after the disastrous failure of

the Bull Moose Party in 1912.
Now you have made my dream of a lifetime
a reality,
and I'm starting work at once
on the Panama Canal."

Ray:

Finally, we have this letter
from a lady in Oregon:
"Life has taken on a new meaning for me
since I became Gladys Knight and the Pips.
I can never thank you enough."
And it's signed "All of Us."

Bob:

Yes, friends, a new identity
can make you feel like a new person.
So why not sign up for membership in the
Bob and Ray Person-of-the Month Club today
and take advantage of
our special bonus offer.

Ray:

If your membership application
is postmarked before midnight tonight,
you will receive at no additional charge
a box of fifty beautiful personalized
Christmas cards.

Bob:

That's right, neighbors.
These are the perfect cards
to fit right in with
your club selection for next December.
Each card bears a photograph
of three lovely children
you've never seen before
frolicking around a Christmas tree.

Ray:

That's not *one*, not *two*,
but a full three children
all handsomely clad in Doctor Dentons
and all opening their packages
with what appears to be obvious glee
on Christmas morning.

Bob:

Each card also carries the heartfelt message:
"Holiday greetings from our house to yours."
And it's signed
"Ernie and Florence Watanaby and family."

Ray:

You'll want a box of these
beautiful greeting cards
for your very own.

So don't delay.
Get that membership application in the mail
before midnight tonight.

Bob:

Just send a check, cash or money order—
but no stamps, please—
to Bob and Ray,
Box 3-2-8-7-6-3-4-5-J-6, New York.

Ray:

Or if you wish, you may address us
as the new people
we're becoming this month.
through the facilities of the club.
That would be
Dolly Madison and Ivan the Terrible—
Box 3-2-8-7-6-3-4-5-J-6, New York.

Bob and Ray Reunite the Whirleys

Bob:

Are the two people all set in opposite studios,
Ray?
Miss Whirley and her brother, Mr. Whirley?
They haven't seen each other
for sixty-seven years.
We have flown Miss Whirley here
and Mr. Whirley lives here in New York.

Ray:

He took a bus.

Bob:

We have them in separate studios
and we think that they really will have
a big surprise in store for them,
thanks to us.

Ray:

Why don't you talk to Miss Whirley first?

Bob:

All right,
will you bring in Miss Whirley, please?

*(SOUND: DOOR OPENS; SLOW
FOOTSTEPS)*

Bob:

Come in, my dear.

Ray:

(Roughly)
Step lively, lady, will you?

Bob:

Ray, she's eighty-seven years old.

Ray:

I don't care, Bob,
we only have . . .

Bob:

Let's be kind to her.

Ray:

Step along,
c'mon, lady.

Bob:

Sit down, if you will.
You are Miss Tabetha Whirley?

Tabetha:

Ta-be′tha.

Bob:

Ta-be′tha.

Tabetha:

A lot of people make that mistake.

Bob:

And where do you make your home?

Tabetha:

I live in Bondurant, Wyoming.

Bob:

That's wonderful country out there.
And you are eighty-seven years young,
is that right?

Tabetha:

That's right.

Bob:

And you were flown here by Bob and Ray.
Do you have any idea why
you are here in this studio today?

Tabetha:

I don't have the remotest idea
why I am here.

Ray:

Speak up, lady, please.

Bob:

She is speaking up, Ray.
Do you have anybody
you particularly would like to see
after a great many years?
Someone you used to know?

Tabetha:

No, I don't suppose . . .

Bob:

Anybody in your family, Miss Whirley,
that you particularly . . . ?

Tabetha:

Let me see.
(Musing)
My family . . .
no, it's been so long
since I saw any of them,
I wouldn't know them
if I fell over them.

Bob:

Do you remember your brother, Frank?

Tabetha:

Sure, sure.

Bob:

How long is it since you saw him?

Tabetha:

Let's see,

it must be about seventy years.

Bob:

Seventy years?

We thought it was only sixty-seven.

Well, we have a little surprise for you,

Miss Whirley.

We like to do this now and then.

Will you open that door over there,

and bring in our next guest?

(SOUND: DOOR OPENS; FOOTSTEPS)

Ray:

(Briskly)

All right, c'mon, pal,

will you step along?

Bob:

(Whispering reverentially)

Now, Mr. Frank Whirley

is facing his sister Tabetha

for the first time in sixty-seven years.

Let's hear what they have to say.

Frank:

What did you want me here for?

Bob:

This is your sister Tabetha, Frank.

Tabetha:

Hello, Frank.

Frank:

Oh, hello, Tabetha.

Bob:

Now, will you go over

and sit down in our studio audience, please.

Knowing that we have made

two people happier . . .

Ray:

Why don't you sit together?

You're not even in the same row.

Bob:

You probably will have a lot to talk over,

won't you, Miss Whirley?

Tabetha:

I suppose,

but it's been so long.

Bob:

Mr. Whirley, you have anything to say?

Frank:

No, no.

You've changed.

Where do you live now, Tabetha?

Tabetha:

Bondurant, Wyoming.

Frank:

Ah, huh.

Bob:

As they exchange anecdotes
of days gone by . . .

Frank:

I have to get out of here,
I have a dental appointment.
Do you mind if I run along?

Tabetha & Bob:

No, no.
Go ahead.

Bob:

And so we have rejoined the Whirleys
and we know that we have added
a little bit of human kindness.

Tabetha:

Is that why you flew me here?

Bob:

Why, yes,
you can go back anytime now.

Tabetha:

Well, I might as well run along home now.
There is probably a plane leaving.
'Bye.

Bob:

'Bye.

(SOUND: FOOTSTEPS)

Ray:

Isn't that heartwarming?

Bob:

It certainly is,
and it did something to me.